Founders and Organizational Development

Founders and Organizational Development: The Etiology and Theory of Founder's Syndrome is designed to help today's researchers, faculty, students, and practitioners become familiar with the etiology and dynamics of founder's syndrome as an organizational condition challenging nonprofit/ nongovernmental, social enterprise, and for-profit and publicly traded organizations. The book uses applied social and psychological theories and concepts to peel away the layers of an organizational enigma, revealing three causes of founder's syndrome and insight into the power and privileges assumed by founders who engage in undesirable and self-destructive behaviors leading to their termination, going from hero status to antihero.

Researchers, instructors, students, and practitioners will find thought-provoking case studies from the real world of organization development practice. Segments from interviews during interventions reveal the type of emotional turmoil experienced in organizations where founder's syndrome is present. Insight is provided into accounts of well-known founders who were terminated or forced to resign. The unique features of this book include the following: integrating theory into practice, describing a new theory about the psychological reaction of founder's syndrome victims, prevention ideas when designing new organizations, strategies for intervention, using content based on research and organization development consultation experiences, and integrating feedback from students who have launched organizations.

Stephen R. Block was a Research Professor and Director of the Nonprofit Concentration at the University of Colorado-Denver's School of Public Affairs, USA.

Katrina Miller-Stevens is an Associate Professor in the Department of Economics and Business at Colorado College, USA.

Routledge Studies in Management, Organizations and Society

This series presents innovative work grounded in new realities, addressing issues crucial to an understanding of the contemporary world. This is the world of organized societies, where boundaries between formal and informal, public and private, local and global organizations have been displaced or have vanished, along with other nineteenth century dichotomies and oppositions. Management, apart from becoming a specialized profession for a growing number of people, is an everyday activity for most members of modern societies.

Similarly, at the level of enquiry, culture and technology, and literature and economics, can no longer be conceived as isolated intellectual fields; conventional canons and established mainstreams are contested. Management, Organizations and Society addresses these contemporary dynamics of transformation in a manner that transcends disciplinary boundaries, with books that will appeal to researchers, students and practitioners alike.

Recent titles in this series include:

Towards the Compassionate University
From Golden Thread to Global Impact
Edited by Kathryn Waddington

Industry 4.0
A Glocal Perspective
Edited by Jerzy Duda and Aleksandra Gąsior

Pierre Bourdieu in Studies of Organization and Management
Societal Change and Transforming Fields
Edited by Sarah Robinson, Jette Ernst, Kristian Larsen and Ole Jacob Thomassen

For more information about this series, please visit: https://www.routledge.com/Routledge-Studies-in-Management-Organizations-and-Society/book-series/SE0536

Founders and Organizational Development

The Etiology and Theory of Founder's Syndrome

Stephen R. Block and
Katrina Miller-Stevens

Routledge
Taylor & Francis Group

NEW YORK AND LONDON

First published 2021
by Routledge
605 Third Avenue, New York, NY 10158

and by Routledge
2 Park Square, Milton Park, Abingdon, Oxon, OX14 4RN

*Routledge is an imprint of the Taylor & Francis Group, an
informa business*

© 2021 Taylor & Francis

Library of Congress Cataloging-in-Publication Data
A catalog record for this title has been requested

ISBN: 978-0-367-47983-1 (hbk)
ISBN: 978-0-367-52375-6 (pbk)
ISBN: 978-1-003-05762-8 (ebk)

Typeset in Sabon
by MPS Limited, Dehradun

Contents

Preface

We all seem to know from anecdotal tales that founder's syndrome is a thorny organizational behavior problem. As a matter of fact, from the reports we receive from ResearchGate, a network of scientists and researchers, the topic has progressively attracted interest among faculty and practitioners from all over the world representing many disciplines including anthropology, economics, sociology, organizational psychology, organizational leadership, organizational behavior, business, management, nonprofit/nongovernmental organizations, healthcare management, arts management, among others. Despite the growing interest, there have been few scholarly investigations, and none have peeled away the layers of this organizational enigma to accurately explain its causation, properties, and significance. For this reason, we approached the writing of *Founders and Organizational Development: The Etiology and Theory of Founder's Syndrome* with a lofty goal of making a timely contribution to help today's faculty, students, and practitioners become familiar with the etiology and dynamics of founder's syndrome as an organizational condition challenging large-size, medium-size, small-size, nonprofit/nongovernmental, social enterprise, and for-profit and publicly traded organizations.

In order to make *Founders and Organizational Development: The Etiology and Theory of Founder's Syndrome* a teaching and learning tool, we used content from our graduate and undergraduate courses on developing and launching organizations, as well as our peer-reviewed research and case studies of founder's syndrome. Additionally, the pedagogical features of this book were selected to balance the coverage and application of concepts and theories, and to share an abundance of ideas from the real world of organization development practice with interventions into companies experiencing founder's syndrome.

In terms of the approach, each chapter begins with study objectives and at its end, we pose questions to encourage critical thinking and vibrant discussions. The book is rich in information from interviews and survey results from staff and board members at different stages of their organizations' founder's syndrome. Additionally, there are segments of interviews with founders who were under pressure while employed and with founders who were terminated or forced to resign. The content from all the interviews serves two purposes. One intention is to illustrate the emotional turmoil that individuals experience with founder's syndrome. The second intent relates to our pedagogy of bringing life to the concepts and theories from the book's chapters.

Throughout the book, we present cases that we believe are thought provoking and afford additional opportunities to demonstrate the application of concepts and theories for analyzing founder's syndrome behaviors and the handling of knotty human problems. Except for Chapters 6 and 7, the names of the organizations and their founders were concealed to honor the requests for confidentiality from the organizational participants. In Chapters 6 and 7, the organizations, the founders, and the nature of the offending behaviors were openly identified because the information came from public records, magazines, journals, and newspaper accounts. In some instances, we reached out to the prominent figures for clarification of details. We were careful not to make personal judgments beyond the existing published statements. However, where appropriate, we asserted explanations of concepts, theories, and propositions drawn from different chapters to match them to the details of the cases from the public domain.

The book is organized into eight chapters. Chapter 1 examines the reasons that individuals have for establishing organizations, which is the starting point for understanding founder's syndrome. Additionally, we present 16 sociological and psychological concepts that get to the heart of how founders think and feel about their organization. This provides an essential perspective on the relational aspect of organizations and human behavior.

A founder's psychological connection with his or her organization is an underlying cause for using powers and privileges to make certain that employees and board members assent to the founder's organizational vision. This becomes clear in Chapter 2, which is a primer on power and control and summarizes the abuses of power that are often attributed to founders engaged in founder's syndrome. The use of power transforms the founder from hero status or entrepreneurial genius to the person that senior managers and board members wish to see terminated.

A founder's undesirable behaviors can cause an employee to have a psychological reaction. In Chapter 3, we introduce a theoretical construct we named Founder's Transformational Reaction Syndrome (FTRS). FTRS is based on the unconscious process of self-protection using a psychological defense mechanism. The unconscious protections can explain how individuals are able to continue to come to work while being the target of founder's syndrome. FTRS also explains how board members, managers, and founders can justify actions that harm other organizational actors. It also represents a process of how unconscious protections can convert into conscious awareness whereby a victim becomes an assertive individual and acts against founder's syndrome.

Chapter 4 draws on the ideas and knowledge of several theorists whose concepts have provided considerable relevance as tools to stimulate our analytic thinking about founder's syndrome. We present 12 theories that we have used as lenses to expand our knowledge of founder's syndrome, helping us to see relevant parts of organizational behavior problems and spark creative ideas for planned change and organization development interventions.

As we explored the causes of founder's syndrome, we discovered two triggers that incite founders to engage in deleterious behaviors in response to staff actions. Consequently, we devoted Chapter 5 to learn about the social behaviors of organizational employees. To accomplish this aim, we explored six theories and three interrelated psychoanalytic concepts. Like Chapter 4, we use social and psychological theories to make sense of reality and find meaning in the personal experiences of staff and board members. The individuals we write about in Chapter 5 are genuinely motivated to get rid of the founding CEO.

Chapters 6 and 7 are interesting case studies of well-known companies that had engaged in founder's syndrome, which led to the dismissal of their founders. Chapter 6 focuses on for-profit companies and Chapter 7 on three nonprofit organizations. The dynamics that are described in both chapters link back to the highlighted concepts and theories that were discussed in the earlier chapters.

Chapter 8 is our concluding chapter, and we address three important questions: (1) Is founder's syndrome inevitable? (2) Can founder's syndrome be prevented? And (3) Once founder's syndrome is observed, are there options for effectively defusing the hostilities, surviving the symptoms, and improving organizational performance?

We endeavored to write this book in a readable style to make it compatible with course textbooks or to be read as a standalone monograph about founder's syndrome. You will be the judge as to its relevance as a learning tool and as an instructive tool for teaching.

We welcome your feedback and inquiries, and you will find our contact information in the summary section, *About the Authors*.

Acknowledgments

The idea for this book has its early roots in the summer of 2002 when Steve Rosenberg and I (SRB) took the subject of founder's syndrome from anecdotal stories into the realm of empirical research. Steve's valued research expertise led to our first peer-reviewed article on founder's syndrome that has been read by more than 20,000 faculty, students, and practitioners and still receives 100 reads per month. I (SRB) am grateful for Steve's friendship and his never-ending support for this book.

Because of the nature of their company problems, we cannot mention by name the nonprofit and for-profit organizations that have called over the years wanting to discuss their founder's syndrome issues and requests for organization development consultation. But their need and willingness to expose their problems provided an unconventional education that deepened our understanding of founder's syndrome that was so vital for writing this book.

From the first contact with Brianna Ascher, we were confident that Routledge was the best choice for publishing this book. Their Editorial Board's insights and constructive ideas were helpful to our objective of creating a book that would be an important and useful tool for the processes of teaching and learning. Furthermore, throughout the writing of the chapters and the preparation at the final stages of the manuscript, the support and input provided by Brianna and by Naomi Round Cahalin were invaluable. We also acknowledge the kind manner in which Helen Evans kept us on track during the production stages, and the copy editing task provided by Neha Shrivastava.

We would also like to extend our appreciation to our colleagues whose feedback provided a meaningful way forward: Judith L. Millesen, College of Charleston; Mary Tschirhart, The George Washington University; and Thomas Duening, University of Colorado-Colorado Springs. In addition, we thank Mia Solberg, a senior at Colorado College for her invaluable work as a research assistant on this project. We would also like to thank the peer reviewers who offered their time and comments.

We also owe our gratitude to many students who took our courses that are referred to in this book. Their questions, comments, stories, and insight were an inspiration for teaching and writing this book.

I (SRB) want to thank my wife, April, for her unwavering encouragement and her comments on my work. I should add that I am also grateful for April's patience and tolerance for my excuses for what I did not get done during the period of writing.

Finally, I (KMS) want to thank my husband and parents for their support and words of encouragement on this project, along with my children who motivated me with their hugs and smiles.

About the Authors

Stephen R. Block, PhD, was a Research Professor and Director of the Nonprofit Management Concentration at the University of Colorado-Denver's School of Public Affairs for 25 years. He has authored seven books and many peer-reviewed journal articles, book chapters, and professional encyclopedia entries. Stephen is a Fulbright Scholar and frequent guest lecturer throughout Europe and the USA, and expert consultant on human behavior and organization management in both the private and public sectors. He has helped launch several organizations and programs and has more than 22 years of experience as CEO of three important human service organizations. He started his career as a social worker in Newcastle-Upon-Tyne, UK, and was Chief of Social Work in Adult Psychiatry, Indiana University Medical Center. Stephen welcomes correspondence at Stephblock@aol.com.

Katrina Miller-Stevens, PhD, is an Associate Professor at Colorado College in the Department of Economics and Business where she has also served as the Faculty Director of three programs including the Public Interest Fellowship Program, Nonprofit Initiatives, and State of the Rockies Project. Previously, Katrina was a faculty member at Old Dominion University's School of Public Service. She is the co-editor and contributing author of *Advancing Collaboration Theory: Models, Typology & Evidence*, also published by Routledge. She has authored numerous journal articles and book chapters in the areas of individual motivations to participate in the nonprofit sector, typologies and frameworks of collaboration, and strategies of nonprofit lobbying and advocacy. Prior to her academic career, Katrina worked in the nonprofit sector for 10 years as a budget coordinator, grants manager, and program evaluator. Katrina welcomes correspondence at kmillerstevens@coloradocollege.edu.

1 Starting an Organization: The Underlying Basis of Founder's Syndrome

Chapter Objectives

When you finish studying this chapter, you should be able to:

- Define the term Founder's Syndrome
- Discuss sociological or psychological concepts that help to explain founder's syndrome
- Discuss how historical changes in management philosophy have contributed to the construct of founder's syndrome
- Explain individual motivations to establish a company
- Identify the different stages of founder's syndrome
- Discuss some of the 16 sociological or psychological concepts that help to explain founder's syndrome

Introduction

The inherent challenge in communicating about any complex subject is to reach a common understanding of the relevant concepts that are used for the purpose of explanation, teaching, learning, or engaging in a dialogue. We embark on our challenging exploration of the subject of founder's syndrome by conveying our understanding of the key concepts associated with this topic and ask each reader to examine the subject and concepts through the same lens.

Most descriptions of founder's syndrome generally start and end with a narrative about the founder's use of abusive power and control. Indeed, power and control are important to understanding the founder's syndrome. However, the exercise of power and control can be personality driven or understood as a relational construct triggering a cause and effect reaction. To fully appreciate how power and control work with founder's syndrome, we need to first comprehend the role, character, and intrinsic motivators of the founder or the organizational stakeholders. As we will explore in Chapter 3, founder's syndrome also requires an encounter by stakeholders that the founder interprets as threatening his or her sense of ownership.

There might be other descriptors used about the founder such as being heavy-handed, a micro-manager, and a self-centered narcissist. This is also where the narrators often find it appropriate to insert a quote from Machiavelli to inform their audience that some founders have evil intentions. If we were to follow with this familiar interpretation, we would be defining founder's syndrome as the reaction of organizational leaders to rid the organization's founder who has blundered, mismanaged, and ill-treated his or her staff who also lost confidence and respect in their founding CEO.

We believe that describing and defining founder's syndrome from this vantage point has been the most common and simplistic approach taken for explanations found online or passed along as anecdotal tales. However, such explanations and definitions do not begin to scratch the surface of the meaning and condition of founder's syndrome. Although we will not take that easy and, perhaps, expected route, we will take some liberties in the conveyance of our ideas and definitional distinctions of founders and founder's syndrome that are presented as a gestalt; our intellectual argument with many parts that are necessary to fully examine the etiology, theory, and processes of founder's syndrome. These parts include several social and psychological concepts that help us gain that essential insight and they include the following:

1. Belongingness
2. Competence
3. Entrepreneurialism
4. Effectance motivation/psychological reactance
5. Internalization
6. Language
7. Management
8. Ownership/psychological ownership
9. Persistence
10. Privilege
11. Resistance
12. Self-efficacy
13. Social identity
14. Stewardship
15. Syndrome
16. Territoriality

After familiarizing ourselves with these foundational concepts, we will be able to discuss the issues of power and control in Chapter 2.

The Founder

It all starts with an individual who has a vision of a type of organization that he or she wishes to create and manage. This individual has taken the additional step of filing Articles of Incorporation to the appropriate state government agency and paying the application fees to create a legal organizational entity and declaring it as either a nonprofit or for profit corporation. Founders take these steps to create their organization that aside from being legally recognized is no more than a construct of the founder's mind. Organizations are after all based on ideas and concepts but do not exist in tangible formats. Organizations cannot be seen or touched because they do not have physical properties. They exist representatively in written form as having a purpose and can succeed by attracting competent individuals who agree with the founder's intentions. The organization may be initially housed in someone's basement, a church, an office, or a stand-alone building. Its physical home is not the organization; it is merely a place that is used for conducting business. Should the founder and/or board choose a different geographical location, the vacated space will remain and could become available for use by a different organization.

Although our interest is in corporate organizations that assemble individuals to take on the purpose of a nonprofit mission or the development of a service or product that is intended to generate profits for its owners, we do acknowledge the existence of other organizational types not constructed for corporate purposes that have founders. For example, some founders have created organizations for the purpose of being a neighborhood book club, or social groups to play softball or volleyball. Some founders have created organizations to bring people together to go on hikes, morning walks, bicycles, or runs. Some individuals gather at someone's home, a restaurant, or a coffee shop to discuss politics or other current events. In each instance, these organizations share commonalities with most other organizations. The participants, for example, know when to meet, where to meet, and how long they are likely to assemble. Additionally, they may have established rules of conduct, collect membership dues, or have instructions on how outsiders can join their organization. Each of these groups depend on the participation of individuals and were founded by someone with a decided vision. These types of organizations are excluded from our investigation of organizational founders.

For this book, we are only interested in founders who have taken the step to create a legal corporate entity. Once created, they are required to adhere to government rules and regulations in addition to any self-imposed bylaws or rules outlined in their governing documents. Once incorporated, the incorporators must follow their State's laws that regulate corporate governance and shareholder rights. Although the Articles of Incorporation are public, a company's bylaws are internal documents. However, a newly formed corporation may not commence their activities without first creating corporate bylaws and affirming who will serve as the initial board of directors, often at the invitation of the founder.

Definition: Syndrome

The use of the word syndrome in the context of describing a founder has a pejorative intent. Almost all medical dictionaries share a common definition for the word 'syndrome.' The general meaning is a display of symptoms that help to define a certain condition or associated symptoms that are common enough to describe a disease. However, founder's syndrome is not a medical anomaly. Whoever first coined the term 'founder's syndrome' was clever to borrow the medical term that conveys the seriousness of ill behaviors and applies it to the behaviors that have an adverse impact on organizations. Applying the word 'syndrome' provides another part of the definitional puzzle, that is, the conditions that are problematic to the organization's health that can or has negatively impacted the culture of the organization.

The group of symptoms that comprise the syndrome can include staff morale problems, higher levels of staff turnover, loss of funding, board member conflict, drop in stock price, and unwelcomed media attention inimical to the interests of the organization. The most common traits of a founder who is responsible for founder's syndrome, whether real or perceived, includes actions that are cunning, deceitful, authoritarian, secretive, underhanded, devious, opportunist, unscrupulous, and amoral.

Most writings about founder's syndrome are based on anecdotal evidence and almost always attributed to the behaviors of one person, the founder. Interestingly, one commonality shared in cases of founder's syndrome is that the founder is initially honored for his or her leadership and his or her vision and commitment to society. They may be considered community heroes who deserve special recognition because they have demonstrated a remarkable feat to translate their visionary ideas into an organizational reality that can address a societal issue with a nonprofit organization or create a for-profit company that fulfills the needs of consumers and creates jobs in the community. Accolades are warranted, but they are time limited.

Some founders are criticized because of their leadership style and propensity to use their position of privilege to influence the course of direction of board decisions or the work of management and line staff. According to BoardSource (2016), the term founder's syndrome is a term used to describe a founder's resistance to change. They also maintain that founder's syndrome evidences the founder's 'misunderstanding' of his or her role (McLaughlin & Backlund, 2008). We do not readily accept the notion that the cause of founder's syndrome is the founder's resistance to change because the notion of resistance to change is such a widespread phenomenon. Kotter and Schlesinger's (1979) Harvard Business Review impactful article stated,

> all people who are affected by change experience some emotional turmoil. Even changes that appear to be 'positive' or 'rational' involve loss and uncertainty. Nevertheless, for a number of different reasons, individuals or groups can react very differently to change—from passively resisting it, to aggressively trying to undermine it, to sincerely embracing it. (p. 3)

Kotter and Schlesinger's (1979) Harvard Business Review article proposed four reasons for resistance to change in organizations, which are as follows:

1. Parochial Self-Interest: People focus on their own interests that conflict with proposed changes.
2. Misunderstanding and Lack of Trust: This occurs when staff are unaware of the implications for change or simply do not trust the initiator of the change.
3. Different Assessments: Here, staff assess the need for change differently from the initiator.
4. Low Tolerance for Change: People have fears; they will not have the skills necessary to perform their work following an organizational change.

The founder may dismiss ideas for organizational change that is put forward by the board or department directors because the ideas are not consistent with the founder's vision. Muriithi and Wachira (2016) similarly assert,

> The main reasons associated with resistance of both internal and external forces are the fact that the organizations are seen as vehicles to fulfilling the founders' dreams. To this end, the founders invest too much time and effort, in terms of time, energy and resources to make their dreams become reality. (p. 3)

In our opinion, it is more likely that the board, department directors, and other managers are resistive to changes because of the founder's exercise of his or her assumed privileges to make unilateral decisions that represent his or her preferences for organizational direction and planned change. The late management guru, Peter Drucker (2006) claimed that organizational resistance was a result of key staff's limited tolerance for change even when they intellectually are aware that it would be beneficial for the organization.

We are also hesitant to accept the notion that when founder's syndrome surfaces, it is a result of the founder's misunderstanding of his or her role. If the founder is indeed the major contributor to founder's syndrome, it is more likely a result of not having an appropriate level of management knowledge and skills. Although some may find the founder's influential or brash behaviors distasteful, it should not come as a surprise because it is motivated by predictable human behavior. It is normal for founders to want to control the destiny of the organization they created. Given their emotional energy and often financial investment, founders start an organization with an aim to accomplish some specific mission, and they have a personal stake to accomplish their organizational goals and vision.

Founder's syndrome is a transformational process that starts from a neutral state when an organization is in the idea phase. After the organization is launched, there are several dynamics that can take place as a result of the founder's personality and extent of management skills, in addition to the internal forces and influential ideas of other key management staff or board members. As the organization evolves with the stressors and pressures on the founder from numerous internal and external forces, it is possible that the founder finds himself or herself incapable of processing all of the input and reacts or overreacts in a way that appears illogical or irrational. The troublesome behavior can be obstructive and inappropriate in the way the founder speaks to the staff, his or her department directors, or even board members. At that point, it could be concluded that founder's syndrome reared its proverbial ugly head. If it gets to that point, the organization will be under siege for control by the founder versus organizational stakeholders, such as the board of directors, department directors, and other key managers. Given these conditions, we prefer to apply Block and Rosenberg's (2002) definition of founder's syndrome as a reaction to the "influential powers and privileges that the founder exercises or that others attribute to the founder" (p. 354).

In the previous sentence, it is important to underscore the word 'attribute.' This is because the characterization and allegations of the founder's power and privileged behavior may be real or perceived. What is more, the assertions about the founder's behavior may be concocted to satisfy some other party's nefarious agenda to take over the role of CEO. Indeed, we have uncovered a few organizations in which one or more board members or senior staff engaged in their own Machiavellian-like behaviors with unscrupulous intentions to sabotage the standing of a founder with the intent to assume the role of CEO or pull strings for their preferred applicant for the CEO position.

Why Become a Founder?

Initially, we wondered why an individual would want to be a founder and what sets an individual apart from others who are not founders.

After all, when we analyze an organization, we find this one person or occasionally a small group who started the company versus the larger number of employees and/or volunteers who inhabit the entity. Why do some individuals strive to start their own organization? We learn that a founder is not satisfied just being a 'boss.' He or she has a motivational drive to create their own organization.

To aid in understanding the concept of organizational founders, we offered graduate courses on starting and launching corporations. We asked the students who were all potential organizational founders why they enrolled in the course. Some students explained that they had unpleasant work experiences and thought learning how to start their own company would give them the knowledge and skills to be in charge. Being in charge meant they would have a happier work-life experience. Some students expressed naivety in believing that starting their own company would provide them with long term if not a lifetime of workplace security. Their goal was to have an executive-level position without having to search, apply, and compete for a job. These students were almost always alarmed to learn that founders can be fired by their boards of directors. Students familiar with the idea of needing a governing or advisory board of directors mainly proposed stacking the board with friends and relatives who would support their ideas. Students were reluctant to conceptualize a governing board comprised of experts rather than friends and relatives. Prior to the discussion, the concept of self-aggrandizement, conflict of interest, or ethical decision-making had been predominantly absent from their organizational vocabulary.

Students who were interested in starting nonprofit organizations had similar security-in-work reasoning, although several were guided by a life experience that captured their imagination to be a community problem-solver. For example, some students had a family member who was either cured of an illness or died from one. The student was motivated to start an organization to support research or treatment of the disease. Some students described a religious experience that inspired them to be more community minded. Other students were motivated by ideological reasons, such as concerns about climate change, conservation, and animal rights. Although their motivations to start organizations seemed authentic, the students' underlying incentives were also based on tangible and psychological benefits they would each derive from starting an organizational entity. Gul and Beysenova (2019) describe the behavior as an "entrepreneurship tendency" and "a self-motivation of persons to employ themselves" (p. 3).

Some students described their interest in launching their own organization as part of the American Dream. They were guided by their interest in the creation of wealth, such as the founders of Microsoft, Apple, and Amazon. The students assumed that starting their own company would bring them closer to that goal, although they had not contemplated the challenges in parting with their own money and finding investors who would want some ownership in exchange for providing a loan or investment capital. Almost all the students were of the belief that they would experience greater advantages in founding a company than seeking employment. These potential founders were focused on acquiring some known or unknown rewards without fully comprehending the risks, sacrifices, and personal hardship that they might encounter to reach their goals.

Most students were surprised when asked how they were going to raise money to launch their organization. They had given little if any thought to the need for funds to seed their new organization and assumed they would get help from family and friends or get a loan from a bank or the Small Business Administration. Many students interested in starting nonprofit organizations thought they could simply write proposals to foundations. Although we are pointing out some of the unrealistic expectations for funding a company, we do so with no critical intent. We were not surprised and held no expectations that students would come to the course with existing experience or knowledge of the ins-and-outs of starting a company. After all, one of the main objectives of the course is to help students fill in the gaps of knowledge on the functional aspects of going from an organizational idea to the legal steps of incorporation and to the developmental stages from locating a physical location for their organizational activities to developing a business plan and the acquisition of resources with the many steps in-between.

When we discussed competition in the external environment, we would point out the likelihood of existing organizations already accomplishing similar missions. We questioned the viability of launching an organization that would provide duplicative services. This reality had no bearing on their goal to form their own organization. Instead of foregoing their vision, they insisted that they would come up with a niche to distinguish their organization from other existing entities. In some cases, the students contended that they need not worry because they were confident that their organization would do a better job than their competitors. Additionally, they were not swayed from the notion that adding another organization into the marketplace would make it more difficult to raise funds from a finite number of funders in the community. Because the primary focus for starting an organization is almost always to benefit the founder, the discussions about barriers to success did not alter the students' mindset. With the warnings and information in hand, the prospective founders believed they would not be caught off-guard by any impediments and unexpected obstacles that could hinder their creating an organization.

Persistence and Ownership

The strength and enthusiasm in which the want-to-be founders persevered to create their organization is a behavioral indicator of persistence.

The fact that the students were only in the idea planning stages, yet resolute in some of the organizational details, is an excellent example of the contingency effect of psychological ownership. Although it may seem obvious, psychological ownership is a cognitive-affect state in which an individual feels possessive of his or her target – in this case, the organization. In their 2015 study, Cardon and Kirk found that passion and goal-directed energy mediated the relationship between self-efficacy and persistence. We interpret their finding to mean that the degree of passion the founder has for their organization will determine how strident the founder will be to protect his or her organization from individuals trying to separate him/her from it. Bao, Zhou, and Chen (2017) used the term 'entrepreneurial passion' to include "intense positive feelings originating from engagement in entrepreneurial activities and the centrality of these activities for entrepreneurs' self-identity" (p. 1211). Entrepreneurial passion is illustrative of how a founder's identity is tied to their organization and triggers goal-directed and possessive behaviors, and we add especially when embroiled in founder's syndrome.

Management and Entrepreneurialism

Clearly having an idea for a for-profit or nonprofit business and even filing articles of incorporation are the easiest steps in the launching of an organization. We cannot stress enough that being entrepreneurial by starting a company and then managing the company require two different skill sets. Even if a new founder can overcome the financial issues that are typical barriers for a startup, the key to their success will be whether they have the management know-how to actualize their vision.

In addition to the importance of management and management sciences to the success of organizations, we include it because the history of management informs us of the etiology of founder's syndrome. The evolution of management as a field of study and research has been responsible for how we expect organizations to operate and that includes the sensitive treatment of employees. This mid-twentieth century turning point altered the practice of human resource management that monitored the legal protections put into place to ensure employees are treated fairly. Additional protections and benefits are often provided to workers in unionized settings. Over the years, public policy changes have increased guarantees of pay through minimum wages. Corporations seeking qualified candidates have added an array of benefits beyond paid sick leave and vacation pay for full-time employees. With all of these changes, today's employees are less tolerable of being treated harshly and expect to have more of a say in the strategic direction of the company. Anything less may result in employees feeling as though they are being ill-treated. With their viewpoint that the workplace milieu starts from the organization's top leader, it is easy to see how founder's syndrome can be pinned to the CEO.

Although management or managing people has been practiced by individuals for centuries, it only became a field of study in the nineteenth century. The École Supérieure de Commerce de Paris has the distinction of being the first business school in 1819. In the United States, the first collegiate business school was founded in 1881 by Joseph Wharton through his generous gift to the University of Pennsylvania. An academic discipline of management has allowed faculty to engage in research and develop sophisticated theories to improve the way organizations are managed.

In fact, several scholars have contributed to the modern practice of management science that has evolved over a hundred years. Toward the end of the nineteenth century, sociologist Max Weber (1947) approached the practice of management emphasizing structure and bureaucracy with leadership principles based on an authoritarian philosophy. In the 1880s, Taylor (1911) advanced his theory of scientific management that also relied on the structure to achieve efficiency. Taylor determined what a factory worker should be able to produce in a day and supervisors monitored to achieve the outcome. Without giving the workers a daily target for them to achieve to keep their job, Taylor was of the opinion the workers would resort to laziness. One of the early books on management was *Administration Industrielle et Générale* written in the French language by Fayol (1917). Fayol presented 14 principles to follow for successful management including the concept of division of labor. In keeping with the scientific management philosophy of the period, Fayol believed the first priority should be the organization and not the employees. In the United States, Gulick and Urwick (1937) advanced a similar list that became especially popular in the early academic study of public administration. His eight-letter acronym POSDCORB stands for Planning, Organizing, Staffing, Directing, Co-ordinating, Reporting, and Budgeting. If the earlier scientific management theories that promoted structure, harsh rules, and domineering managers remained the norm of organizational life, there would be no phenomenon as founder's syndrome. Instead, we would all be complacent workers accustomed to harsher working conditions and a top-down management approach with a philosophy that endorses the idea that if you do not like your work or work environment, then quit.

The idea of a CEO demonstrating more care, concern, and inclusive management input is a result of researchers Elton Mayo and Fritz Roethlisberger of the Harvard Business School who conducted scientific management productivity studies at the Hawthorne plant of the Western Electric Company in Chicago. The researchers purposefully altered the working environment to determine how it would impact worker outcomes and productivity. What they discovered was a surprise. The employees who were subjected to the altered work environment were of the belief that the researchers were sent by management to determine how to be helpful to the employees. Consequently, the changes to the physical environment did not adversely impact the employees. Their productivity improved because the employees were satisfied based on their (incorrect) belief that their employer was attempting to improve their working conditions.

Mayo's (1933) findings are credited with leading to an understanding of the psyche of workers and humanistic management approaches. As an ideology, humanistic management takes into consideration that workers are human beings with multifaceted social and personal needs and their feelings matter. The implementation of this style of management requires managers who are compassionate and capable of providing a style of situational leadership that is consistent with the needs of the employees (Hersey, Blanchard, & Johnson, 2012). In addition to Mayo, there were other prominent scholars who contributed to humanistic management. An early theorist and social worker, Mary Parker Follett (2013; Metcalf & Urwick, 1942) was one of the first management scholars who wrote about the importance of management and staff working cooperatively. The pursuits of psychologist Abraham Maslow's (1943, 1954) well-known Hierarchy of Needs, and Chester Bernard's (1938) ideas of supervisors' respecting employees and the importance of organizations operating as cooperative systems were also integral to the development of humanistic management approaches (Herzberg, Mausner, & Snyderman, 1959; Likert, 1961, 1967; McGregor, 1960).

In 1947, Herbert Simon, who three decades later would become a Nobel Laureate, was critical of scientific management principles as nothing more than 'myths' and 'proverbs.' In his assessment of scientific management, he observed that decision-makers were not completely rational and were more likely to accept a decision that was satisfactory but not necessarily the best decision, which could be reached if more time and effort were devoted to the decision-making process. Of particular importance, Simon (1947) equated decision-making and management as synonymous.

Humanistic management introduced a more positive approach to the treatment of staff. Consequently, as humanistic management became the preferred management approach, the mindset of employees shifted. Instead of being treated as human cogs who were replaceable if they could not keep up with the demands ordered by their supervisors, organizational staff have become acculturated to a management philosophy that claims employees are the most important asset to a company's success. Workers have learned to expect to be treated fairly, to become part of the decision-making process, and give input to the strategic direction of the company.

A founding CEO that is unschooled in management is less likely to follow a theoretical framework about best decision-making practices. This same CEO may set a tone that is not consistent with the employee's expectations of how they should be treated in today's modern organization. The result may lead to charges of founder's syndrome.

However, if the founding CEO knew how to practice humanistic management and was open to explore staff's various ideas that could lead to better decisions, it is unlikely that founder's syndrome would emerge in his or her organization.

It is difficult to predict who among new organizational founders will be successful in integrating a humanistic management philosophy to their day-to-day management operations. Although we can instruct individuals in the finer points of entrepreneurship and starting a company and explain the differences between traditional scientific management versus humanistic management, what is truly needed is skill acquisition. Translating knowledge into practical skills can be attained through a mentorship, apprenticeship, or an educational practicum for experiential learning and appropriate supervision to ensure certain lessons are learned. Second best to actual field-based learning would be using a case study methodology. Case studies can be used to help students apply practical knowledge and theory.

Arpat, Yesil, and Kocaalan (2019) have been promoting entrepreneurship courses in Turkey to generate new business enterprises and encountered barriers. They state,

> The fact that students are unable to carry out practical activities throughout the entrepreneurship courses prevents them from observing the mistakes/deficiencies in the business ideas that they design. As such, even when a student takes action after graduation, s/he may not turn out to be successful because of lack of experience. (p. 157)

Cao and Zhou (2018) have also been researching the education of entrepreneurship in China and reached similar conclusions:

> At present, there are many drawbacks and limitations in the development of innovation and entrepreneurship education in colleges and universities. There is relatively large amount of theoretical teaching while small amount of practical operation, which is not conducive to the improvement of the quality of innovation and entrepreneurship education in colleges and universities and the cultivation of innovative and entrepreneurial talents. (p. 1613)

In his article on organization development and talent management, Church (2013) studied the level of engagement of highly capable employees whose talent can help an organization become successful. He refers to those employees as 'high potentials,' and made three astute observations that have applicability for our topic of founder's syndrome:

> One, for high potentials the quality of the management running the company was far and away the most important predictor of engagement,

followed by their belief in their own career and their pride for the organization. (p. 45)

Two, as management heads in the wrong direction and/or the high potentials lose faith they are more likely to be disengaged and/or leave the organization for greener pastures. (p. 46)

Three, if the company is indeed poorly managed there is not much that can be done short of changing leaders to impact the overall level of engagement of high potentials. (p. 46)

Ownership and Language

Consistent with the findings of Brown, Lawrence, and Robinson (2005) and Pierce, Kostova, and Dirks (2001), we found that it did not take long for students to think like soon-to-be founders as exhibited by their use of possessive language of ownership, and interrelated their self-identity when discussing their proposed organization. The ownership concept that extends to possessiveness is a key distinguishing variable among founders versus non-founders. The longer in years a founder directs their organization, the deeper will become their possessive feelings.

During founder's syndrome, when a founder struggles to retain his or her ownership coupled with the duration they have been CEO of the organization, the greater will be the degree he or she will feel wronged. When engaged in a founder's syndrome struggle with the board and/or key managers and department directors, it is the founder who feels victimized, mistreated, and experiences the absence of support as a personal betrayal. The founder especially feels injured by the managers and department directors that he or she hired and by the board members that were hand-picked. Goodenough (1997) expounds on the idea of moral outrage as "an emotional response to what other people do, not to what we do ourselves" (p. 1).

Many founders demonstrate their strong sense of psychological ownership with language, and they describe their organization as their 'baby' or use similar nurturing language. This is exactly the language used when the founder's struggle to hold on to their organization, and it is not dissimilar to the emotional feelings individuals experience and express when going through a marital divorce or an ending to a re-lationship. Zhu, Hsu, Burmeister-Lamp, Heine, and Fan (2018) state, "the stronger the possessive feelings, the stronger the sense of belonging, and the stronger are the individual's emotional attachment to the own-ership target" (p. 141).

During the 1930s, a hypothesis about language and identity was ad-vanced, known as linguistic relativity or the Whorfian hypothesis. There has been some skepticism about its validity because of lack of scientific proof, although research experiments continue searching for answers. Nevertheless, it should hold some academic interest and especially for our topic of founder's syndrome. The idea is that language shapes how one thinks and influences decisions. Consequently, should a founder be accused of engaging in founder's syndrome, the founder would internally associate the words and how he or she perceives the organizational environment around him or her. The founder's response to his or her understanding of language would result from cognition. To observers, the founder's response reflects his or her identity. The same holds true for the employee who interprets the meaning of the directives and feedback provided by the founder. In the 1930s, Korzybski (1995/1933) developed his theory of general semantics, which is based on the idea that individuals are limited by their nervous system and language. He wrote, "we read unconsciously into the world the structure of the language we use" (p. 60).

Psychological Ownership and Territoriality

Although Pierce et al. (2001) believe that psychological ownership is a cognitive-affective construct, Avey, Avolio, Crossley, and Luthans (2009) observed a behavioral relationship between territoriality and the strength of psychological ownership. Founder actions that are territorial stem from an attempt to prevent infringement by stakeholders. They state,

> Territoriality leads people to become too preoccupied with 'objects of ownership,' at the expense of their performance or other pro-social behaviors. Furthermore, the fear of losing one's territory and associated self and social identity may promote politicking and prohibit transparency, collaboration, and information sharing. (p. 176)

These potentially negative outcomes identified by Avey et al. (2009) share uncanny similarity with the type of complaints about founders exhibiting founder's syndrome. The complaints include the founder not sharing an array of strategic information, micromanagement and the absence of collaboration, and game-playing by testing staff loyalty. Another way of looking at the complaints is to recognize that the founder is being territorial and the sharing of information or allowing collaboration is a 'lessening of self' (Belk, 1988, p. 142). Staff and board members are merely the founder's organizational guests.

In their study, Kirk, Peck, and Swain (2018) clarify the two concepts of psychological ownership and territoriality. They state, "Whereas psychological ownership refers to feelings of possession of a target, territoriality refers to behaviors, often motivated by psychological ownership" (p. 150). Henkin, Dee, and Vineburgh (2010) offer the following definition, "territoriality as an organizational construct, examines how people negotiate issues of space, ownership, identity, and power" (p. 53).

Although the founder's behavior can be explained by psychological ownership and territoriality, it is possible that department directors, other managers, and board members may also express through communication and behavior similar characteristics of ownership and territoriality. This would especially be a reasonable response for those individuals who were associated with the organization at its earliest inception. After all, getting up in the mornings to spend the day at a worksite or visiting to volunteer weekly or monthly as board members over a period of years creates a feeling of personal association and psychological ownership. Any threat or belief of the potential loss of that relationship may create a territorial battle reflected in words, lawsuits, or firing. The winner of the battle is the person or persons who control the organizational territory. Kirk et al. (2018) refer to control as an "important form of marking" territory (p. 50).

In Mayhew et al.'s (2007) study on psychological ownership, they report that,

> Researchers have identified two distinct types of psychological ownership. Organization-based psychological ownership is concerned with individual members' feelings of possession and psychological connection to an organization as a whole. Several characteristics may influence this state, including organizational culture and climate, attitudes of senior management, corporate goals and vision, reputation of the organization, and corporate policies and procedures. (p. 477)

The constructs of psychological ownership and territoriality provide us with another viewpoint in our understanding of a founder's behavior and reaction when he or she believes that some members of the organization are infringing on his or her territory. Once engaged in reactionary behavior, it is predictable and comprehensible that founder's syndrome behavior will become evident.

Effectance Motivation

One of the characteristics that we observed in the students enrolled in the course on launching corporations has also been observed to exist among many founders, that is, effectance motivation. White (1959) introduced the concept of effectance motivation to describe how personal competence motivates oneself to enhance one's abilities. Instead of being driven to succeed by an internal or external motivator, the motivational drive stems from an accomplishment that was very challenging, such as launching a new organization. In the case of the students, we observed in them a significant sense of achievement to continue after they accomplished the assignment of filing articles of incorporation. They actually created their organizational entity and secured a document issued by the Secretary of State that indicates their organization is in good standing with the State of Colorado.

Self-Efficacy and Internalization

Social cognitive theorist, Bandura (1997), has similarly described his social-learning approach as observational learning or self-efficacy. The high degree of enthusiasm exhibited by the students can be described as displaying competence or confidence based on the social reinforcement and reciprocal experiences in the classroom from the positive reactions of students hearing about the successes of establishing corporations. Although students may not have had prior experience with starting and launching a corporation, they have internalized their enrollment in the course and filing of articles of incorporation as a major step toward their success as an organizational founder. Their belief in their own abilities coupled with the instructor's review of the course objectives that align with their learning needs, enhance the student's belief that they will learn the ins and outs of being a founder and what competencies are necessary to achieve organizational success. Albert, Ashford, and Dutton (2000) would suggest that by internalizing organizational identity, individuals gain meaningfulness or psychological ownership.

Building on Bandura's form of self-efficacy and social learning theory, each semester the course is given there are some former students invited to attend as guests to "show & tell" where they are in the process of their own organization. The objective in bringing in the former students is aimed as demonstrating that it is possible to gain some mastery from the course and overcome obstacles that could get in the way of becoming an organizational founder. Although we are realistic that the course will not prevent the fledgling founders from a future foray into founder's syndrome, we would anticipate that by building on their self-efficacy experiences, it may help them make sound organizational development choices that would lessen their exposure to founder's syndrome behaviors.

Psychological Reactance

There are situations beyond the control of a founder that may leave the founder feeling threatened. For example, in a situation where one or more persons are collaborating or conspiring to find a way to get rid of the founding CEO, psychological reactance can come into play. According to Nail, Van Leeuwen, and Powell (1996), when an individual's behavioral freedom is threatened, he or she will experience an aversive motivational state toward reestablishing the threatened freedom. One way to restore a freedom is to move in a direction opposite to that advocated by the source of the threat. Support for this reactance theory prediction has been found in numerous studies demonstrating negative or boomerang attitude change in response to threatening communications. ... The idea here is that a threat to one's behavioral freedom really represents a threat to one's competence in dealing with the environment. Thus, when threatened, an individual will be motivated to reaffirm effective control. (pp. 573–574)

In the founder's attempt to gain effective control, there are different strategies or psychological reactance effects (Brehm, 1966; Dowd, Milne, & Wise, 1991). However, almost all the options open to the founder can be characterized as founder's syndrome behaviors. Among the actions include the retaliatory firing of the employees that are known to be involved in the planning. Another is to engage in aggressive behavior with legal threats toward the board members that are known to be engaged in planning efforts to terminate the CEO.

Stewardship and Empowerment

Stewardship and empowerment are two well-known relational constructs that focus on the accomplishment of organizational goals through shared responsibility and personal efficacy. The concept of stewardship assumes that the focus of organizational managers is on protecting their organization above self-interest. Empowerment is about management enabling staff to be self-reliant to take initiatives to solve problems and having authority to access resources and make independent decisions. Taken together, the organizational values would encourage autonomy, reinforce feelings of belonging, organizational connectedness, and commitment.

According to Block (2013, 2016), who authored two important organizational behavior books focused on empowerment and stewardship, most organizations do not achieve the ideals of stewardship or empowerment. Block (1996) writes, "Holding on to privilege is an act of self-interest, the antithesis of service and stewardship" (p. 47). The term privilege denotes a class structure within governance settings and self-interest refers to using one's power (through the exercise of privilege) to ascertain an objective that may not be in accord with other managers, board members, funders, and investors.

Block claims that most organizations are established as patriarchal and foster narrow self-interest. Similarly, Tjosvold and Sun (2006) refer to this viewpoint as a "fixed sum," where managers sabotage self-initiative efforts of staff to protect their own power (p. 219). Consequently, Block looks to the practice of Organizational Development (OD) to succeed over the organizational forces that promote caution, isolation, dependence, conformity, and lack of trust.

If founders have developed their organization with a fixed sum mentality and promote a patriarchal supervisory style, there is a greater likelihood that the founder will eventually face scorn and allegations of founder's syndrome. Depending on how long and deep-seated the negative behaviors exist, it may not be possible to save the CEO position held by the founder even with a successful OD intervention. Success may be limited to bringing about a change to the value system and other organizational culture norms and beliefs (Schein & Schein, 2016), but the founder will have either been forced to resign or fired.

Target and Belonging

Among their research findings, Avey et al. (2009) use the term 'target' as an object of attachment which is consistent with its use in the psychological ownership literature. If a target of attachment is the organization, then the founder will personally identify with the target. Additionally, the founder will experience a sense of belongingness toward the organizational target and will take responsibility to protect it. The founder will also hold others accountable for any behaviors intended to influence the target that do not meet his or her requirements or desires.

The concept of belongingness is essential to our understanding of founders and founder's syndrome. Although founders experience the sense of ownership and identity with the organization, paradoxically they need to distance themselves from the employees they supervise. From early research interviewing 1,000 executive directors of nonprofit organizations over a five-year period, Block (1998) discovered many who revealed a sense of loneliness in their role as CEO. The loneliness issue is a by-product of being the boss as a non-founder, and even a greater sense of alienation experienced by the founder in their role as boss. No matter how close one feels toward the individuals working in their organization, by necessity of being the CEO some personal detachment is required. One CEO remarked that,

> unless I am having a business lunch with one of my department directors, I don't go out with the directors who frequently will get together for lunch. They may even be getting together for social time after work hours. I must be careful since I supervise them, can fire them and I make decisions about their salary. I can't get emotionally attached to anyone in the event I have to downsize or fire them for some cause.

From another,

> My decisions have a direct bearing on their family's well-being.

Similarly, it is important to maintain professional relationships with board members because the Board has responsibility for the CEO's contract, salary, and bonuses. We assume the experienced board member has an impression of how a CEO should comport themselves when interacting with board members. Attempting to become chummy with a board member is not the norm. However, getting to know board members' interests, knowledge about their families and their employment may be key to understanding what motivates them to serve on the board. Once the motivational factors are known, the CEO should look for ways to meet the interests of the board members to maintain their motivation to serve on the board (Block, 1998; 2016).

Organizational Identification and Social Identity Theory

Ashforth and Mael (1989) start their article on Social Identity Theory (SIT) stating,

"Organizational identification has long been recognized as a critical construct in the literature on organizational behavior, affecting both the satisfaction of the individual and the effectiveness of the organization" (p. 20). The two researchers found that strong bonds emerge between individuals and their assigned workgroups. In many instances, the workgroups have a stronger social identity than an individual employee has with the organization. However, their findings would not apply to the founder whose sense of belonging is limited to the organizational entity but not bonded to any individual or subgroup.

If a subgroup member expresses his or her adverse opinion about the founder's decisions, attitudes, or behavior, it is likely that other subgroup members will support the member's opinions. This can be one way for negative comments to begin to circulate throughout the organization. Because subgroups are permeable, a member can transfer to another work group and bring the opinions of the former subgroup with him or her. This is another way of spreading criticism about the founder.

If the founder traces the injudicious rumors back to the staff member or the subgroup and singles them out with derisive comments and perhaps termination, it would be a warning to others that it is not safe to make imprudent remarks about the founder. If the staff member or subgroup are not fired, the milieu of the workplace will remain suppressed for some period. If the staff do not leave their positions, then they are likely to experience social identity threats (Branscombe et al., 1999; Holmes et al., 2016). Although they were singled out by the founder in retaliation for what was said, identity threat may also be experienced by other staff in the organization. The threat stems from fear of the founder and feeling vulnerable for what they may have said or thought in the past, even though they were not caught.

There are two avenues for resolving social identity threats that emanate from the founder. One way is to quit one's job. The other way is to undermine the founder with a significant number of staff complaints to the board of directors. If the board is receptive to addressing the complaints of no confidence as a response to founder's syndrome, the organization will be in turmoil for a while, but eventually will calm with new leadership. The risk to the staff is if the board does not intervene or the board delays in making a decision and the founder responds with mass firings.

First Stage of Founder's Syndrome

If we think of founder's syndrome as an evolutionary process, the first stage occurs when discussions and rumors emerge about the founder's character and competency. Given the most common top down management model, discontent with the founder can emerge at any age or life cycle of an organization. If department directors and other senior managers believe their ideas are considered and input appreciated and even applied, then there will be personal and organization-wide satisfaction and limited turnover. However, when senior staff make recommendations that are decidedly dismissed whether consistent with the direction of the founder or an outright rejection of novel ideas, discontent among senior staff is probable. Dissatisfaction is even more likely to happen depending on the tone and way the founder dismisses the ideas. If the founder does not have the skill to offer positive feedback for the generation of ideas intended to improve the organization, and the ideas are simply ignored or verbally rejected, then the staff person may feel belittled, disparaged, humiliated and will psychologically disengage. Psychological detachment is often the first step toward quitting.

Consequently, articulating negative feelings about the founder is almost always introduced by individuals who work closest to the founder such as disgruntled department directors or other senior managers. Comments made to one's peers with the expectation of confidentiality usually spawns more anti-founder sentiment. This is a result of subgroup cohesion. Occasionally, an offhanded comment made by a manager about a policy directive or new organizational objectives that were set by the founder without any input from department directors or other senior staff is enough to set in motion a grapevine of expressed discontent about the vision and behavior of the founder. Such rumors always find their way to one or more board members, especially to those board members serving on committees that are staffed by employees.

As discontent becomes more evident and spreads like an epidemic, the founder is left isolated with no supporters. In the meanwhile, subgroups of board members, managers or department directors have strong affiliations with their own group members which reinforces a division between them and the founder. Rumors, accurate or inaccurate information that goes unchecked in the subgroups will influence the opinions held by each subgroup member. Furthermore, when subgroup members are unanimous with their shared opinions, it reinforces the bond among its members and strengthens each members' self-confidence. Consequently, the psychological and social aspects of belongingness and social identity can drive a wedge between the alienated founder and the other inhabitants of the organization. Feeling isolated and with no organizational allies, the founder cannot fully trust anyone associated with the organization.

Every founder has his or her own idiosyncratic characteristics which colors their approach to management and leadership. Their approach can either be interpreted favorably by staff and management or met with disdain. For instance, management styles and expectations of founder-led organizations tend to be particularly more demanding than non-founder led organizations. In non-founder led organizations, board members and key staff may feel freer to express their ideological differences about direction and mission of the organization, because the CEO does not have the same deep personal investment that a founder has to a mission they created. The non-founder has less reason to feel offended since he or she did not create the organizational mission.

Predicting Founder's Syndrome

Given the fact that most employees engaged in organizational life have not been formally trained in decision-making sciences, change management theory, or problem resolution techniques, they are unlikely to know when the organization is in its earliest stages of founder's syndrome. Evidence or symbols of founder's syndrome might appear during verbal exchanges that occur in the boardroom or during management meetings. Detecting the early warning signs of founder's syndrome requires keen observation abilities and knowledge of organizational behavior and pragmatic communication (Watzlawick, Beavin Bavelas, & Jackson, 1967). For example, in some organizations, we can point to problematic communication styles and faulty decision-making models as fundamental elements contributing to unsatisfactory outcomes that will contribute to confusion and founder's syndrome. Another sign is when the outcome of management staff meetings always results in unanimous agreement with the founder's ideas and without any significant challenges, it is inevitable that feelings of discontent will emerge among some, if not all, department directors. The same applies to boards of directors that merely rubber-stamp the policy ideas of the CEO, especially without a substantive discussion.

Summary

Founders are risk takers with a high need to succeed after creating their organization. In some situations, a founder's behavior is characterized as overbearing and even heavy-handed. On the one hand, it is possible that the officious behavior is personality driven. On the other hand, the behavior may be the result of a founder who asserts and defends his or her ideology that prompted the founding of the organization.

It may also be the case that being a visionary does not equate to a knowledgeable and effective manager. When a board of directors, senior staff, or even outside funders begin to challenge the direction or decisions of the founder, some founders may feel threatened. Rather than explore the criticisms, a founder may become discouraged and try to defend his or her decisions and protect his or her territory. The receiver of the founder's communications may interpret the founder's language as a defensive response, characterizing it as self-centered, narcissistic, unreasonable, and an unwillingness to tolerate a participative organizational environment.

Board members and key staff may conclude that they have ideological differences from the founder about the direction and mission of the organization. In a safe environment, they would be comfortable in sharing their opinions. In an environment of founder's syndrome, they will alter their discourse and either say nothing or claim to share in the strategic ideas of the founder. The staff's or board members' behaviors of apathy and indecision are symptoms of organizational dysfunction. Eventually, these organizational players may internalize their actions as a lack of commitment and loyalty to the organization and react accordingly. A change in their disposition means challenging the founder. The challenge may exacerbate the founder's feelings of being threatened and cause more egregious language and behaviors aimed at the board of directors and department directors and any other individuals involved in activities that the founder believes to be an attempt to rid him or her of their CEO position. The resolution of this founder syndrome conundrum resides with those individuals in decision-making positions that hold influence. Whatever the outcome, the lesson learned is that organizational effectiveness or organizational dysfunction are by-products of human behavior in the for-profit or nonprofit corporation.

Discussion Questions

1. What is the definition of founder's syndrome? Explain the different stages of founder's syndrome.
2. How might a founder's identity with his or her company lead to symptoms of founder's syndrome?
3. Think about the management theories discussed in this chapter. Then, reflect on the definition of founder's syndrome. Which management

theories provide the best foundation for our understanding of founder's syndrome? Explain your answer.

4. In your opinion, which three of the 16 social or psychological concepts provided you with the greatest insight into examining founder's syndrome?
5. What historical events have contributed to changes in employee expectations of how they should be treated in the workplace? In your opinion, are such expectations limited to the labor force in the United States of America?
6. What motivates individuals to become organizational founders?
7. What is the meaning of the term 'syndrome' and why is it coupled with the word 'Founder's?'
8. It has been said that Founder's syndrome is the outcome of a transformational process. Explain.
9. Drawing on your own experiences, or the experiences of someone you know, or what you have read, why do you think the authors chose the following definition of founder's syndrome? *A reaction to the influential powers and privileges that the founder exercises or that others attribute to the founder.*
10. What do you think are the differences between an Entrepreneur and a Manager?
11. What does human behavior have to do with an organization's success, failure, or founder's syndrome?
12. Some CEOs claim that being in the organization's top job is alienating and lonely. Why?
13. Without naming names, can you think of someone (or yourself) who might have behavioral tendencies to engage in founder's syndrome if they were an organizational founder? Explain using some of the concepts from this chapter.

References

Albert, S., Ashford, B., & Dutton, J. (2000). Organizational identity and identification: Charting new waters and building new bridges. *Academy of Management Review, 25*(1), 13–17.

Arpat, B., Yesil, Y., & Kocaalan, M. L. (2019). A longitudinal study on the effect of entrepreneurship courses taught at the vocational colleges in Turkey on students' entrepreneurial tendency. *Eastern Journal of European Studies, 10*(2), 127–161.

Ashforth, B. E., & Mael, F. (1989). Social identity theory and the organization. *The Academy of Management Review, 14*(1), 20–39.

Avey, J. B., Avolio, B. J., Crossley, C. D., & Luthans, F. (2009). Psychological ownership: Theoretical extensions, measurement and relation to work outcomes. *Journal of Organizational Behavior, 30*(2), 173–191.

Bandura, A. (1997). *Self-efficacy: The exercise of control.* Worth Publishers.

Bao, J., Zhou, X., & Chen, Y. (2017). Entrepreneurial passion and behaviors: Opportunity recognition as a mediator. *Social Behavior and Personality*, *45*(7), 1211–1220. https://doi.org/10.2224/sbp.6492

Barnard, C. (1938). *The functions of the executive*. Harvard University Press.

Belk, R. W. (1988). Possessions and the extended self. *Journal of Consumer Research*, *15*(2), 139–168.

Block, P. (1996). *Stewardship: Choosing service over self-Interest* (1st ed.). Berrett-Koehler Publishing.

Block, P. (2013). *Stewardship: Choosing service over self-interest* (2nd ed.). Berrett-Koehler Publishers.

Block, P. (2016). *The empowered manager: Positive political skills at work* (2nd ed.). John Wiley & Sons.

Block, S. R. (1998). *Perfect nonprofit boards: Myths paradoxes & paradigms*. Simon & Schuster.

Block, S. R., & Rosenberg, S. (2002). Toward an understanding of founder's syndrome: An assessment of power and privilege among founders of nonprofit organizations. *Nonprofit Management & Leadership*, *12*(4), 353–368.

BoardSource (2016, June 21), Founder's syndrome. Retrieved March 2, 2020, from https://boardsource.org/resources/founders-syndrome/

Branscombe, N. R., Ellemers, N., Spears, R., & Doosje, B. (1999). The context and content of social identity threat. In N. Ellemers, R. Spears, & B. Doosje (Eds.), *Social identity: Context, commitment, content* (pp. 35–58). Blackwell Science.

Brehm, J. W. (1966). *A theory of psychological reactance*. Academic Press.

Brown, G., Lawrence, T. B., & Robinson, S. L. (2005). Territoriality in organizations. *Academy of Management Review*, *30*(3), 577–594.

Cao, Z., & Zhou, M. (2018). Research on the innovation and entrepreneurship education mode in colleges and universities based on entrepreneurial ecosystem theory. *Educational Sciences: Theory & Practice*, *18*(5), 1612–1619.

Church, A. H. (2013). Engagement is in the eye of the beholder: Understanding differences in the OD vs. talent management mindset. *OD Practitioner*, *45*(2), 42–48.

Dickson, W. J., & Roethlisberger, F. J. (1966). *Counseling in an organization: A sequel to the Hawthorne researches*. Harvard University Press.

Dowd, E. T., Milne, C. R., & Wise, S. L. (1991). The therapeutic reactance scale: A measure of psychological reactance. *Journal of Counseling & Development*, *69*(6), 541–545. https://doi.org/10.1002/j.1556-6676.1991.tb02638.x

Drucker, P. F. (2006). *The practice of management*. Harper and Row. (Original work published 1954.)

Fayol, H. (1917). *Administration industrielle et générale; prévoyance, organisation, commandement, coordination, controle*. H. Dunod et E. Pinat.

Follett, M. P. (2013). *Dynamic administration: The collected papers of Mary Parker Follett* (H. C. Metcalf & L. Urwick, Eds.). Martino Fine Books. (Original work published 1940.)

Goodenough, W. H. (1997). Moral outrage: Territoriality in human guise. *Zygon: Journal of Religion and Science*, *32*(1), 5–27.

Graham, P. (Ed.). (2003). *Mary Parker Follett prophet of management: A celebration of writings from the 1920's*. Beard Books.

Gul, H., & Beysenova, A. (2019). Evaluation of thesis on leadership properties in Turkey by content analysis. *Journal of Economics & Administrative Sciences, 20*(1), 438–446.

Gulick, L. H. (1937). Notes on the theory of organization. In L. H. Gulick and L. F. Urwick (Eds.), *Papers on the science of administration* (pp. 1–46). Institute of Public Administration.

Gulick, L. H., & Urwick, L. F. (Eds.). (1937). *Papers on the science of administration*. Institute of Public Administration.

Hagerty, B. M. K., Lynch-Sauer, J., Patusky, K. L., Bouwsema, M., & Collier, P. (1992). Sense of belonging: A vital mental health concept. *Archives of Psychiatric Nursing, 6*(3), 172–177.

Henkin, A. B., Dee, J. R., & Vineburgh, J. H. (2010). Territoriality: Defining the construct in the organizational context of schools. *Educational Research Quarterly, 33*(3), 52–75.

Hersey, P., Blanchard, K., & Johnson D. E. (2012). *Management of organizational behavior: Leading human resources* (10th ed.). Prentice Hall.

Herzberg, F., Mausner, B., & Snyderman, B. B. (1959). *The motivation to work.* John Wiley & Sons.

Holmes IV, O., Whitman, M. V., Campbell, K. S., & Johnson, D. E. (2016). Exploring the social identity threat response framework. *Equality, Diversity and Inclusion, 35*(3), 205–220. https://doi.org/10.1108/EDI-08-2015-0068

Kirk, C. P., Peck, J., & Swain, S. D. (2018). Property lines in the mind: Consumers' psychological ownership and their territorial responses. *Journal of Consumer Research, Inc., 45*(1), 148–168.

Korzybski, A. (1995). *Science & sanity: An introduction to non-Aristotelian systems and general semantics* (5th ed.). Institute of General Semantics. (Original work published 1933.)

Kotter, J. P., & Schlesinger, L. A. (1979, March). Choosing strategies for change. *Harvard Business Review, 57*(2), 106–114.

Likert, R. (1961) *New patterns of management.* McGraw-Hill.

Likert, R. (1967). *The human organization: Its management and value.* McGraw-Hill.

Maslow, A. H. (1943). A theory of human motivation. *Psychological Review, 50*(4), 370–396.

Maslow, A. H. (1954). *Motivation and personality.* Harper and Row.

Mayhew, M. G., Ashkanasy, N. M., Bramble, T., & Gardner, J. (2007). A study of the antecedents and consequences of psychological ownership in organizational settings. *The Journal of Social Psychology, 147*(5), 477–500.

Mayo, E. (1933). *The human problems of an industrial civilization.* The Macmillan Co.

McGregor, D. (1960). *The human side of enterprise.* McGraw Hill.

McLaughlin, T. A., & Backlund, A. N. (2008). *Moving beyond founder's syndrome to nonprofit success.* BoardSource.

Metcalf, H. C., & Urwick, L. (Eds.). (1942). *Dynamic administration: The collected papers of Mary Parker Follett.* Harper & Row.

Muriithi, S., & Wachira, D. (2016). The Founders' syndromes, challenges and solutions. *Journal of Entrepreneurship, 4*(4), 1–11.

Nail, P. R., Van Leeuwen, M. D., & Powell, A. B. (1996). The effectance versus the self-presentational view of reactance: Are importance ratings influenced by anticipated surveillance? *Journal of Social Behavior & Personality*, *11*(3), 573–584.

Pierce, J. L., Kostova, T., & Dirks, K. T. (2001). Towards a theory of psychological ownership in organizations. *Academy of Management Review*, *26*(2), 298–310.

Schein, E. H., & Schein, P. A. (2016). *Organizational culture and* leadership (5th ed.). John Wiley & Sons.

Simon, H. A. (1947). *Administrative behavior: A study of decision-making processes in administrative organization.* The MacMillan Co.

Taylor, F. W. (1911). *Scientific management.* Harper & Row.

Tjosvold, D., & Sun, H. (2006). Effects of power concepts and employee performance on managers' empowering. *Leadership & Organization Development Journal*, *27*(3), 217–234.

Watzlawick, P., Beavin Bavelas, J., & Jackson, D. D. (1967). *Pragmatics of human communication: A study of interactional patterns, pathologies, and paradoxes* (1st ed.). W. W. Norton & Co.

Weber, M. (1947). *The theory of social and economic organization* (A. M. Henderson & T. Parsons, Trans.). Collier Macmillan Publishers. (Original work published 1922.)

White, R. W. (1959). Motivation reconsidered: The concept of competence. *Psychological Review*, *66*(5), 297–333.

Zhu, F., Hsu, D. K., Burmeister-Lamp, K., Heine, H., & Fan, S. X. (2018). An investigation of entrepreneurs' venture persistence decision: The contingency effect of psychological ownership and adversity. *Applied Psychology: An International Review*, *67*(1), 136–170.

2 Power and Control

Chapter Objectives

When you finish studying this chapter, you should be able to:

- Discuss different types of power as they relate to founder's syndrome
- Understand why the founder's power and control may result in negative consequences for a company
- Discuss how employees and the board of directors might react to negative forms of power exerted by the founder
- Discuss the construct of power and control and its significance to founder's syndrome
- Identify French and Raven's five bases of power and Raven's sixth base
- Summarize why founder's syndrome would not exist without power
- Discuss McClelland's Achievement Motivation Theory

Introduction

We are curious why most anecdotal descriptions of founder's syndrome generally start and end with a narrative about the founder's use of abusive power and control. Could it be that most people view life in terms of a zero-sum game where there must be an equal number of losers to winners? The preferred power principle would be, 'I win, and you lose.' Or, could it be that although possessing power can be used for good purposes, society has mixed emotions about powerful people. In this same line of academic curiosity, consider the following question: If individuals have negative feelings about power, is it because they do not view themselves as powerful, or is it based on centuries of history upon which powerful people have caused political terror and exploitation? We lean toward the belief that most of society is suspicious about people in positions of power and control, especially in the workplace. If there were high levels of trust, there would be no need for unions, labor contracts, labor laws, or personnel attorneys.

Orwell (1949) gave us all a succinct lesson on power in his best-selling novel *1984*, writing "the object of power is power" (p. 179). The concepts of power and control are also important to our understanding of founder's syndrome. We acknowledged that fact by citing Block and Rosenberg's definition of founder's syndrome in Chapter 1, as a reaction to the "influential powers and privileges that the founder exercises or that others attribute to the founder" (2002, p. 354). We can add the Latin term sine qua non to that definition, meaning *without it, it could not be*. In other words, power and controlling behavior are intrinsic qualities of founder's syndrome. It is as though an organizational founder is encoded with an innate and reflexive trait to become controlling, demanding, destructive, and unreasonably powerful; whether they use those traits is situational. Without power and control, founder's syndrome could not exist.

Interest in the concepts of power and control is not just an American phenomenon. Our review of the professional literature revealed many variations on the concept of power, depending on the professional discipline, country setting, or location of the authors (see, e.g., Barua & Haukanes, 2020 in Norway; Leburu-Masigo, Maforah, & Mohlatlole, 2019 in South Africa; Ballon, 2018 in United Kingdom; Rodrigues, Menezes, & Ferreira, 2018 in Portugal; Arnold, 2016 on medical education; Pixley, 2015 on Legal matters; Van Voorhis & Hostetter, 2006 on social justice and social work; and Zimmerman, 1995 on community psychology). In her book *Empowerment & Community Planning*, Israeli author Sadan (1997) provides a historical review of the concept of power and recognizes several disciplines that have an interest in power. She writes, "Karl Marx influenced the conceptualization of power in all the social sciences; Alfred Adler, following Marx, opened a discussion on power in psychology; Friedrich Nietzsche influenced thought about power in philosophy" (p. 34). Giddens advanced a social theory of power known as the duality of structure, declaring,

> Power is exercised by human agents and is also created by them, influences them, and limits them. In other words, power is not a quality or a resource of people, or a position in the social structure, but a social factor which influences both these components of human society and is also created by them. (Sadan, 1997, p. 38)

As stated in Chapter 1, the descriptions of founder's syndrome frequently include some reference to Machiavelli because of a widespread belief that Machiavelli is synonymous with evil. In their book *Machiavelliana*, Jackson and Grace (2018) take exception to the constant pairing of Machiavelli with malevolent intent and abusive power. They review several examples of books and book titles that use 'Machiavelli' and claim many authors have distorted the real character of Niccolò Machiavelli. In their words,

The only conclusion we can draw is that attaching his name to something routine and even banal, like a case study, provokes curiosity and makes a work stand out on the shelf. Whatever else it does, such labeling seldom takes Machiavelli seriously and, worse, it perpetuates the mythical Machiavel. (p.188)

A supporting interpretation about Machiavelli's advices comes from Harris (2007) who reminds us that when reading Machiavelli, we need to consider the context and timeframe of Machiavelli's writings. Harris notes that,

Machiavelli advocated behavior which we might consider amoral only in limited circumstances, i.e., when the liberty of the state was threatened. In effect he was supporting the granting of what we would now call emergency powers to the government, except the sort of actions permitted in those times were more appropriate to volatile and violent sixteenth century Italy than to comparatively stable twenty first century liberal democracies. (p. 185)

Although our intent is not to mock or mischaracterize Niccolò Machiavelli, we cannot ignore the rate of occurrence the Machiavelli name is synonymously brandished as founder's syndrome. It is also true that the content of his best-known book, *The Prince*, written in 1513, is replete with unprincipled political behavior although couched as being pragmatic guidance for the benefit of Florence's ruler, Lorenzo de' Medici, during a period of political unrest. Writing about and construing the implications of Machiavelli's recommendations as devious and deceitful, Ayyildiz (2019) notes that "as a significant political rule, the ruler may disregard all his virtuous and moral values and that a ruler should be concerned just with ensuring his own survival through the use of power" (p. 1038).

A distinction could be made between leadership influence and behaviors that are based on a CEO's political performance that uses a Machiavellian-type power edict. The power that comes from being an influential leader is a result of the followers' beliefs in their CEO. Followers also generally feel respected and believe in the organizational mission and vision. Should followers withdraw their support, the CEO would not have influence over them, unless the CEO switches his or her tactics and introduces coercive power. The use of Machiavellian power also creates followership and compliance in response to feelings of fear and intimidation and not based on mutual respect. A famous sixteenth-century quote from *The Prince* (Machiavelli, 1992) exemplifies the tone of unprincipled behavior and intimidation that is suggestive of founder's syndrome:

> it is much safer to be feared than loved because ... love is preserved by the link of obligation which, owing to the baseness of men, is broken at every opportunity for their advantage; but fear preserves you by a dread of punishment which never fails. (p. 68)

Instead of love being linked by obligation, Papadimos and Marc (2004) found a similar and interesting obligation linkage about generosity. They state that "if CEOs want to keep a reputation for being generous, they will have to give time and money to the staff or employees and the community on an ongoing basis." They draw this conclusion based on Machiavelli's deduction that generosity cannot go on forever. Upon ending or reducing one's munificence, the CEO will be reviled. Like the Machiavellian idea that being feared is better than being loved, they conclude that "being parsimonious with one's attention and allocations is a better thing" (p. 14). As a warning to CEOs, Papadimos and Marc quote Machiavelli,

> there is nothing that is so self-consuming as generosity: The more you practice it, the less you will be able to continue to practice it. ... Therefore, it is shrewder to cultivate a reputation for meanness, which will lead to notoriety, but not hatred. This is better than being considered generous, which will lead to notoriety and hatred as well. (2004, p. 14)

Another writer following the period of Machiavelli was the English political philosopher Hobbes (1994). Hobbes believed that human beings are by nature prone to aggression and writes in Leviathan the idea that we are inclined to want power,

> The passions that most of all cause the differences of wit are principally: The more or less desire of power, of riches, of knowledge, and of honor. All which may be reduced to the first, that is, desire of power. For riches, knowledge, and honor are but several sorts of power. (p. 41)

Another description was advanced by Mann (2012), the author of *The Sources of Social Power,* who declares power "the ability to pursue and attain goals through mastery of one's environment" (p. 6). Additionally, "social power [is] mastery exercised over other people" (p. 6). Although many characterizations of power are about controlling people, Fairholm (1993) presents an interesting outlook on the behavioral reaction to power who writes that people resist power tactics by:

> (a) using a countervailing power tactic; (b) striving to destroy or limit the base or bases of power we control; (c) seeking to wrest

power bases held by us from us; and (d) trying to disengage from the relationship, thereby destroying not only our power, but the underlying relationship itself. (p. 67)

Fairholm's comments remind us of the hardline response and surreptitious acts by managers resisting founder's syndrome who counter with plans to get rid of the founding CEO.

An unexpected observation revealed by Haslam, Reicher, and Platow (2020) is that power that organizational founders display may have been reinforced through formal management education programs. The researchers paint an interesting picture of the organizational leader as manifesting heroic qualities, whereby we read their use of the word heroic as a euphemism for the adjective, powerful. The authors argue that leadership education has indoctrinated potential leaders to believe that "they are a special breed that can do no wrong" (p. 15). Their opinion about management education is in line with a critical assessment espoused by Mintzberg (2004) who is the Cleghorn Professor of Management Studies at McGill University in Montreal. He argues that business schools have incorrectly equated management and entrepreneurship as similar. Thus, they have underrepresented the difficulties of starting new organizations and created a disturbing message about organizational leadership. Mintzberg writes about the comparison between startup organizations and managing existing business entities:

> To treat the two together is to repeat the major mistake business schools have been making all along: Seeing management as something general, generic, removed from context. On the personal shoulders of the entrepreneur falls the enormous burden of getting a company going. To equate that with the managing of a large established business – being there, compared with getting there – is to belittle the task of entrepreneurship. And it perpetuates that cult of heroic leadership, that the chief executive is responsible for everything. (p. 131)

Founding CEOs with or without formal management education do believe that they are responsible for all facets of the organization's operations. This provides them with the belief or at least the assumption that they have an organizational advantage with their hiring and firing powers and by one of the most important initial acts of establishing the originating board of directors. Founders are empowered by hierarchical design. Empowerment or the power one asserts from feeling sanctioned as the founder is not just relegated to structural design. Certain environmental conditions may embolden individuals to act in ways that can have social consequences. For example, we have all observed individuals who have a favorite sport team feel empowered when their team wins, especially when winning a major tournament. Some fans feel so empowered that they act emboldened and with impunity run on to the field, engaging in aggressive behaviors such as tearing down goal posts and trying to evade stadium staff in an attempt to follow the players into the locker rooms. Such actions may seem out of character and attributed to impulsivity, which Kopetz, Woerner, and Briskin (2018) note has conventionally been theorized as a "disregard for consequences, lack of deliberation, or poor executive control" (p. 3). They also propose an alternate view in their belief that impulsivity,

> does not necessarily reflect deficiencies, or lack of ability. The fact that the behavior appears unplanned, reckless, or that it may have negative consequences is not necessarily indicative of poor self-regulation. Rather, it reflects the person's motivational priorities and her willingness to respond to those priorities with the best available means. Thus, we propose that impulsive behavior could be strategic in that it is enacted to achieve a goal and could therefore be understood according to the principles of goal pursuit, even when the goal that it serves is not immediately accessible to the person or the outside observers. (p. 4)

Founder's syndrome behavior may also seem like an overreaction and indicative of poor self-regulation by a founder who is motivated in pursuit of a goal to achieve his or her organizational vision. But even if we understand founders' behaviors to be in accordance with the principles of goal pursuit, there is no mistaking the results as founder's syndrome.

Goal pursuit is a result of a motivational drive. Psychologist McClelland (1953) is influential for developing Achievement Motivation Theory that describes individuals as having a learned motivational drive for either achievement, affiliation, or power. During his research, McClelland (1953) found,

> individuals are proud of having a high need to Achieve, but dislike being told they have a high need for Power. It is a fine thing to be concerned about doing things well (*n* Achievement) or making friends (*n* Affiliation), but it is reprehensible to be concerned about having influence over others (*n* Power). The vocabulary that behavioral scientists use to describe power relations is strongly negative in tone. (p. 32)

The negative association with power could not be more exampled than with the research of social psychologist Milgram (1974). While a professor at Yale, Milgram devised an experiment in which two individuals are introduced in a laboratory. One is an insider playing a victim role, but the other is unaware. The two individuals are separated into different rooms. The actor-victim is to receive a shock that is to be intensified by each wrong answer. Shocks are given by the unaware participant by pushing a lever that ranges from 15 volts to 450 volts. The victim is truly not receiving any shocks, but the participant is not aware of that fact. The actor begins to express his discomfort and eventually screams from pain as the voltage increases for each wrong answer. In some of the experiments, the victim yells about his troubled heart. When the unwitting participant wants to quit pushing the lever, the researcher exhibits his forceful positional power and tells the participant that they signed up for the experiment and must continue. The wary participant succumbs to the power of the authority figure in the white lab coat. (For deeper insight as to why participants would continue to obediently listen to the authority figure, Milgram's book provides keen insight.) Even among those subjects that eventually refused to go any further, they appeared distressed to defy the authority figure, and some offered apologies as though they were failures for stopping their participation.

Applying the power differential that is observed in Milgram's experiment for purposes of understanding founder's syndrome, we can see similar ambiguities among board members and/or department directors who take a considerable amount of the time, sometimes years, to mount a formidable reaction to a founder's edicts. In some cases, the founder has not exercised any abhorrent behavior. However, the founder has what French and Raven (1959) would describe as legitimate power from his or her position as the founding CEO. Given the perceived and legitimate power as the founder, subordinates might ascribe negative feelings to the founder because of the objectionable idea that someone has control and influence over them. As employees of organizations, almost all of us are dependent on CEOs for our financial resources that enable us to provide for ourselves and family the necessities of shelter, food, and medicine. Many workers fear the loss of employment, and accordingly will act deferentially or obsequiously when encountered by their CEO, like the subjects did to the man in the white lab coat.

The employees' reverent behavior reminds us of one of our interviews with an organizational founder who had a practice of meeting with new employees after 30–60 days of starting their jobs. In her interviews, she would ask the new employee how well the organization performed in welcoming and acculturating him or her into the organization and job responsibilities. Besides providing a positive response about their new job and the helpfulness of staff, almost every new employee dutifully thanked the CEO for founding such a wonderful organization. Given the eventual 'overthrow' of this founding CEO from her position, we asked her what she did differently that employees would go from acting admiringly to becoming either neutral or impudent. She stated that she had not changed anything about her manner or practices in the 12 years she was the CEO. We believe that this founding CEO was correct in her assessment of her organizational behaviors. The sharp difference was that the new employees had not yet experienced or become familiar with the power and control that the CEO exercised in the daily operations of the organization. When they did experience the CEO's organizational power and control, they did not like it and neither did their supervisors, department directors, or board members.

Kanter's (1979) writing in the Harvard Business Review presents an interesting statement on society's negative view of organizational power:

> Power is America's last dirty word. It is easier to talk about money – and much easier to talk about sex – than it is to talk about power. People who have it deny it; people who want it do not want to appear to hunger for it; and people who engage in its machinations do so secretly. (p. 65)

Kanter also offers another view that should give pause as to whether founders accused of founder's syndrome are exercising real power, or are they figures of powerlessness? She writes, "Powerlessness, in contrast, tends to breed bossiness rather than true leadership. In large organizations, at least, it is powerlessness that often creates ineffective, desultory management and petty, dictatorial, rules-minded managerial styles" (p. 65).

There are other CEO power characteristics that were noted in Block and Rosenberg's (2002) study on founder's syndrome in nonprofit organizations. Power is demonstrated through the focal point of board meetings, where the agenda is more often established by the founding CEO and thereby controlling the meeting. Also, the founder is more likely to review and edit the minutes of prior board meetings and thus control the historical and official records adopted by the board of directors. The CEO is also the most influential person during board meetings and can influence board members to vote in the way he or she wants the outcome of a policy decision.

Kahan and Rock's (2010) Texas Law Review article found similar power characteristics in for-profit companies. They write,

> First, CEO power includes the CEO's ability to control whether an issue is even presented to other potential decision makers, i.e., the power of the CEO to control the agenda of these other decision-making bodies. Second, it includes the ability of the CEO to determine the outcome of an issue that is presented to these other bodies, i.e., the power to determine the decision outcome. Third, it

includes the ability of the CEO to act if the issue is not presented to these other bodies, i.e., the power to act independently. CEOs have the greatest power if they either (i) have both agenda control and the power to act independently or (ii) have the power to determine the decision outcome. (p. 993)

Additionally, Denhardt, Denhardt, and Aristigueta (2016) note that various approaches are used to gain power and manipulate organizational staff. They suggest that some strategies can be used for good purposes, but such tactics could be employed for unethical reasons. They provide a sampling of organizational tactics that exhibit some similarities to the devices identified by Kahan and Rock (2010) and Block and Rosenberg (2002). The following six were selected from the nine chosen by Denhardt et al., because they are strategies common to founder's syndrome:

1. *Controlling the agenda* – determining in advance what issues will and will not be discussed or decided on.
2. *Controlling information and using ambiguity* – keeping communications and meanings unclear so that others will be less able to act; not divulging all information, particularly information that can be used against you.
3. *Forming coalitions* – securing alliances with people who are willing to support or agree with you.
4. *Developing others* – increasing the capacity of those around you, thereby increasing overall power.
5. *Incurring obligations* – doing things for people, knowing that such favors will create an obligation for them to repay the favors.
6. *Selecting decision criteria* – controlling the criteria by which decisions are made, allowing you to influence the outcome without personally deciding (pp. 237–238).

Pulitzer prize winning political scientist James MacGregor Burns' (1978), the author of *Leadership*, contrasts his view of power to the views of other scholars as follows:

Lasswell and Kaplan hold that power must be relevant to people's valued things; I hold that it must be relevant to the *power wielder's* valued things and may be relevant to the *recipient's* needs or values only as necessary to exploit them. Kenneth Janda defines power as "the ability to cause other persons to adjust their behavior in conformance with communicated behavior patterns." I agree, assuming that those behavior patterns aid the purpose of the power wielder. (p. 19)

In this glimpse of Macgregor Burn's thinking, we see a connection with his viewpoint of power and a founder exercising founder's syndrome behavior. The focal point in using power is to satisfy the aim of the founder. Burns does draw a distinction between an individual using power from the act of leadership. In other words, a founder engaged in founder behavior would not meet his conceptualization of a leader. He writes,

> Some define leadership as leaders making followers do what *followers* would not otherwise do, or as leaders making followers do what the *leaders* wants them to do; I define leadership as leaders inducing followers to act for certain goals that represent the values and motivations – the wants and needs, the aspirations and expectations – of both leaders and followers. And the genius of leadership lies in the manner in which leaders see and act on their own and their followers' values and motivations. (p. 19)

Two decades before MacGregor Burn's treatise on differentiating types of social and political dimensions of leadership, French and Raven (1959) distinguished five types of power including referent power, expert power, reward power, coercive power, and legitimate power. A few years later, Raven (1965) added a sixth type, information power. According to Raven, the impetus for their research was a presidential address to the Society for the Psychological Study of Social Issues by Dorwin Cartwright, stating that 'social power' was a neglected variable in social psychology (Raven, 2008, p. 10). We take note in their statement of purpose and how their ground-breaking research is important to our understanding of founder's syndrome:

> The phenomena of power and influence involve a dyadic relation between two agents which may be viewed from two points of view: (o) What determines the behavior of the agent who exerts power? (h) What determines the reactions of the recipient of this behavior? We take this second point of view and formulate our theory in terms of the life space of P, the person upon whom the power is exerted. In this way we hope to define basic concepts of power which will be adequate to explain many of the phenomena of social influence, including some which have been described in other less genotypic terms. (p. 259)

French and Raven's (1959) ground-breaking study illuminates power alternatives that can be adapted by founding CEOs. Reward power is the recognition that the CEO can incentivize employees with the ability to provide wage increases, bonuses, extra paid leave, and public recognition. For reward power to be effective, employees must recognize the opportunity to be rewarded and they must feel that rewards are within their reach and meaningful to receive. This reward type is unlikely to be exercised during a state of founder's syndrome unless it is used to manipulate staff. We are aware of several examples of organizations in which founding CEOs were very generous with their employees with bonuses and holiday pay and several unique benefits such as memberships to health clubs, time off during the day for walking, bonuses to stop smoking, tickets to shows and sporting events, internet availability at home, among others. Despite the use of reward power and high levels of support among line staff, these CEOs were eventually terminated by their board due to key stakeholders who were well-compensated company vice presidents providing negative feedback to board members and threats of their leaving if the board did not terminate the founder.

The opposite of reward power is coercive power. This type of power is reminiscent of the power held over workers during the height of scientific management promoted by Frederick Taylor (1911), a period when workers were required to achieve a prescribed level of productivity. The view held by Taylor was that without requiring targets, workers would resort to being lazy. This type of mindset represents a founder's syndrome work environment in which employees may not feel safe given a negative organizational culture with a greater number of firings, threats of firing, unrealistic productivity expectations for some employees, scapegoating, and an overall off-putting milieu.

According to French and Raven (1959), legitimate power is the most complex of power-types (p. 264). This is due to certain cultural views in which power may be a result of age, educational degree, professionalism, belonging to a certain caste or tribe, level of intelligence, or physical characteristics. Legitimate power is also the result of the authority of position in the organization. A founding CEO has legitimate power as the boss of the organization. Organizational power, however, is not absolute and is subject to modification based on whether the scope of power is defined through bylaws, an employment contract with a board of directors that sets out the extent of the CEO's authority. A board of directors also has the positional power and clout to force a change in the decisions promulgated by its Chief Executive. Undoing the decisions made by a founding CEO is a thorny process. The challenge and hardship of social interactions that will manifest in the boardroom between the board and CEO often make the attempt to change a decision a futile endeavor. In other words, sometimes a decision will stand rather than board members exercising their authority to avoid the tension and hostilities of challenging the founder. This is an important point because the symptoms associated with founder's syndrome may prevail because a board simply chooses to avoid a battle with the founder. This same avoidance dynamic can occur when a directive is grudgingly accepted by department and program directors who may fear either the legitimate or coercive powers of their CEO.

A CEO has legitimate power but may also have referent power that is more attractive to others internal or external to the organization. For example, referent power may result from being closely identified with organizational board members who have considerable wealth, or a celebrity such as a movie star or a Nobel laureate or a Pulitzer Prize author. In such situations, the CEO might take on some of the beliefs and opinions held by the admired, well-known individuals. Despite the level of identification by way of reference, if the founding CEO is engaged in any founder's syndrome behaviors, their referent power would be diminished.

Expert power is the fifth type of power. Expertise must be recognized by others for power to exist. It also requires a belief that the individual with expertise has more knowledge than others. French and Raven (1959, p. 267) give an example of attorneys providing legal advice as an example of expert power. However, the researchers also clarify that the 'validity of the content' is only considered as acceptable because of the belief and recognition of the person as an expert who made the statements (p. 267).

According to Raven (2008), he had wanted to include informational power in the original work with his mentor John French. However, French did not consider it as a power, but more as an influencing factor because the source of the power was the content of information and not necessarily a person (p. 12). However, Raven did reveal informational power in a separate publication in 1965. This form of power comes from the internalization of information that is understood by the receiver of the communication. Not only is the information understood, but also as a result of obtaining knowledge the recipient changes his or her behavior. This is differentiated from expert power where the information might not be understood, but the information is accepted because it was generated from a recognized expert. Informational power can come from a wide range of sources from individuals, videos, and reading material. It only becomes powerful when the information generates a new cognitive framework for the participant who accepts the logic of the information. In organizations, instructions on how to do a specific task in the most efficient and effective way would be considered informationally powerful for the employee.

Another form of power is referred to as political power. According to Zaleznik (1970), "organizations operate by distributing authority and setting a stage for the exercise of power" (p. 47). Landelles and Albrecht (2017) note that definitions of political power are varied from both positive and negative perspectives, although negative viewpoints dominate the political power literature (p. 44). Reminiscent of the organizational environment where founder's syndrome is present, Ishaq and Khalid (2014) found that, "organizational politics is mostly perceived as negative and presence of organizational politics in the work environment have many negative job outcomes which include low job involvement, job anxiety, turnover, absenteeism and job dissatisfaction" (p. 70).

An interesting approach to the topic of power comes from McLagan's (2013) article 'Emerge from the Shadows.' Her characterization of a CEO that has a shadow trait is similar to elements observed in founder's syndrome. McLagan explains that she uses the word shadow as described by the famous Swiss psychiatrist Carl Jung who equated the word shadow with an individual's negative personality. She warns that followers will become guarded and submissive when CEO's display their shadowed power and behave like tyrants. Additionally, "when left unchecked, these dynamics damage morale, squash innovation, focus behavior on defensiveness rather than strategy implementation, and ultimately alienate talent and destroy people and organizations" (p. 36).

McLagan's aim in writing the article is for leaders to become in tune with their own shadow personality for self-enlightenment and to change their leadership style and dynamics. Although her recommendations may be sound for the CEO who has had an epiphany about his or her negative side and wants to change, it seems that most CEOs would view their power as appropriate to their position. In organizations that evidence founder's syndrome, it is even less likely that the CEO would seek to change especially if they are embroiled in a struggle to hold on to their job. It may sound counterintuitive that the CEO would not want to change to save their job, but at the stage of being confronted by the board of directors and any other organizational stakeholders who suggest that the CEO resign or has been warned of potential termination, the CEO is not likely to become obsequious and beg for their job. The level of trust that the CEO may have once held for those stakeholders will have withered, much like the married individual who is instantly stunned when served with a divorce petition and reacts with a surge of anger, disillusionment, and world-weariness. The founding CEO is more likely to threaten legal action and fight the board, much like a parent seeking full custody of their child.

A common complaint among individuals who have direct contact with a CEO engaged in founder's syndrome is the oversight of their work and negative and unconstructive comments about their work styles. Micromanagement is a form of (unnecessary) supervision in which a founder asserts his or her power by attending to the details of work methods and work products of staff members. Although a founder may communicate their interest in helping, the recipient staff may view the offer as a form of control or a backhanded attempt to categorizing their work as unacceptable. Similarly, staff may receive the CEO's communication as a challenge to their knowledge and skills. Staff who are micromanaged often feel fearful and powerless to contradict the founder's supervision and advice.

Marino (1998) writes about his own experiences as an employee and a victim of a CEO's micromanagement. He asserts that the result of the CEO's interference results in the staff ceasing to contribute because their thinking and contributions are not encouraged. He wants CEO's to know that those who micromanage are gameplayers and not leaders, stating "leadership inspires freedom, not serfdom. Employees must be free to think, to talk, to act, to suggest, to solve, to invent, to dare, and even to err" (p. 22). Marino's personal account of being micromanaged makes real the sense that individuals who are micromanaged are emotionally injured and experience a reduction of self-confidence. We know that staff who are micromanaged are often discouraged and pessimistic about their work life. In fact, Delgado, Strauss, and Ortega (2015) claim that,

> Micromanaging can lead to employee disengagement. An actively disengaged employee has a negative impact on both service and productivity, which ends up costing the organization money. Furthermore, his or her performance is undoubtedly limited because the manager has in effect chosen to remove any incentives for the employee to demonstrate effort and creativity. There is an implied lack of trust ... (p. 772)

Nearly all types of relationships are comprised of affirming and deleterious interpersonal encounters. However, daily work relationships with chronic micromanagement will diminish those positive events and become a persistent source of stress for staff. Another way that micromanagement behavior can be described is based on the relationship research of Vinokur and Van Ryn (1993) who found a greater adverse effect on the mental health of individuals who experienced undermining communication than reassuring messages. Berscheid and Regan (2005) labeled the undercutting behaviors as "social undermining" (p. 55). Furthermore, they define social undermining as,

> behaviors toward another that display (1) negative affect, such as anger; (2) negative evaluation or criticism of the person in terms of his or her attributes, actions and efforts; and (3) behaviors that interfere with the attainment of the individual's goals. (p. 55)

When examining undermining behavior in the workplace as a facet of founder's syndrome, another related concept emerges in the form of bullying. Lo Presti, Pappone, and Landolfia (2019) define workplace bullying as a "severe form of harassing people in organizations and, theoretically, it is an extreme form of social stressor at work" (p. 808). A single incident of negative behavior would not constitute workplace bullying. However, founder's syndrome as bullying behavior is sustained over a period and may resemble any number of founder syndrome symptoms. According to Ali (2019), for example, the bullying symptoms can be displayed in many forms from micromanaging, meaningless assignments, ignoring of ideas, lack of clarity in policies, idealistic goal setting (p. 179).

Workplace incivility is another form of founder syndrome behavior that can affect employee motivation that affects staff performance. It can also be a contributing factor for somatic and/or psychological symptoms among staff who are victims of the behavior. It can manifest between the CEO and employees or as a reaction to the CEO's behavior it can be redirected between employees or between employees and organizational customers. Porath, MacInnis, and Folkes (2010) describe the behavior in the following way,

> When one is uncivil, one acts in a way that lacks consideration and is disrespectful of another's feelings or sensibilities. These rude and discourteous actions can be verbal (making snide or derogatory comment toward another) or nonverbal (snatching an item out of someone's hand or pushing in front of another person). (p. 293)

In some organizations, the uncivil behavior may not be as overt as in other organizations where founder's syndrome behavior is evident. Marchiondo, Cortina, and Kabat-Farr (2018) contend that workplace incivility is a low-level form of deviance in which workplace norms for respect are violated (Anderson & Pearson, 1999). By definition, incivility is both subtle and ambiguous (Anderson & Pearson, 1999), which may lead targeted employees to engage in greater cognitive efforts to 'make meaning' of these rude encounters, compared to more overt forms of mistreatment that contain clearer intentions. (p. 370)

Research on workplace incivility informs us that staff need time off to recover from the stressors of uncivil founder syndrome type behavior. The toxic effect of this form of power over employees can have an impact on an employee's physical or psychological well-being. According to Nicholson and Griffin (2017),

> early fade-out effect of weekend recovery has been identified, potentially due to one's anticipation of work on a Monday acting as a stressor (Brosschot, Pieper, & Thayer, 2005). Indeed, the finding that workers have elevated cortisol levels on Monday mornings (when compared to Sunday) demonstrates the negative effect that anticipating an impending workday has on stress (Devereux, Rydstedt, & Cropley, 2011). (p. 3)

An interesting concept written by a Turkish academician (Akar, 2018) who examined 31 research studies written primarily for an education audience also seems applicable to our task of communicating about power, control, and reactions to founder's syndrome. Akar discusses the idea of organizational silence, a model first introduced by Morrison and Milliken (2000) as a choice made by employees not to share their thoughts. Feeling fearful of the reaction to their ideas, employees prefer to remain quiet. One aspect of organizational silence is that its occurrence is not limited to a few employees, but the fear of retribution causes more of an organizational wide silence among line staff (Akar, p. 1079). Silence is often a result of management behaviors that message their lack of interest in receiving feedback, according to Morrison and Milliken (2000, p. 708), who also assert that research suggests that management believes subordinates cannot be trusted to provide accurate feedback (p. 710). In founder syndrome terms, the CEO knows best, and all other opinions do not matter. Consequently, suppression of alternative possibilities starts at the top:

> We expect in most cases, when cues from the top indicate that the organization is not open to employee input, the attitudes of senior managers will trickle down and affect the behaviors of middle managers (Floyd & Wooldridge, 1994) and that they, too, will send cues to those below them that voice is not welcome. (Morrison 2000, p. 714)

The research literature on job insecurity is another path of information that is relevant for understanding the implications of power and control in founder's syndrome, especially its adverse impact on organizational employees. Staff who feel threatened about job loss either the result of micromanagement or voicing their opinion in an environment that prefers organizational silence may experience anxiety, depression, headaches, neck pain, back pain, or other symptoms from stress (Vander Elst et al., 2014, p. 145). According to Vander Elst et al., research on job insecurity demonstrates that a key factor as to whether an employee engages in psychological withdrawal is whether the individual believes they have any control over their work situation. In their research on work-related stress to determine differences in stress among workers with temporary versus full-time contracts and differences in gender response, De Sio et al. (2018) quote the World Health Organization, "(WHO) defines work related stress as a condition characterized by physical, psychological, or social suffering or dysfunction, which arises from the feeling of not being able to respond to requests or to live up to expectations" (p. 1). Their survey findings indicate higher levels of perceived stress among workers with temporary contracts and female respondents were more susceptible to stress than their male counterparts.

It is evident that the negative use of power characterized as founder's syndrome emerges from one or more varying behaviors in a workplace such as micromanagement, bullying and incivility, social undermining, silence, job insecurity, or other coercive means. As we mined the organizational behavior research literature to understand the weight that these powerful forces have on the workplace milieu, our interest turned to the function of organizational culture and whether cultural variables can be used to help explain founder's syndrome. Schein (2010) has clarified the barriers and difficulties in accurately deciphering organizational culture through research methods of demographics, experimentation, action research, ethnography, interviews, projective tests, process consultation, and other clinical research techniques (pp. 180–181). Schein affirms our understanding that founders create an organizational culture, which are the rules and unwritten rules of a company. He also refers to the elements of culture as being comparable to an individual's personality. Schein notes the importance of observation to understand cultural elements of language, espoused values, environmental climate such as physical layout of the workplace, the history of shared meaning, company rituals, and actual behaviors compared to stated beliefs (pp. 14–16). Schein informs us that,

> Culture is an abstraction, yet the forces that are created in social and organizational situations deriving from culture are powerful. If we don't understand the operation of these forces, we become victim to them. Cultural forces are powerful because they operate outside of our awareness. We need to understand them not only because of their power but also because they help to explain many of our puzzling and frustrating experiences in social and organizational life. (p. 7)

One of the frustrating experiences in social and organizational life was identified by renowned sociologist Goffman (1966). He describes the concept of involvement obligation in which an individual is enjoined by another individual in an obligatory expressive event, "projecting through them a proper image of himself, an appropriate respect for the others present, and a suitable regard for the setting" (p. 104). These occasions can be a window into witnessing the impact of organizational founder's syndrome. Consider a scenario of an employee on his or her way back to their workstation following a lunch break and is unexpectedly encountered by the CEO. The CEO decides to engage the employee in conversation. The employee is suddenly burdened by social etiquette to respond politely and informatively in response to the questions posed by the CEO. The employee is now involved and constrained by an involvement obligation and cannot escape without being discourteous to the CEO. What appears as a spontaneous event becomes paradoxically a threatening event in which the employee is not a free and naturally willing participant. When the CEO frees the employee from conversation, the employee is not free from the emotional toll taken and will likely spend time wondering what type of impression he or she made with the CEO. This will likely take the form of reviewing the interaction, what was said, what the employee wished he or she would have said and would not have said. The anxiety experienced by the employee is a result of his or her consciousness that the CEO holds power in the interaction, the relationship, and any depreciative or positive impressions formulated by the CEO which is out of the control of the employee. More than likely, the employee is transfixed on the potential negative impressions he or she left. In some situations – depending on the evolution of founder's syndrome in the organization – the interaction can leave the employee temporarily incapacitated.

In organizations with more advanced evidence of founder's syndrome, the founding CEO might be categorized as a toxic leader. According to Matos, O'Neill, and Lei (2018), this type of toxicity will taint an organizational culture including its norms, rituals, and beliefs. The organizational culture will be personified by a CEO who uses

> social dominance, prioritizing work above all other parts of life, gratuitous displays of physical strength, and the avoidance of weakness. In such workplaces, masculine ideals warp into a culture where mistakes are irreparable, emotional vulnerability must be avoided at all costs, and displays of strength and stamina are a requirement for success. ... This becomes 'a win or die culture.' (p. 501)

Toxic leadership includes behavioral insensitivity and detrimental displays of power in the form of bullying and criticizing employees. Some authoritarian-style CEOs who have a deep-seated need to exercise their toxic power also share attributes with individuals diagnosed with narcissistic personality disorder (Matos et al., 2018, p. 504). The disorder is a psychiatric condition with a range of symptoms that can include an exaggerated sense of self-importance, a preoccupation with power, lacking empathy, envious and exploitive of others, and seeks excessive admiration (American Psychiatric Association, 2013).

Conclusion

Our objective in this chapter was to explore the multiplicity of concepts of power and control in organizations and concentrate on its usage primarily by founders who by their nature or happenstance contribute to the symptoms of founder's syndrome. Linking power and control to founder's syndrome is significant because it plays a vital role in its existence. From a functionalist perspective, power and control has ex-emplified undesirable and sometimes harmful social behaviors. We purposefully avoided attention to how power and control can be used for positive and constructive purposes because founder's syndrome is not associated with beneficial and productive behaviors in organizations.

Although much negativism can be attributed to the founders who engage in socially undermining behaviors, we assert that many have a completely different mindset about their behaviors. In fact, Hershcovis, Reich, Parker, and Bozeman (2012) inform us that "research suggests that high-powered people do not spend as much time processing in-formation in their relationship with employees as low-powered people because their outcomes are not dependent on the low-powered in-dividual" (p. 15). In other words, founders may engage in founder's syndrome behavior without being aware of their deleterious behavior or its injurious impact on employees.

We also assume that the founder's behaviors are a function of two aspects of their human nature. First, they engage in intrusive or ag-gressive behaviors because they want their organization to be successful and they do not have the management or strategic know-how to for-mulate appropriate decision criteria; and, second, although staff may perceive the founder as spying on them, not trusting them, acting rude or inconsiderate, the founder is merely demonstrating a greater need to control what takes place in the organizational environment. On the second point, most observers of founder's syndrome do not appreciate the founder's personal, emotional, and financial stake in the success of their creation. Like a parent's overly involved behavior, some founders have a harder time 'letting go' and allowing their brainchild to be en-trusted to others. Regardless of the founder's personal motivations or unintended consequences from their behaviors, their display of coercive or abusive power toward employees can lead to intervention by the board of directors. Presutti (2006) warns the CEO that "an involved board of directors may need to intervene by directing or replacing their chief executive so that the detrimental individual and organizational effects may be identified and corrective measures implemented for the facility to thrive and prosper" (p. 34).

All organizational founders possess legitimate power as a result of their organizational position. However, it is their use of coercive or author-itarian abilities that will expunge their standing as an entrepreneurial hero. With few exceptions, founders who become targets for removal by their board of directors or through subterfuge by other stakeholders such as department directors or corporate vice presidents will retaliate. All parties involved will resort to tactics and strategies that they did not realize they were capable of employing, some ethical and some unethical.

In the next chapter, we will discuss goal achievement and the roles employed by the founder, the board of directors, and other stakeholders.

To accomplish this objective, we will expand on the concept of Founder's Transformational Reaction Syndrome, first introduced by Block (2016).

Discussion Questions

1. Name and define five types of power and explain how each one relates to founder's syndrome.
2. How does the founder's power impact his or her relationship with the board of directors? How might employees react to a founder who is exerting power over them?
3. In this chapter, the authors note that Kanter (1979) asks whether founders accused of founder's syndrome are exercising real power, or whether they are in fact exhibiting powerlessness. Explain what Kanter is asking and then offer your own opinion as to whether founders accused of founder's syndrome are exercising real power or exhibiting powerlessness.
4. Do you agree with the statement that *most of society is suspicious about people in positions of power and control, especially in the workplace?* Explain.
5. Think of an organization where you have been employed or affiliated in some way. Of the five bases of power identified by French and Raven, recall an event in which the CEO or a supervisor used one of the bases of power. Describe.
6. Bertram Raven added a sixth base of power. Identify that additional power and explain what makes it a base of power.
7. In Dr. Stanley Milgram's experiments, why would an individual continue to increase the electric shock level on another participant who is yelling from pain?
8. What is meant by the concept of power and privilege in the Block and Rosenberg's definition of founder's syndrome?
9. Answer from the standpoint of an organizational founder: Explain why engaging in micromanagement or ignoring advice from other managers is an appropriate management practice.
10. Imagine you are a senior manager in Organization ABC, explain to your founding CEO why founder's syndrome behaviors may not be the best managerial approach?
11. Machiavelli writes that *it is safer to be feared than loved.* Look at this statement from both sides and explain first, why it would be safer to be feared than loved. Second, explain why it would not be safer.
12. When you do not get agreement from friends or family, do you ever try to use your influence to change their minds? What tactics have worked?

References

Akar, H. (2018). Organizational silence in educational organizations: A meta-analysis study. *International Journal of Eurasia Social Science*, *9*(32), 1077–1098.

Ali, Z. (2019). Workplace bullying: A sad reality, too costly to be ignored. *Journal of Postgraduate Medical Institute*, *33*(3), 179–181.

American Psychiatric Association. (2013). *Diagnostic and statistical manual of mental disorders* (5th ed.). American Psychiatric Publishing.

Anderson, L. M., & Pearson, C. M. (1999). Tit for tat? The spiraling effect of incivility in the workplace. *The Academy of Management Review*, *24*(3), 452–471.

Arnold, K. C. (2016). Impact of one training session on improving advocacy, knowledge, and empowerment in medical students. *Education in Medicine Journal*, *8*(2), 79–82.

Ayyildiz, N. E. (2019). An evaluation of the evil characters in Shakespeare's four main tragedies in terms of Machiavellian principles. *Gaziantep University Journal of Social Sciences*, *18*(3), 1037–1049.

Bachrach, P., & Baratz, M. S. (1962). Two faces of power. *The American Political Science Review*, *56*(4), 947–952.

Ballon, P. (2018). A structural equation model of female empowerment. *Journal of Development Studies*, *54*(8), 1303–1320.

Barua, P., & Haukanes, H. (2020). Organizing for empowerment: Exploring the impact of unionization on domestic workers in India. *Studies in Comparative International Development*, *55*(1), 27–47.

Berscheid, E. S., & Regan, P. C. (2005). *The psychology of interpersonal relationships*. Pearson Education, Inc.

Block, P. (2016). *The empowered manager: Positive Political skills at work* (2nd ed.). John Wiley & Sons.

Block, S. R., & Rosenberg, S. (2002). Toward an understanding of founder's syndrome: An assessment of power and privilege among founders of nonprofit organizations. *Nonprofit Management & Leadership*, *12*(4), 353–368.

Brosschot, J. F., Pieper, S., & Thayer, J. F. (2005). Expanding stress theory: Prolonged activation and perseverative cognition. *Psychoneuroendocrinology*, *30*(10), 1043–1049.

Burns, J. M. (1978). *Leadership*. Harper & Row.

Dahl, R. A. (1958). Critique of the ruling elite model. *The American Political Science Review*, *52*(2), 463–469.

De Sio, S., Cedrone, F., Trovato Battagliola, E., Buomprisco, G., Perri, R., & Greco, E. (2018). The perception of psychosocial risks and work-related stress in relation to job insecurity and gender differences: A cross-sectional study. *BioMed Research International*, *2018*, 1–8. https://doi.org/10.1155/2018/7649085

Delgado, O., Strauss, E. M., & Ortega, M. A. (2015). Micromanagement: When to avoid it and how to use it effectively. *American Journal of Health-System Pharmacy*, *72*(10), 772–774.

Denhardt, R. B., Denhardt, J. V., & Aristigueta, M. P. (2016). *Managing human behavior in public and nonprofit organizations* (4th ed.). Sage.

Devereux, J., Rydstedt, L. W., & Cropley, M. (2011). An exploratory study to assess the impact of work demands and the anticipation of work on awakening saliva cortisol. *Psychological Reports*, 108(1), 274–280.

Fairholm, G. W. (1993). *Organizational power politics: Tactics in organizational leadership* (2nd ed.). Praeger.

Floyd, S. W., & Wooldridge, B. (1994). Dinosaurs or dynamos? Recognizing middle management's strategic role. *The Academy of Management Executive*, 8(4), 47–57.

French, J. P., & Raven, B. H. (1959). The basis of social power. In D. Cartwright (Ed.), *Studies in social power* (pp. 150–167). Institute for Social Research.

Goffman, E. (1966). *Behavior in public places: Notes on the social organization of gatherings*. The Free Press.

Harris, P. (2007). Machiavelli, marketing and management: Ends and means in public affairs. *Journal of Public Affairs*, 7(2), 181–191.

Haslam, S. A., Reicher, S. D., & Platow, M. J. (2020). *The new psychology of leadership: Identity, influence and power* (2nd ed.). Routledge.

Hershcovis, M. S., Reich, T. C., Parker, S. K., & Bozeman, J. (2012). The relationship between workplace aggression and target deviant behavior: The moderating roles of power and task interdependence. *Work & Stress: An International Journal of Work, Health & Organizations*, 26(1), 1–20.

Hobbes, T. (1994). *Leviathan: With selected variants from the Latin edition of 1668* (E. Curley, Ed.). Hackett Publishing. (Original work published 1668.)

Ishaq, S., & Khalid, S. (2014). Job satisfaction, commitment and perceived organizational in politics in employees of a public sector university. *Journal of Behavioral Sciences*, 24(2), 69–82.

Jackson, M., & Grace, D. (2018). *Machiavelliana*. Brill Rodopi.

Kahan, M., & Rock, E. (2010). Embattled CEO's. *Texas Law Review*, 88(5), 987–1051.

Kanter, R. M. (1979). Power failure in management circuits. *Harvard Business Review*, 57(4), 65–75.

Kopetz, C. E., Woerner, J. I., & Briskin, J. L. (2018). Another look at impulsivity: Could impulsive behavior be strategic? *Social & Personality Psychology Compass*, 12(5), 1–16.

Landelles, E. M., & Albrecht, S. L. (2017). The positives and negatives of organizational politics: A qualitative study. *Journal of Business and Psychology*, 32(1), 41–58. https://doi.org/10.1007/s10869-015-9434-5

Leburu-Masigo, G. E., Maforah, N. F., & Mohlatlole, N. E. (2019). Impact of victim empowerment program on the lives of victims of gender-based violence: Social work services. *Gender & Behavior*, 17(3), 13439–13454.

Lo Presti, A., Pappone, P., & Landolfia, A. (2019). The associations between workplace bullying and physical or psychological negative symptoms: Anxiety and depression as mediators. *Europe's Journal of Psychology*, 15(4), 808–822.

Machiavelli, N. (1992). *The prince* (N.H. Thomson, Trans.). Dover Publications. (Original work published 1532.)

Mann, M. (1986). *The sources of social power: Volume 1, a history of power from the beginning to AD 1760*. Cambridge University Press.

Mann, M. (2012). *The sources of social power: Volume 3, global empires and revolution, 1890-1945*. Cambridge University Press.

Marchiondo, L. A., Cortina, L. M., & Kabat-Farr, D. (2018). Attributions and appraisals of workplace incivility: Finding light on the dark side? *Applied Psychology: An International Review, 67*(3), 369–400.

Marino, S. (1998). Micromanagement leads to mismanagement. *Industry Week/ IW, 247*(14), 22.

Matos, K., O'Neill, O. M., & Lei, X. (2018). Toxic leadership and the masculinity contest culture: How "win or die" cultures breed abusive leadership. *Journal of Social Issues, 74*(3), 500–528. https://doi.org/10.1111/josi.12284

McClelland, D. C. (1953). *The achievement motive.* Appleton-Century-Crofts Inc.

McLagan, P. A. (2013). Emerge from the shadows. *T+D Magazine, 67*(9), 36–40.

Milgram, S. (1974). *Obedience to authority: An experimental view.* Harper & Row.

Mintzberg, H. (2004). *Managers not MBAs: A hard look at the soft practice of managing and management development.* Berrett-Koehler Publishers.

Morrison, E. W., & Milliken, F. J. (2000). Organizational silence: A barrier to change and development in a pluralistic world. *Academy of Management Review, 25*(4), 706–725.

Nicholson, T., & Griffin, B. (2017). Thank goodness it's Friday: Weekly pattern of workplace incivility. *Anxiety, Stress, & Coping, 30*(1), 1–14.

Orwell, G. 1984. Penguin Group.

Papadimos, T. J., & Marc, A. P. (2004). Machiavelli's advice to the hospital chief executive officer. *Hospital Topics, 82*(2), 12–17.

Pixley, S. (2015). Lawyering with challenges: Disability and empowerment. *Professional Lawyer, 23*(1), 1–6.

Porath, C., MacInnis, D., & Folkes, V. (2010). Witnessing incivility among employees: Effects on consumer anger and negative inferences about companies. *Journal of Consumer Research, 37*(2), 292–303.

Presutti, M. (2006). Is micromanagement killing your staff? *Nursing Homes: Long Term Care, 55*(2), 34–38.

Raven, B. H. (1965). Social influence and power. In I. D. Steiner & M. Fishbein (Eds.), *Current studies in social psychology* (pp. 371–382). Holt, Rinehart, Winston.

Raven, B. H. (2008). The bases of power and the power/interaction model of interpersonal influence. *Analyses of Social Issues and Public Policy, 8*(1), 1–22.

Rodrigues, M., Menezes, I., & Ferreira, P. D. (2018). Validating the formative nature of psychological empowerment construct: Testing cognitive, emotional, behavioral, and relational components. *Journal of Community Psychology, 46*(1), 58–78.

Sadan, E. (1997). *Empowerment and community planning: Theory and practice of people-focused social solutions* (R. Flantz, Trans.). Hakibbutz Hameuchad Publishers.

Schein, E. H. (2010). *Organizational culture and leadership* (4th ed.). John Wiley & Sons.

Taylor, F. W. (1911). *The principles of scientific management.* Harper & Brothers.

Vander Elst, T., Richter, A., Sverke, M., Näswall, K., De Cuyper, N., & De Witte, H. (2014). Threat of losing valued job features: The role of perceived control in mediating the effect of qualitative job insecurity on job strain and psychological withdrawal. *Work & Stress: An International Journal of Work,*

Health & Organizations, 28(2), 143–164. https://doi.org/10.1080/02678373.
2014.899651

Van Voorhis, R. M., & Hostetter, C. (2006). The impact of MSW education on
social worker empowerment and commitment to client empowerment through
social justice advocacy. *Journal of Social Work Education, 42*(1), 105–121.

Vinokur, A. D., & Van Ryn, M. (1993). Social support and undermining in close
relationships: Their independent effects on the mental health of unemployed
persons. *Journal of Personality and Social Psychology, 65*(2), 350–359.
https://doi.org/10.1037/0022-3514.65.2.350

Weber, M. (1947). *The theory of social and economic organization* (A. M.
Henderson & T. Parsons, Trans.). Collier Macmillan Publishers. (Original
work published 1922.)

Zaleznik, A. (1970, May). Power and politics in organizational life. *Harvard
Business Review, 48*(3), 47–60.

Zimmerman, M. A. (1995). Psychological empowerment: Issues and illustrations. *American Journal of Community Psychology, 23*(5), 581–599.

3 Founder's Transformational Reaction Syndrome

Chapter Objectives

When you finish studying this chapter, you should be able to:

- Explain how defense mechanisms play a key role in the sufferers of founder's syndrome
- Discuss Founder's Transformational Reaction Syndrome and how it differs from traditional explanations of founder's syndrome
- Discuss the theoretical construct Founder's Transformational Reaction Syndrome
- Explain the purpose of a defense mechanism
- Describe the defense mechanism known as reaction formation, rationalization, projection, and denial

Introduction

In their introductory paragraphs on ecological rationality, Todd and Gigerenzer (2007) state, "prevailing explanations of behavior are still expressed most often in terms of personality traits, cognitive styles, brain-region activation patterns, preferences and utilities, and other assumed entities 'inside' the mind" (p. 167). In this chapter, we explore the state of mind of the victims of founder's syndrome. Because founder's syndrome behavior is anomalous to the humanistic management styles of leadership that employees expect, how do we explain the uninterrupted attendance of employees who are the object of unwanted and objectionable behaviors? Our explanation is based on a psychological theory that draws on the concept of defense mechanisms that acts to safeguard the employees or even board members who are targets of founder's syndrome.

We introduce you to Founder's Transformational Reaction Syndrome (FTRS), which is a theoretical construct grounded in over 20 years of observing the behavior of individuals in organizations where founder's syndrome has been reported to exist, coupled with interviewing founders, board members, and senior management staff and executives. It was introduced by Block (2016) who recognized missing details about the reason that individuals will continue to subject themselves to founder's syndrome day after day, week after week, month after month, and so on. The word *syndrome* was intentionally assigned to this paradigm in the same way that *syndrome* is used in traditional accounts of founder's syndrome.

As will be explained in this chapter, FTRS differs from the traditional explanations about founder's syndrome. The foundation of the construct stems from an obvious factor of logic that founder's syndrome can only exist under the following conditions:

1. There must be a founder of an organization
2. The founding CEO generates assaultive behaviors
3. There must be one or more employees or board members who are harmed by the founder's behaviors

The additional step represented by FTRS is an individual's psychological reaction to the founder's deleterious decisions and behaviors. The individual may be a board officer, board member, company vice president, department director, senior manager, or any employee that has regular exposure to the founding CEO. In most cases, the victim is an employee.

Given the psychological nature of FTRS, the employee who is maltreated by the founder unconsciously conceals their reaction initiated by a defense mechanism (Hentschel, Smith, Draguns, & Ehlers, 2004).

Defense Mechanisms

Defense mechanisms are a psychoanalytic concept that has become more widely used among psychotherapists from different mental health disciplines to explain an unconscious mental process that provides protection for an individual from recognizing their undesirable thoughts, feelings, or memories. Defense mechanism terminology is sometimes used in the broader society among individuals knowledgeable about mental health or by devotees of pop-psychology. Although not always applied in the technical sense of their meaning, some of the defense mechanism concepts have become part of idiomatic language, such as accusing someone of 'projecting' their feelings or being in 'denial' or argumentatively accusing someone of being 'defensive,' or a plea to stop 'rationalizing.'

Although such terms may be freely bandied about, its clinical application is more complex. On this point, Kreitler and Kreitler (2004) explain that "Defense mechanisms (DMs) are a unique set of mental operations, first described by Freud (1913, 1962, 1964a), elaborated by Anna Freud (1966), and further developed in recent decades" (p. 195). However, in writing about defense mechanisms in this chapter, we have no intention of interpreting or diagnosing the employee's or founding CEO's thoughts and behaviors as pathological, neurotic, or psychotic as in the framework of the Freudian School of Psychoanalysis. Moreover, we draw a distinction between the typical unconscious reliance on defense mechanisms that occurs in the general population compared to the function that defense mechanisms occupy in FTRS. The key differences with FTRS are:

1. The link between founder's syndrome behavior and its victims in a workplace setting
2. It is a common occurrence in organizations with founder's syndrome

In constructing the FTRS paradigm, Block, a former practitioner of adult psychotherapy and marriage and family therapy, chose the defense mechanism concept because of a prevalent acceptance of the model of mental processes that incorporates a conscious and unconscious mind. Thus, defense mechanisms are an essential part of FTRS for analyzing and explaining the reactions, protections, and developments that:

1. Motivate a staff member to continue their affiliation with an organization while personally being targeted with founder's syndrome behaviors.
2. If there is a triggering event that leads the employee to gain conscious awareness of their symptoms, and after developing psychological strength and confidence, the employee will intervene against the founder and founder's syndrome behavior.
3. If the employee's attempt at creating change is unsuccessful, the employee will resign their position and leave the organization.

Defense mechanisms are triggered by an individual's unconscious mind as a barrier to guard against psychological distress, frightening ideas, memories of traumatic experiences, protection from anxiety or other forms of extreme stress and emotional conflict, as well as to prevent acting on unsavory or objectionable impulses. Defense mechanisms are considered a theoretical construct because we are unable to see the actual workings of the mind, but we trust in the explanation. However, we can observe an individual's calm behaviors that are attributable to the defense mechanism process. The diversion from both ill thoughts and from acting on extreme feelings of anger and hostility serves a function to keep the employee emotionally and physically safe during interactions with the CEO and makes it possible to go to work.

However, under certain conditions, the suppressed thoughts and feelings have the potential of surfacing into consciousness. Consequently, as the hidden thoughts and feelings approach the surface of consciousness, the employee may feel worried, uneasy, and experience physical signs of ailing without understanding the reasons for his or her feelings of angst. Additionally, the mind and body must continually use energy to keep the undesirable thoughts repressed. This depletion of energy to keep thoughts and feelings hidden can express itself through different symptoms. In their interpretation of defense mechanisms, Cullari and Kusché (2010) write:

> repressed energy must be released if the organism is to remain healthy … sooner or later, something has to give in. Symptoms serve as a compromise, because they allow the repressed ideas to be expressed indirectly in a disguised form … either psychological or physical. (p. 65)

We glean from Cullari and Kusché's understanding that an individual's psyche undergoes a psychological reaction that causes the person to exhibit different forms of behaviors or expressions. Additionally, the energy it takes to repress thoughts and feelings may convert into symptoms of fatigue, headaches, anxiety, depression, or generalized dysphoria. The symptoms are internally directed as the substitutes for the actual thoughts and feelings that remain repressed. Although the symptomatic feelings and thoughts are uncomfortable and potentially harmful, these symptoms may be less destructive or detrimental to an individual's career than the fallout one would experience if the actual thoughts and feelings were directly expressed to the founding CEO.

Although some psychological studies use coping strategies as a substitution for defense mechanisms, we draw a distinction between the two. Defense mechanisms remain at the unconscious level and coping strategies are at the conscious level. The trigger that sparks defense mechanisms or coping strategies may be the same set of events, but the employee's psychological readiness will determine whether they rely on defense mechanisms or coping strategies. Coping strategies occur when a staff member feels safer to consciously acknowledge and respond to undesirable events and stressors that initially required protection in the form of unconscious reliance on defense mechanisms. Lazarus writes in his essay on a theory of emotions (2006) that,

> If we regard emotions as having major significance for adaptation, then the traditional tripartite division of the mind into cognition, motivation, and emotion must be supplemented with another concept, the coping process. Coping is concerned with our efforts to manage adaptational demands and the emotions they generate. (p. 10)

The ability to cope with the pressures of working in a founder's syndrome environment may be the difference between feeling ill or feeling satisfied. Kent, Devonport, Lane, Nicholls, and Friesen (2018) point out that employees without adequate coping skills to regulate physiological and psychological states affected by pressure may underperform, relative to their skill level (DeCaro, Thomas, Albert, & Beilock, 2011). Coping strategies that help an individual regulate perceived demands in an important moment could enhance an individual's ability to attend, concentrate, and perform effectively under pressure (Jensen & Wrisberg, 2014). (p. 40)

Type of Defense Mechanism

Reaction Formation

Sarnoff (1960) explains, "a person who employs reaction formation against a consciously unacceptable motive will tend to behave in a manner which is diametrically opposed to that motive" (p. 132). Reaction formation, as a defense mechanism, in an individual employed in an organization with recognizable founder's syndrome would suppress his or her feelings of anger and hostility in reaction to the way they are treated and, instead, would communicate in the opposite way of how they feel. The defense will remain in place until such time that the individual is able to cope with the underlying motive.

The following case example stems from an interview with Gary L., a Vice President of Marketing for a Dallas-based chain of restaurants who began his position within six months after the organization was founded by Jonathan M., and before it went public. With the company in its fourth year, Gary was the target of Jonathan's ridicule and sarcasm during management team meetings. The antagonistic behavior was sporadic and gradually became a standard founder's syndrome symptom. The other managers in the group were relieved that they were passed over and not the target of the CEO's public ridicule. Rather than confront Jonathan during the management team meetings or in a private setting, Gary repressed his feelings through the defense mechanism known as reaction formation evidenced by smiles and chuckling. In fact, for Jonathan's birthday, Gary wrote in a Birthday card, "To a great boss who possesses wit and humor ...."

At an after-work social gathering for drinks at a nearby restaurant, Milton, the Vice President of Finance, pulled Gary aside to have a private conversation. Milton expressed his bewilderment how Gary was able to simply laugh off Jonathan's nasty comments during management team meetings. Gary was surprised by Milton's question and in his defense replied that he thought it was Jonathan's way of joking to lighten up the seriousness of the meetings. Milton shrugged his shoulders and said there was nothing funny about Jonathan's critical remarks nor being treated 'like a doormat.'

Following the exchange between Milton and Gary, the next few months proved to be a metamorphic experience for Gary. During management team meetings, the more he tried to ignore Jonathan's comments, the more aware he became of the undertones of derision in Jonathan's remarks. He also became acutely cognizant of the nonverbal reaction among the other managers in the room and for the first time he felt embarrassed. Following the meetings, Gary began having periods of confusion and depression in addition to experiencing physical symptoms such as headaches and digestive upset. Consequently, he consulted his physician who prescribed some medication and suggested that his ailments were a result of stress. They discussed ways of mitigating the stress including a referral to a psychologist. After several weeks of exercising and yoga at his health club, Gary admittedly found only minor relief and decided it was time to meet with a psychologist.

After three therapy sessions with the psychologist, Gary acknowledged that his stress and physical symptoms were caused by his anger at how he was being treated by Jonathan in front of his colleagues. Gary discussed his options with the psychologist and decided that he was going to meet with other management team members to determine if he was the only target of Jonathan's bullying behaviors. Some refused to discuss the relationship they have with the boss but three of the managers revealed in confidence that Jonathan was a tyrant during their one-to-one meetings and would frequently enter their offices to micromanage their work. Gary also discovered that the two senior managers that had resigned in the previous six months did not leave for a better career opportunity as Jonathan had announced. Instead, they quit because they felt harassed by Jonathan.

Given Jonathan's acerbic style, Gary decided that it would not be productive to confront Jonathan and ask him to stop his caustic treatment, although his psychologist suggested that being direct would be a healthier way to deal with his anger. Instead, with support from two of the Vice Presidents, Gary contacted a few members of the board of directors and asked for their intervention. He informed them that Jonathan's maltreatment and harassment led to the loss of two key managers, and if there were no changes in how Jonathan comported himself, he and other company's Vice Presidents would quit the company. It was not lost on the board members that if several Vice Presidents departed the company at the same time, it could cripple the company's business. In response to the threat, the board of directors brought in an organizational development consultant to evaluate the organizational culture, the dynamics of the workplace, and the allegations of Jonathan's founder syndrome behaviors. The board of directors did not inform Jonathan of the potential loss of the key managers but did inform him that the consultant was engaged to evaluate the organizational culture and evaluate the company's effectiveness and efficiencies and whether any training was warranted to shore up any weaknesses. As a result of receiving confirmation about the morale problems based on their CEO's mediocre management abilities, the Board negotiated a settlement package with Jonathan who made a public announcement that he was leaving the company.

Case Analysis

Gary's experience with FTRS is an example triggered by the founder's syndrome behavior. Until being confronted by a curious colleague, Gary endured being the target of intimidation and harassment by the founding CEO. When we discussed this case in a seminar with doctoral and graduate students and asked them to analyze the case, several said they never would have put up with the torment that Gary endured. This is a common reaction among individuals who never experienced founder's syndrome behavior and especially coupled with the dilemma of quitting a job and sacrificing a better than average or high-level salary versus tolerating the browbeating in the workplace.

After all, human beings find different ways of living with disturbing events and will especially endure hardships if their income is at stake, and even more so if they have a family that is dependent on that income and company benefits. Furthermore, despite civil protections from discrimination, one's age, sexual orientation, race, and ethnicity are all factors individuals consider whether to stay in a job or leave without transitioning into a new job in hand. These are also the types of predicaments that trigger a reliance on psychologically based defense mechanisms or consciously oriented coping strategies. Baumeister, Dale, and Sommer (1998) writing in the *Journal of Personality* point out that a

> particular crisis in self-perception may arise when an internal or external event occurs that clearly violates the preferred view of self. In such cases, it is necessary for the self to have some mechanism or process to defend itself against the threatening implications of this event. Such processes are commonly called defense mechanisms. (p. 1082)

The case of Gary and Jonathan is a textbook example of FTRS. Additionally, there were coincidental events that contributed to the outcome. The dynamics of Jonathan's behavior with his management team resulted in a longstanding practice of organizational silence. As the target of founder's syndrome, Gary repressed his feelings and thoughts with the defense mechanism of reaction formation and laughed away Jonathan's sarcasm and belittling remarks. It was fortuitous that Gary's colleague was compelled to inquire about Gary's state of mind and how he tolerated being mistreated during management team meetings. That one event led Gary to struggle with maintaining the unconscious defense mechanisms that provided him with safety from Jonathan's verbal assaults. Gary's unconscious needs for a defense mechanism did not immediately wither away. As his true feelings of anger surfaced into consciousness, his attempt to cope and suppress them required energy that turned into stress-related headaches and other somatic symptoms.

Gary's decision to begin therapy sessions with a psychologist gave him a safe outlet to come to terms with his feelings of anger and to decide on his next steps. Over a period of months, Gary went through a personal transformation and became psychologically healthier which gave him the strength and courage to discuss his personal situation with several senior managers. The fact that some of his colleagues also shared information was vital to Gary's problem resolution. Had the three managers refused to discuss their plight and maintain their silence as did some other managers, the outcome might have been quite different for Gary and for the organization. Gary might have quit rather than continue to take the brunt of Jonathan's callous comments, and the organization would have continued to be imperiled by founder's syndrome.

The board members' receptivity to listen to Gary and his two colleagues was fortunate and seemed propitious. The outcome would have been different if the board members were unwilling to listen, which has occurred in other organizations. Or, had the board members listened but decided not to engage an organizational development consultant with the aim of assessing the health of the organization, a different ending would also have transpired.

This last point requires additional clarification. In other organizations, we have observed hurried board members make quick decisions to fire CEOs without any tangible evidence of wrongdoing. With some other boards, we witnessed abrupt decision-making to place their CEOs on paid leave without any discussion with their CEOs, who might have been able to shed some light on the allegations that were hailed against them by disgruntled managers. In those instances, the firings and job suspensions were reckless decisions. They presumed a conclusion that the CEOs were guilty of the allegations made against them.

Firing the CEO or suspending the CEO's position of authority completely undermines the CEO's credibility and integrity by removing his or her legitimate control and power. In those circumstances, if the board does do an investigation and finds that the allegations were not justified, it would be an untenable situation for a fired CEO to return to their former position and equally embarrassing to return from a suspension. The primary issue is not that employees circumvent their CEO-supervisor to complain to the board; it is the board's assumption that their CEO is guilty because his or her subordinates say so.

Consider what would happen if a CEO does return, the management staff know they have a path to bypass the CEO to complain and a board that is willing to terminate their CEO or place him or her on suspension on the basis of hearsay. A CEO cannot successfully manage without the trust of the board of directors or trust in his or her senior managers. Consequently, a returning CEO must fire all the employees he or she suspects of having betrayed him or her. The CEO's action of firing some of his or her management staff is likely to bring charges of retaliation and lawsuits and it certainly will adversely impact the morale of the staff that report to those managers. Depending on how many senior staff are fired might also jeopardize the workflow of the organization until key management talent can be found and hired. The reality is that if a CEO is asked to return to their position, very few would do so. A competent CEO must preserve his or her integrity and try to negotiate a departing settlement in line with his or her contract.

In this case example, the board took a mature and responsible governance position by bringing in an organizational development consultant without informing the CEO that their decision was prompted by employee rumors or allegations, although it would have been reasonable to inform the CEO that they heard rumors of dissatisfaction in the workplace. Had the allegations against the CEO proven false, there would not have been any harsh results to the CEO. Instead, the organizational consultant would have been able to make workplace quality improvement recommendations for the board and the CEO to consider. This would have included recommendations on how to identify problematic supervisory relationships and best practices to resolve differences, which might include improved personnel appraisal practices, staff development and goal setting, training, or even practical methods for terminating subordinates when all attempts to improve the fit of the employee to their job responsibilities fail.

In the case of Jonathan, the board of directors received a report with an objective finding and testimonies that the CEO had engaged in detrimental founder's syndrome behavior. The board did not want intervention to see if the CEO's behavior could change, but they also wanted to prevent a public relations fiasco. The board of directors took a wise course of action by offering a departure settlement. It was a smart decision that the board acknowledged Jonathan's role in founding the organization and he was deserving of some financial settlement for a history of success, albeit they had cause to terminate him for his behavior toward staff. Had the board refused to negotiate a departure settlement, it is highly likely that Jonathan's termination would have escalated into hostilities with bad public relations and a lawsuit that might have led to devaluing the financial worth of the company.

Would it be correct to consider the idea of a settlement of an ethical dilemma? The idea of giving money to the CEO who engaged in founder's syndrome seems like rewarding him or her for their disturbing behavior. Truly, there is no sense of reward for the founder of an organization who considers the company his or her baby and has it taken away. The organization that he or she founded has been their identity and a source of pride. There is no replacement for that type of loss. Also, the CEO loses salary and company benefits. The settlement is not a gift, it is a means to expedite the CEO's removal with a signed document of indemnification to avoid a more costly lawsuit. Although not completely foolproof, it offers some protections for the stockholders from the degree of devaluation of the for-profit company, and some protection from the loss of reputation of a nonprofit company that is dependent on grants and donations.

Rationalization versus Intellectualization

Rationalization is a common defense mechanism that operates at the level of unconsciousness to assist an individual to justify their own or someone else's unacceptable behavior or ill thoughts. In their paper on rationalization and political corruption, Gannett and Rector (2015) describe how individuals engage in rationalization to explain their bad behavior as being good. The following quote is reminiscent of a Robinhood tale, "corporate actors typically rationalize corrupt behavior after the fact, and tend to do so most often in ways that highlight their own good intentions instead of in ways that minimize the harmful consequences of their choices" (p. 165). These authors also identify the work of Rabl and Kühlmann (2009), who have an eight-item typology of rationalization that has application for our explanations of FTRS, as follows:

1. Legality: "Corrupt actors excuse their behaviors by claiming that as long as an act is legal it is not specifically wrong" (Rabl & Kühlmann, 2009, p. 272).
2. Denial of Responsibility: "Corrupt actors construe that they had no other choice than to participate in corrupt activities due to circumstances which are beyond their control" (Rabl & Kühlmann, 2009, p. 272).
3. Denial of Injury: An individual "concludes that the corruption did not have any victims" (Gannett & Rector, 2015, p. 169).
4. Denial of Victim: "Rather than denying that any person has been harmed, the corrupt actor denies the very existence or ethical standing of the victim … the victim was a lower class of person and thus might have deserved it" (Gannett & Rector, 2015, p. 169).
5. Social Weighting: "occurs when corrupt actors compare themselves to other, presumably worse, actors, including their accusers" (Gannett & Rector, 2015, p. 169).
6. Appeal to Higher Loyalties: Individuals "claim that the corrupt acts they committed were in pursuit of a higher goal or greater loyalty" (Gannett & Rector, 2015, p. 169).
7. Metaphor of the Ledger: "Corrupt actors claim they have earned a certain right to commit corrupt acts because of the credit they have

gained for previous good works" (Gannett & Rector, 2015, p. 169–170).

8. Good Will Ambassador: "Corrupt actors deemphasize, compartmentalize, or suppress the knowledge of their acts in favor of more normatively redeeming features of their work" (Rabl & Kühlmann, 2009, p. 273).

Through the review of the aforementioned typology, we can see the possibilities of founders engaging in a form of mental calisthenics to argue how their immoral behavior should be condoned as moral conduct. Brown et al. (2011) capture that essence in their following statement:

> Rationalization can enable immoral behavior to be reinterpreted as moral (or at least as neutral) and can allow people to erect a psychological barrier between their misbehavior and the self-concept, enabling them to see themselves as 'decent human beings' while they engage in immoral or unethical behavior. Thus, rationalization can free people to misbehave without being plagued by the dissonance and guilt that would otherwise stem from their contradicting their moral values. (p. 2)

As a defense mechanism operating at an unconscious level, intellectualization uses the process of an emotional detachment relying on thinking and citing facts to block feelings and undesirable thoughts. According to Zepf (2011),

> Intellectualization refers to the handling of the outcome of a process in which instinctual wishes are isolated from the feelings that accompany them. By virtue of further defensive mechanisms, they are then transferred into substitutive ideas that are situated on a higher level of abstraction. (p. 156)

As implied in the word intellectualization, an individual views an event in an intellectual manner and may present him or herself by philosophizing, being brainy or analytical. This differs from rationalization in which an individual uses justification as a primary defense tool to block feelings and disturbing ideas and other upsetting thoughts. Burgo (2012) also distinguishes rationalization from intellectualization stating,

> While rationalization as a defense mechanism offers explanations for *specific facts* that are more plausible than true, intellectualization seeks to keep the entire spectrum of *disturbing emotion* at bay ... Rationalization is a discrete, occasional defense, whereas intellectualization pervades and defines one's entire character. (p. 148)

With rationalization as a defense mechanism, the complication for the receiver of a message is to determine whether the content is truthful. In many situations, there is no attempt to ascertain the legitimacy of the message especially if the originator is an individual that seems to be of upstanding character. Because the message is formulated at an unconscious level and spoken aloud or in writing as a statement of truth, there is no question of accuracy unless the message is from someone known to be of questionable make-up. Keep in mind that in situations where the content of a rationalized message is untrue, the originator of the message believes in its veracity and is not conjuring a lie on a conscious level, they are unconsciously using logic to excuse their situation.

The following FTRS case exemplifies the use of rationalization. Dr. Leonard, a board member of a large nonprofit organization in Florida's panhandle, had a personal connection to a private foundation. During a board of directors meeting, Dr. Leonard reported that he will be contacting his friend who is a foundation trustee and happens to owe him a favor. To everyone's satisfaction, Dr. Leonard announced that he will be requesting a $250,000 dollar donation for a new homeless and mental health project targeted for veterans of the Vietnam War. Despite the level of personal acquaintanceship with the foundation director, his grant request was denied.

To offset the anxiety and embarrassment of informing the board of his failure after such bravado at the last board meeting, the board member rationalizes that,

> it is just as well we did not get the funds since I have come to realize that our executive director and staff are not really up to taking on the added responsibilities of a new project. Although not directly said, I got the distinct impression from my friend at the Foundation that our organization may have outgrown our executive director's abilities to expand the organization with new programs. (Source: Private discussion)

The organization's founding executive director, Margaret K., immediately stood up and declared that the statement about her is not only ridiculous, but also insulting, and she plans on meeting with the foundation director to find out why he would have such a belief. The board member responded saying that the foundation trustee is his personal connection and that Margaret may not contact anyone at the foundation. Most of the board of directors verbalized their agreement that it would be a mistake to allow their executive director to have contact with the foundation.

Over the weekend, Margaret was seething with anger. She was certainly not going to accept that she was not capable of starting new programs, after all she started the company. She sent out an email to her department directors asking that they clear their schedule for the following Friday for a review of their strategic plan and each department's status to meet their plan objectives. At Friday's meeting, Margaret informed her managers of what was stated at the last board meeting. Still upset, she was unusually hostile in her response to hearing the strategic plan updates reported by each department director. One of the department directors, David B., said, "Margaret, I understand why you are upset because of what was said at the board meeting, but it is not fair to take your anger out on us." Although David might not have been wrong about Margaret's anger, his comment just compounded her feelings of hostility. She responded, "don't confuse my anger with the board for my disappointment after hearing today's reports from you and the other department directors." It was an unforgiving tone that was appreciatively different than Margaret ever used in prior management meetings and retreats. She said, "the board expects to see excellence from my work, and I expect to see it in your work. Maybe I have been to lax with everyone, but that's going to change."

Indeed, Margaret altered her supervisory style and continued in ensuing months to be belligerent and started micromanaging the work of her department directors. Six months later, David wrote a letter of resignation addressing it to Margaret with copies to the department directors and each member of the board of directors. In the letter, he stated he would no longer work for an executive director who micromanaged his work and was a bully. He wrote,

> your pessimistic and unappreciative attitude toward your department directors who helped make this organization successful is evidence that you are no longer up to the task to manage this organization. I now understand why Dr. Leonard's request for a grant was denied from the Billings Family Foundation. (Source: Private discussion)

Case Analysis

An effort to garner funds by a board member for a new organizational project eventually led to the dismissal of Margaret, the founding CEO. It was as though the statement of rationalization by Dr. Leonard, allowing him to save face from an embarrassing attempt to acquire a foundation contribution turned into a self-fulfilling prophecy.

Rationalization was the defense mechanism that allowed Dr. Leonard to feel better about himself. Many nonprofit organization executive directors and fund development directors would be grateful that a board member would use his or her time to contact a potential funder. However, a turning point in this case was the added statement by Dr. Leonard, "Although not directly said, I got the distinct impression from my friend at the Foundation that our organization may have out-grown our executive director's abilities to expand the organization with new programs." It is unfortunate that none of the board members raised questions about the qualifying beginning of Dr. Leonard's statement and intuitive deliberation. He admitted what he was stating was not some-thing he heard. On that basis, we can speculate that Dr. Leonard was shielded from being challenged because of his standing on the board of directors.

The potential trouble that the organization eventually experienced could have been foretold by the immediate emotional reaction of the founding CEO. Instead of her protestations, she could have asked the board of directors whether anyone on the board required information to dispel such a belief that she was unqualified to successfully expand the organization's programming. Instead, over the next several days and months, Margaret's style of management changed from a supportive leadership style to a founder's syndrome behavior model. Her behavior at subsequent board meetings was professional but she acted cool and distant toward board members.

Thus, the organization underwent a transformation that started with one board member's good intentions, to his rationalizing why he was unsuccessful in obtaining a grant, and it led to the resignation of a competent department director who had the strength to take it upon himself to point out the CEO's problematic behaviors. It concluded with the dismissal of the founding CEO for founder's syndrome behavior.

Projection

If you recall in the explanation about reaction formation, an individual unconsciously blocks their true feelings and takes on an opposite per-sona. In the defense mechanism of projection, an individual also takes on a different persona by blocking their true feelings and thoughts and as-signing them to another person, 'I'm not like that at all, you're like that!' Baumeister et al. (1998) wrote the following about projection:

> In its simplest form, it refers to seeing one's own traits in other people. A more rigorous understanding involves perceiving others as having traits that one inaccurately believes oneself not to have ... projection can be seen as defensive if perceiving the threatening trait in others helps the individual in some way to avoid recognizing it in himself or herself, and indeed this is how Freud (e.g., 1915/1961a) conceptualized projection. (p. 1090)

In 1997 and 2005, Newman et al. described a viable hypothesis of projection. As a result of suppressing thoughts about one's own negative traits and behaviors, an individual is more likely to be sensitive to those types of traits and, therefore, "especially prone to interpret other people's behavior in terms of those (and not other) unfavorable traits" (2005, p. 260).

The following instance of projection is a summary from a founder's syndrome case study about a sports organization with details and a theory-based explanation presented by Block (2004, pp. 135–154). An interesting aspect of this case is that the employee is also the organization's founder who exhibits the defense mechanism in addition to his display of founder's syndrome behaviors directed toward board members.

The organization had grown from a small club into an international membership organization with subsidiary companies that sold sports insurance, certification training programs, magazines, and a travel agency. The original board of directors comprised of the founding CEO, Justin R., his wife and two of their family members. In addition, the board consisted of five nonfamily members hand-picked and invited by Justin to serve. As with many founder-led organizations, the board did not have term limits (Block & Rosenberg, 2002).

By its 12th year, three new board members had joined the board replacing three who had left for various reasons. Among the newer members was a banker who was surprised to learn that the board had not established Justin's compensation that apparently grew from the streams of revenue from the subsidiary companies. Recognizing that the board of directors had a fiduciary responsibility to the membership, the banker board member raised his concerns at a board meeting and indicated that the board was required to perform an evaluation of their CEO and establish his compensation.

Justin was caught off-guard by the banker's authoritative statement. Justin replied that it had been his practice to set all salaries including his own since he started the company and he had not taken advantage of that privilege. He also said that it sounded as though he was being accused of having done something wrong. The banker replied that Justin may not have intentionally handled his compensation inappropriately, but it was considered self-dealing and a conflict of interest to set his own salary and his family members' salaries. Justin stated he did not agree that he engaged in a conflict of interest but would certainly abide by the outcome of a vote of the board of directors.

A vote of the five nonfamily board members prevailed over Justin and his three family members. Justin became outraged and accused the banker of being untrustworthy and a conniving plotter who only had his self-interest in mind. He accused the banker of engaging in a conspiracy by somehow promising the other board members that they would benefit by siding with him and against Roger and his family members. Justin stood and while storming out of the boardroom he ordered his family members to follow him to his office. Justin locked his office door and called his attorney. He told the lawyer that he needed a restraining order against the five board members claiming he had been threatened by them and feared for his safety and his three family members. In response to a question by the attorney, Justin said, "yes, I am certain that it could become physical."

The restraining order prohibited the board members from entering the organization's headquarters for 60 days. When the five board members met elsewhere, they took board action to fire Justin. In response to their letter informing Justin of their action to terminate his employment due to his egregious behaviors, Justin's attorney wrote the five board members and informed them that their action was not binding because they did not follow the bylaws in providing proper notice for the board meeting and were required per the bylaws to have seven board members in attendance for a quorum.

The entire matter became litigious and the parties were Court ordered to engage in dispute resolution. The parties met with a retired Judge at a firm that engages in mediation. The exact terms of the settlement were confidential, but we do know that Justin was no longer the CEO and none of his family members remained on the board or in the employ of the company.

Case Analysis

This was an interesting case that started with a new board member wanting to limit the board's liability and properly assume its fiduciary responsibility. In announcing to the board of directors that there existed a problem that needed to be rectified, the founding CEO took offense and reframed the problem as a trust issue, expressing his feelings of being insulted by an accusation of wrongdoing.

We know from the history of the company that it started as a club and grew into a large international membership organization. When he was the club president, Justin's management responsibilities were limited. Like many organizations that become large, there may be gaps in the CEO's knowledge about governance and management practices. However, in this case with governing documents, available legal representation, and the significant growth of the company, we can speculate that Justine was aware of the board's responsibilities to set his compensation and provide him with a written agreement or formal employment contract. Even if we were to believe that Justin did not know that the board should have set his compensation, he recruited a board member with expertise in finances and should have respected the banker's knowledge.

Justin's statement of disagreement with the banker's revelation was not simply a difference of opinion. Had Justin approached the situation ethically, he would not have disputed the banker's remarks. Instead, he would have accepted the banker's statement and/or sought a legal opinion from the company's attorney. Justin's assertions were motivated by his need to remain in control of the organization and its monies. Accordingly, Justin acted agreeably for a vote on the matter because he was convinced that he could defeat the banker's call for a motion to establish an annual evaluation and assume their responsibility to establish a reasonable executive compensation package.

As onlookers, we can witness Justin's efforts as a manipulator and game player believing he can outwit the board of directors. He was confident that he would win with his own vote, his family members' votes, and the votes of two other board members that he confidently thought were aligned with him.

To his surprise, he lost with a tally of five votes in favor of establishing a system of evaluation and executive compensation, and four votes against the motion. The two veteran board members knew that the banker was correct, and they could be found culpable of liability for past mistakes and allow Justin to continue to set his own salary and benefits.

How does Justin reconcile the fact that he will no longer manage the company without some level of accountability? He panics. Justin tries to recover his loss of control and gain back his dominance over the governing board of directors by accusing the banker of the very traits that he embodies. He denounces the banker as a conniver, a plotter to get his own way, and untrustworthy. In his projection, he also accuses the five board members of taking advantage of him and alleges they formed an alliance to personally benefit from the company. Prior to the vote, it was Justin who took advantage of the board of directors and used his alliance with his family members and friends on the board as a tool to help him pass governing policies and other board decisions that benefitted him and family. Consider Beresford's (2012) explanation about this form of defense mechanism:

> If anxiety can be politely tucked away in fantasies, or immediately acted upon without thinking or sent inside to torture the body, it can easily be directed outward – aimed at others whom we regard as the cause of all our troubles ... . In models of the mind that posit the unconscious as part of human makeup ... humans project their own unwanted attributes onto others in this way. (p. 125–126)

The findings, in this case, show Justin as having a high motivation for power and control as reflected in a history of manipulating the board and controlling his family members to achieve his organizational and personal goals. Besides recognizing Justin's propensity for self-protection using projection as a defense mechanism, it is not surprising that his negative affectivity correlates with founder's syndrome behavior of power and control, such as disrupting a board meeting by storming out of the boardroom and ordering his family to follow. His act of seeking a restraining order is a clever tool to control who can enter the organization's headquarters and indirectly uses the court system to cast a label onto the board members as deviants that Justin and his family need protection from.

Given Justin's intemperate outbursts and restraining order scheme to keep board members away from the headquarters, a clinical psychologist colleague asked whether we thought that Justin's behavior was a result of defense mechanisms or a more disturbing personality disorder. The query is one we have contemplated in several cases for certain founders as well as for staff and board members who have plotted to rid of a founder who has not displayed founder's syndrome behavior. As we stated earlier, our intention is not to diagnose mental illness in any of the individuals we have come to know or have studied, other than to point out more common symptoms of anxiety or depression. Although the question will go unanswered, we can say without compromise that even a person with a personality disorder or other mental incapacity issue is still capable of a reliance on an unconscious use of defense mechanisms (Perry, Presniak, Olson, & Trevor, 2013; Schueler, Herron, Poland, & Schultz, 1982).

Denial

Denial is a frequently used word to contradict or accuse someone of their stated beliefs or interpretation of events. We hear people say it, and many of us have said it to others, 'you're in denial!' The literature on denial is vast with examples of individuals with serious illness. We can easily understand why a patient who is told of a terminal diagnosis sinks into denial. Also, individuals close to a terminal patient may want to block the awful reality that death is imminent for their loved one. But denial is not relegated just to sick patients. We also witness it in the workplace and in organizations that exhibit founder's syndrome.

Although the meaning of denial in the simplest sense is used to prevent dealing with a horrific reality, psychological experts provide a more thorough explanation. For example, Cramer (1999) states, "Denial, a defense that is based on dichotomous thinking in which a negative marker (no, not) is attached to an anxiety-arousing perception in order to turn it into something less threatening …" (p. 736).

Baumeister et al. (1998) explain that denial is the "simple refusal to face certain facts. Insofar as these facts are highly upsetting or represent potential damage to self-esteem, denial can in principle be a very useful defense mechanism" (p. 1107). Among the most common use of denial other than illness is individual failure. It could occur when someone fails a test or at work when an individual receives a poor personnel evaluation. Instead of accepting the results of the evaluation, individuals find fault with the evaluation procedures or attribute the results to prejudice. According to Baumeister et al. (1998) and Weinstein (1980), research has demonstrated that individuals tend to be hopeful to the point of being unrealistic about their futures. In fact, most "think they are less likely than the average person to suffer various misfortunes, such as career failure" (p. 1109).

The following FTRS case study is about a mid-size business head-quartered in Torrance, California, that manufactures and retails boutique soaps, shampoos, body oils, and creams in the South Bay region of Los Angeles County. Our contact with this company was prior to it going public after successfully opening its 40th outlet in malls throughout the western region of the United States. In this case, we determined the existence of the defense mechanism denial in the founder and the defense mechanism intellectualization in an employee who was a division director. The founding CEO, Leslie N., successfully grew the company from homemade products sold at Farmer's Markets into a profitable company with a vision of nationwide outlets and perhaps competing internationally.

After eight years of a typical style of annual personnel evaluations, the director of Human Resources (HR), Bryce W., introduced a new annual evaluation method, a 360 Assessment for all full-time and part-time employees. A 360 review provides feedback from multiple sources including peers, subordinates, and supervisors. It can also include feedback from individuals outside the organization such as funders, consultants, suppliers, or customers that have interacted with an employee.

Leslie thought it would motivate her employees to see the results of her 360 review. She wanted to demonstrate how resourceful and inspiring she was to her senior managers and board members and thought it would be an ideal and 'down to earth' segment to include in an infomercial that was in a planning stage and to be released just prior to launching an initial public offering. In view of her plans, she had her HR director distribute the forms and instructions to 16 managers and board members. The aggregated results of her 360 review were shared with Leslie. After reviewing the results, she ripped up the report and notified the HR director that there was a serious blunder with the 360 computation.

After Bryce arrived at her office, she informed him that there must have been a mix-up with her forms and other managers that altered the accuracy of her report. Bryce said he reviewed the raw data and was certain there were no mix-ups. She persisted stating that if the forms were not mixed-up then there was something wrong with the software. She was adamant. "I don't know why you can't see the problem, there is no way on earth I'm a micromanager, and those leadership results are ridiculous. I've been such a successful entrepreneur that to have results saying I am not an imaginative problem-solver is a joke." She then asked Bryce whether he fooled with the results as a stupid prank, manufacturing write-in comments such as "bad-mouthing employees," "giving unreasonable ultimatums," and "seemed proud to make a staff member cry," and "Leslie is brilliant in her business ideas but doesn't seem to know how to build a culture of trust." Although his integrity and ethics were being questioned, Bryce responded matter-of-factly, stating "the results were tabulated by the software."

Leslie stated, "see, it proves my point. You say you didn't alter the results, then either you aren't being straight with me or something was wrong with the program. You chose this program; did you do any kind of due diligence before spending all that money on what turned out to be a piece of crap?" Bryce replied, "the program came highly recommended by several members of the Society for Human Resource Management and I personally reviewed the program for its content. I even had our IT director examine the software requirements for compatibility with our computer system. Everything checked out before I authorized the expenditure."

"You still don't get it do you?" and then she ordered Bryce to shred all the employee results of the 360 reviews and to cease circulating the forms to the employees. Additionally, she demanded that he send out a company-wide memorandum to all staff and copy the board members that there is a problem with the tabulation part of the software and to disregard any of their evaluation results and return them to HR. She also said to include a note that until the software company that supplied the 360 could fix their problems, we will forego 360 reviews and will be going back to our old more reliable personnel review system. Bryce insisted that the software company had hundreds of satisfied clients with unfailing testimonials, and he did not think it was ethical to allege their software as untrustworthy. So, Leslie fired him.

Leslie prepared her own two memos. One noted the software issue with the undependable 360 results. The day after, she sent out another company-wide memorandum announcing that the Assistant Director of HR was being promoted to Director of Human Resources. She asked everyone to wish Bryce well and thanked him for his years of dedicated service.

Case Analysis

It would be incorrect to merely assume that Leslie simply did not agree with the appalling results of her 360 review. Her perception of self and her beliefs about the type of relationships she has with the individuals in her company simply did not compute with the scores on the 360 assessment. Therefore, in her state of denial, she searches for a logical explanation. There can only be three possible reasons for the results. Leslie went through the options of human error, a purposeful prank, and faulty software.

Trevithick (2011) reminds us that "Denial describes a defense where information or events are rejected or blocked from awareness if considered threatening, frightening or anxiety provoking – irrespective of the incontrovertible nature of evidence to the contrary" (p. 396). Given her mindset, Leslie had no alternative but to have all results destroyed and seek some other evaluation tool.

At no time did Bryce get excited in response to Leslie's hysterics. Instead, he continued to use reasoning to avoid confrontation and anger and resorted to facts to explain how he reached a decision to invest in the 360-evaluation program. Additionally, he was straightforward in stating that it would be unethical to follow Leslie's directive and he could not imagine that there was anything wrong with the program. Interestingly, besides insisting something was wrong with the program, Leslie used insults to belittle Bryce. He in return never commented about the insults nor did he return any to her.

Leslie experienced his refusal to do as she directed as being in-subordinate and was an affront to her credibility and belief system. Because Bryce would not agree with her, she took his actions to mean that he must believe the disparaging comments about her management style were accurate. To her way of thinking, she had no choice but to terminate him from the company.

While reviewing this case with graduate and doctoral students, more than one pointed out the written statements about Leslie and in particular the one that said she was "brilliant in business but did not know how to build a culture of trust." The students raised an excellent point that write-in information could not be tabulated like averaging her other results on a Likert scale. Wouldn't the write-in messages convince Leslie that the results were valid? Not at all! With the protections of the unconscious mind, Leslie believes that some words were changed or left out while the informant was entering their remarks into the computer program. Her belief is not completely unreasonable. Almost all of us have left out a word or doubled up on a word or misspelled a word while typing into a computer or smart device. Also, many of us have experienced words changing as we typed them into a smart device that was programmed to anticipate what word we were intending to write. Besides, Leslie was convinced that there was a problem with the software. She could reason that the first part of the sentence was about her, but the second part was about someone else that got combined due to the quirks of the software. Although we may consider Leslie's analysis about a tangle of sentences to be implausible, in her state of denial it would be a reasonable and sound explanation. Leslie's beliefs and pronouncements are reinforced by self-deception, a concept related to denial. Blumenthal-Barby and Ubel (2018) explain,

> Self-deception occurs when a person has a desire for a certain outcome and actively lies to herself or tells herself a narrative about the probability that is in tension with the actual evidence but in line with the desired outcome. (p. 5)

It is easy to imagine that a founding CEO, such as Leslie, can have a fallible belief system. Her company has been successful, and she attributes its growth to her strategic decision-making and her style of management. In preparation for an informercial, we get a glimpse of her belief system that she is adored by all her managers and board members. Although that is what Leslie believes about herself, we learn from the interaction with Bryce's FTRS events and the 360 review findings that Leslie has engaged in founder's syndrome behavior. Because of Bryce's intellectualization, his demeanor remained aloof.

By collecting and destroying the completed reviews, the board of directors was never enlightened about Leslie's founder's syndrome behaviors. The sporadic turnover of management staff did not raise concerns among the board and was merely explained away by Leslie as natural attrition and the need for 'new blood' in the wake of the continued growth of the company. Leslie continues to run the company as its founding CEO.

Conclusion

Despite the challenging behaviors displayed by the individuals protected by defense mechanisms described in this chapter, almost all can be considered emotionally healthy compared to individuals with more profound personality issues. Our selected case examples of FTRS are of the type to be more commonly encountered by consultants.

Other types of cases are exceptional and consist of founders and/or employees that are ill with mental health disorders. For example, a founder relying on the defense mechanism known as Displacement (Massoglia, 2006) is compelled to demonstrate socially unacceptable feelings or impulses toward someone, and they act out inappropriately, perhaps physically, toward a substitute person or animal. Or, consider what happens when a founder enters a state of blankness or blackouts to avoid a psychologically painful event or memory. That defense mechanism is known as Dissociation (Seligman, 2016). Another defense mechanism that is sometimes discussed as part of hypnotherapy treatment is known as Regression. This is when a person reverts to thought processes and behaviors reflective of an earlier stage of life that was safer. A rare defense condition is Somatization or Conversion Disorder (Miller, Archer, & Kapoor, 2020) in which a person experiences physical distress that can include blindness, paralysis, or other symptoms that do not appear to have a neurological root cause. In the event that a consultant without mental health credentials encounters a person displaying any of these or other more unusual defenses, the consultant would be wise to either withdraw from the case or engage a mental health professional to be part of the intervention team.

As a constructed paradigm emanating from our understanding of founder's syndrome, FTRS demonstrates how the unconscious mind alters perceptions and protects individuals from undesirable and distressing thoughts, memories, and objectionable behaviors. FTRS provides an explanation as to how individuals manage to function in unpleasant environments. Although some individuals display disturbing and intolerable behaviors, FTRS gives us a tool to understand that without the aid of unconscious defense mechanisms, the impulsive behaviors of perpetrators or the reactions of victims would be harsher and possibly volatile. FTRS also provides insight into the evolving process that a target of a founder's microaggressions experiences to arrive at the point of asserting themselves against the founder or resigning from the workplace.

In the next chapter, we explore founder's syndrome from the viewpoint of multiple theories of personality, behavior, and organization.

Discussion Questions

1. What is Founder's Transformational Reaction Syndrome (FTRS)? Explain a circumstance where an individual board or staff member would experience FTRS.
2. How does Founder's Transformational Reaction Syndrome differ from the traditional explanations about founder's syndrome?
3. Think about a situation at work where one of the defense mechanisms described in this chapter can be used to explain the behavior of a co-worker or board member. Describe the situation, the defense mechanism, and how the situation impacted other staff or board members in the company.
4. In this chapter, we identify several different defense mechanisms. Explain the purpose of a defense mechanism.
5. Why might an employee who is a target of founder's syndrome experience a defense mechanism?
6. Is it possible for a founder who engages in founder's syndrome to also experience a defense mechanism?
7. What is the difference between a defense mechanism and coping strategies?
8. In the case example of Gary, his boss said some unkind things to him in front of his colleagues during management team meetings. Why didn't Gary become upset about being the target of the remarks? What were the important events that led Gary to become assertive?
9. Explain how a defense mechanism might curb a founder's impulsivity and extreme volatility but not interfere with his or her founder's syndrome behaviors.

References

Baumeister, R. F., Dale, K., & Sommer, K. L. (1998). Freudian defense mechanisms and empirical findings in modern social psychology: Reaction formation, projection, displacement, undoing, isolation, sublimation, and denial. *Journal of Personality, 66*(6), 1081–1124.

Baumeister, R. F., Leary, M. R. (1995). The need to belong: Desire for interpersonal attachments as a fundamental human motivation. *Psychological Bulletin, 117*(3), 497–529.

Beresford, T. P. (2012). *Psychological adaptive mechanisms: Ego defense recognition in practice and research.* Oxford University Press.

Block, P. (2016). *The empowered manager: Positive political skills at work* (2nd edition). John Wiley & Sons.

Block, S. R. (2004). *Why nonprofits fail: Overcoming founder's syndrome, fundphobia, and other obstacles to success.* Jossey-Bass Publishers.

Block, S. R., & Rosenberg, S. (2002). Toward an understanding of founder's syndrome: An assessment of power and privilege among founders of nonprofit organizations. *Nonprofit Management & Leadership, 12*(4), 353–368.

Blumenthal-Barby, J. S., & Ubel, P. A. (2018). In defense of 'denial': Difficulty knowing when beliefs are unrealistic and whether unrealistic beliefs are bad. *American Journal of Bioethics, 18*(9), 4–15.

Brown, R. P., Tamborski, M., Wang, X., Barnes, C. D., Mumford, M. D., Connelly, S., & Devenport, L. D. (2011). Moral credentialing and the rationalization of misconduct. *Ethics & Behavior, 21*(1), 1–12. doi: 10.1080/10508422.2011.537566.

Burgo, J. (2012). *Why do I do that? Psychological defense mechanisms and the hidden ways they shape our lives.* New Rise Press.

Cramer, P. (1999). Ego functions and ego development: Defense mechanisms and intelligence as predictors of ego level. *Journal of Personality, 67*(5), 735–760.

Cullari, S., & Kusché, C. A. (2010). Ego defense mechanisms. In N. A. Piotrowski (Ed.), *Salem Health: Psychology & Mental Health* (Vol. 2, pp. 652–658). Salem Press.

DeCaro, M. S., Thomas, R. D., Albert, N. B., & Beilock, S. L. (2011). Choking under pressure: Multiple routes to skill failure. *Journal of Experimental Psychology: General, 140*(3), 390–406.

Freud, A. (1966). *The ego and the mechanisms of defense.* Routledge.

Freud, S. (1913). *The interpretation of dreams.* MacMillan.

Freud, S. (1966a). Further remarks on the neuropsychoses of defense. In J. Strachey, A. Freud, A. Strachey, & A. Tyson (Eds.), *The standard edition of the complete psychological works of Sigmund Freud* (Vol. 3, pp. 162–185). Hogarth Press. (Original work published 1896.)

Freud, S. (1966b). Repression. In J. Strachey, A. Freud, A. Strachey, & A. Tyson (Eds.), *The standard edition of the complete psychological works of Sigmund Freud* (Vol. 14, pp. 141–158). Hogarth Press. (Original work published 1915.)

Freud, S. (1966c). The unconscious. In J. Strachey, A. Freud, A. Strachey, & A. Tyson (Eds.), *The standard edition of the complete psychological works of Sigmund Freud* (Vol. 14, pp. 159–216). Hogarth Press. (Original work published 1915.)

Freud, S. (1977). *Inhibitions, symptoms and anxiety* (J. Strachey, Ed.). W.W. Norton. (Original work published 1926.)

Freud, S. (1990). *The ego and the id* (J. Strachey, Ed.). W.W. Norton. (Original work published 1923.)

Gannett, A., & Rector, C. (2015). The rationalization of political corruption. *Public Integrity, 17*(2), 165–175.

Hentschel, U., Smith, G., Draguns, J. G., & Ehlers, W. (2004). *Defense mechanisms: Theoretical, research and clinical perspectives.* Elsevier.

Jensen, P. R., & Wrisberg, C. A. (2014). Performance under acute stress: A qualitative study of soldiers' experiences of hand-to-hand combat. *International Journal of Stress Management*, 21(4), 406–423.

Kent, S., Devonport, T. J., Lane, A. M., Nicholls, W., & Friesen, A. P. (2018). The effects of coping interventions on ability to perform under pressure. *Journal of Sports Science & Medicine*, 17(1), 40–55.

Kreitler, S., & Kreitler, H. (2004). The motivational and cognitive determinants of defense mechanisms. *Advances in Psychology*, 136, 195–238.

Lazarus, R. S. (2006). Emotions and interpersonal relationships: Toward a person-centered conceptualization of emotions and coping. *Journal of Personality*, 74(1), 9–46.

Massoglia, M. (2006). Desistance or displacement? The changing patterns of offending from adolescence to young adulthood. *Journal of Quantitative Criminology*, 22(3), 215–239.

Miller, L., Archer, R. L., & Kapoor, N. (2020). Conversion disorder: Early diagnosis and personalized therapy plan is the key. *Case Reports in Neurological Medicine*, 1–4. https://doi.org/10.1155/2020/1967581

Newman, L. S., Caldwell, T. L., Chamberlin, B., & Griffin, T. (2005). Thought suppression, projection, and the development of stereotypes. *Basic and Applied Social Psychology*, 27(3), 259–266. https://doi.org/10.1207/s15324834basp2703_7

Newman, L. S., Duff, K. J., & Baumeister, R. F. (1997). A new look at defensive projection: Thought suppression, accessibility, and biased person perception. *Journal of Personality and Social Psychology*, 72(5), 980–1001. https://doi.org/10.1037/0022-3514.72.5.980

Perry, J. C., Presniak, M. D., Olson, & Trevor R. (2013). Defense mechanisms in schizotypal, borderline, antisocial, and narcissistic personality disorders. *Psychiatry: Interpersonal & Biological Processes*, 76(1), 32–52.

Rabl, T., & Kühlmann, T. M. (2009). Why or why not? Rationalizing corruption in organizations. *Cross Cultural Management: An International Journal*, 16(3), 268–286.

Sarnoff, I. (1960). Reaction formation and cynicism. *Journal of Personality*, 28(1), 129–143.

Schueler, D. E., Herron, W. G., Poland, H. V., & Schultz, C. L. (1982). Defense mechanisms in reactive and process schizophrenics. *Journal of Clinical Psychology*, 38(3), 486–489.

Seligman, S. (2016). Regression, dissociation, self-states, and the developmental dimension in therapeutic action. *Psychoanalytic Dialogues*, 26(3), 273–279.

Todd, P. M., & Gigerenzer, G. (2007). Environments that make us smart: Ecological rationality. *Current Directions in Psychological Science*, 16(3), 167–171. https://doi.org/10.1111/j.1467-8721.2007.00497.x

Trevithick, P. (2011). Understanding defenses and defensiveness in social work. *Journal of Social Work Practice*, 25(4), 389–412.

Weinstein, N. D. (1980). Unrealistic optimism about future life events. *Journal of Personality and Social Psychology*, 39(5), 806–820.

Zepf, S. (2011). About rationalization and intellectualization. *International Forum of Psychoanalysis*, 20(3), 148–158.

4 Founder's Syndrome: The Theoretical Perspective

Chapter Objectives

When you finish studying this chapter, you should be able to:

- Discuss how theories help us to understand founder's syndrome
- Understand the differences between first-order and second-order changes in organizations
- Explain how theories provide a lens to understand human conditions and behaviors in organizations
- Discuss different theories, paradigms, and models that help us understand founder's syndrome
- Discuss what is meant by the Theory of Logical Types
- Explain up to 12 different theories
- Describe what is meant by a structural change

Introduction

Like many of our social science colleagues, we approach the use of theoretical constructs and the application of theory into practice from knowledge gained from the scholarly work advanced by Kuhn (2012) in his classic and often cited book, *The Structure of Scientific Revolutions.* Our objective in using theories and paradigms is to help broaden our understanding of the behavioral phenomenon known as founder's syndrome that impedes the development and progress of organizational intentions. Within the context of our subject, we considered Kuhn's (1977) five characteristics in selecting theories to help explain founder's syndrome. They include the following: (1) accuracy, (2) consistency, (3) scope, (4) simplicity, and (5) fruitfulness (pp. 321–322). Also, as Kuhn understood, there is always room for disagreement. Therefore, we are also mindful that our selections may be challenged, and we are comfortable with any disputable argument over our selections and applications of theories, paradigms, or models. Our only proviso is that a challenge should further the pursuit of knowledge about founder's syndrome.

Kuhn's (2012) use of sarcasm into his serious contribution was an epiphanic moment for applying theories:

> Led by a new paradigm, scientists adopt new instruments and look in new places. Even more important, during revolutions scientists see new and different things when looking with familiar instruments in places they have looked before. It is rather as if the professional community had been suddenly transported to another planet where familiar objects are seen in a different light and are joined by unfamiliar ones as well. (p. 111)

Compared to earlier periods of examining and re-examining our subject through observation and surveys, we achieved a breakthrough when examining founder's syndrome in a different light. Each time we used the lenses of various theories and paradigms, we increased our comprehension of the breadth and depth of the issues that founder's syndrome encompasses.

Besides being enlightened by Kuhn's work and recalling Reynold's (1971) theory construction treatise which was required reading for many as graduate students, our theoretical understanding of founder's syndrome was propelled by the work of Watzlawick et al. at the Mental Research Institute in Palo Alto, California (Watzlawick, Weakland, & Fisch, 1974). The Palo Alto researchers developed an application of Change Theory on problem formation and problem resolution. Their writings and training sessions on the distinction between the Theory of Groups and the Theory of Logical Types drawn from the field of mathematical logic emphasized the duality of the concepts of persistence and change. Their model for understanding a problem and seeking a resolution is more impressive when examining the concepts of persistence and change together and not individually. Also, they found that becoming well-informed about the complementary Theory of Groups and the Theory of Logical Types helped them answer the questions of "how does an undesirable situation persist?" and "what is required to change it?" (p. 2), which are two primary questions for the study of founder's syndrome.

Given our interest in the persistence of founder's syndrome behavior in organizations and the queries we receive about it, we found the theoretical and practical applications advanced by Watzlawick and his associates provided an essential framework for thinking about the nature of change in the practical management of human problems. Additionally, in terms of the theory of groups, their simple lesson is that all changes within a group remain within the group. Watzlawick et al. refer to within organizational changes as a first-order type change that often promotes the persistence of a problem or status quo. They wittingly use the French proverb, *"plus ça change, plus c'est la même chose,"* which means the more something changes the more it remains the same (p. 1).

For a glimpse into their reasoning, let us consider all the employees of an organization, inclusive of all roles from the receptionist to the founding CEO. Include the board members as well. Everyone in the organization comprises a class of individuals. It is a class because the members all share a common characteristic, that is, their current association with the organization. The class is the totality of the members of the organization and it is also a logical type, applying Bertrand Russell's Theory of Logical Types (Whitehead & Russell, 1910). Furthermore, there exists a hierarchy of logical levels such as members being components of a class at one level and the class itself being of a higher level of logical types. To achieve a resolution of a problem that exists at one level requires a shift to a higher level of logical types. The change to a higher level is a structural change.

If some members of an organization are promoted or demoted or work assignments are altered, the class of members remains the same. If members leave or new members join the organization, the class still remains the same because all the members of the organization comprise the totality of the class and a class contains only members of one logical type. Moreover, a class cannot be a member of itself (which is reminiscent of the old Groucho Marx line, "I don't want to belong to any club that would have me as a member!"). This last point of a class not being able to be a member of itself is a significant part of Russell's Theory of Logical Types that he formulated to avoid paradoxes and antinomies in logic and communication (Whitehead & Russell, 1910, pp. 37–65). We can conclude that if changes within an organization evidencing founder's syndrome does not alter the structure of that organization, nor transform the class or alter the structure of the problem, then organizational founder's syndrome will persist in that organization. We can basically conclude that Group Theory informs us of the immutable nature of organizations when the organizational structure does not change.

Perhaps an analogy about a class as a logical type (of an educational class of students and instructor) will help clarify what may be required for structural change: 15 students have enrolled in a university French I language course. On day 1, all students who enrolled in the course are members that comprise the class, a logical type. On day 2, three new students enroll in the course. On day 3, two students withdraw. Although individual students have come and gone, the course remains the same and whether the members increase or decrease in numbers does not alter the fact that all associated with the course are members of the class, a logical type.

On week 2, a new instructor enters the classroom announcing that the assigned faculty member became ill and will no longer be teaching for the semester. The instructor noted that she would be teaching French I and there are no changes to the course. Here again, even a change of instructor does not change the class because the structure of the course does not change and the properties of instruction does not change since the new instructor along with the previous instructor are members of the same class of French 1 instructors. Consequently, the instructor becomes a member of the existing class, another logical type, because she is associated with the same French 1 course.

However, to create a structural change, the new instructor announces that French I will not be taught during the semester and everyone who was enrolled in the course will now be taught Introduction to the Japanese language. The change from a course of the French language to the Japanese language is obviously an altogether different condition. It amounts to a structural change to a different logical type. The instructor is now a member of a different class and anyone who remains in the new course is now a member of that new class of members, the new logical type. An alternative example of a structural change would be the cancellation of the course altogether and with no substitution of language courses to be offered during the semester. By that action, there would no longer be members. Without members, that class no longer exists. The previous members of the (language) class may now seek alternative course subjects. Of course, if the students do not drop out of the university, they remain a member of a higher class of a logical type that is comprised of all students enrolled in that university.

To simplify matters of this theory's application, we should consider how to go from one level to a higher level for the strategic effort of creating structural change. As a practical application, we use theory as a lens to look upon all the dimensions of founder's syndrome and discover there are different logical types that can be used for this purpose:

1. All founding CEOs that engage in founder's syndrome can be one logical type.
2. All staff experiencing the undesirable effects of founder's syndrome can be another logical type.
3. All staff of one entity in which the founder is engaged in founder's syndrome behavior can be another logical type.
4. An added logical type can be all the individuals in organizations who conspire to sabotage their founding CEOs.

The use of theory allows us to see different facets of founder's syndrome that we did not see when simply looking at it from a single dimension of severe behavior. As a tourist on Kuhn's alternative planet, we can see founder's syndrome in a different light: Its behaviors, its victims, its perpetrators, its implications, its rules, its outcomes, its boundaries, its powers, its destructions, and so on. Examining different vantage points may trigger various ideas for constructing intervention strategies that will lead to a change in group structure that, in turn, alters the structure of the persistent problem of founder's syndrome behaviors.

When we are engaged as organization development consultants to create a change in an organization where founder's syndrome exists, our effectiveness rests with our ability to cause a change in the structure of the class of members of that organization. We contend that without being able to alter our perception of the reality of observed behaviors within the organization, we will not derive an appropriate intervention strategy. Of course, the simplest solution is to recommend the firing of the founder which if the board of directors agreed, would immediately change the class structure of the organization. Once the founder is gone, the organization can never be the same because a newly hired person, while being able to succeed as the CEO, can never be its founder. Additionally, if our objective is to acquire knowledge about founder's syndrome, firing the founder leaves us at an impasse of learning. Also, if our engagement was for the purpose of finding a solution that eliminates founder's syndrome behavior but leaves the founding CEO in charge of the organization, our recommendation to fire the CEO is a failure of engagement. Another important matter is the consideration of the remaining members of the class (staff and board members). We have an obligation to ensure we have not intervened in a way that creates even greater turmoil and has no logical end.

Because we spend a great deal of time and attention on the importance of theories, paradigms, and models, one doctoral candidate that we overheard amusingly wondered aloud that it appeared to him that we get great pleasure from dealing in the abstract. Perhaps 'pleasure' is not exactly the concept that we would use. It would be more accurate to admit to feeling a sense of satisfaction when investigating organizational and social systems issues through the lenses of different theorists that lead to intervention strategies. The use of theories and paradigms is akin to looking into the prisms of a kaleidoscope. Each turn of the lens alters the reality of what we see. Using a theory to alter the perception of reality is certainly a healthier approach compared to the chemically induced kind! Thinking abstractly in search of solutions to human problems is a creative undertaking and it is a challenge worth pursuing if the objective is to assist an organization to resolve its founder's problem or other types of organizational issues that remained stagnant with attempts at first-order change. Watzlawick et al. describe the process of structural change as a second-order type (pp. 75–90) (see Block (2004) or other editions for case examples of using theories for second-order change in organizations).

Imagine seeing the world through the eyes of a theorist, such as Maslow (1943) and his Hierarchy of Needs. One of the stages in his theory is belonging. If you overlay the need for belonging when assessing an organization engaged in founder's syndrome, you will see and think of the founder and his or her behaviors differently than when viewing the same founder by overlapping the next hierarchical level of Maslow's theory, esteem needs. In the second instance, the esteem needs elements of Maslow's theory influence a different motivational drive and corresponding set of behaviors. Imagine using Maslow's theory to fathom what an organization might look like if the founder who had engaged in founder's syndrome achieved actualization. Or imagine looking into Maslow's kaleidoscope and at every turn of the changing prisms were the next stage of the theory's drives and behaviors of organizational members who had been affected by founder's syndrome. Ultimately, you would see a multitude of changes and reactions and your vicarious experiences could spark creative thinking for planning an intervention.

The frame of reference utilized in this chapter recognizes theories or their variant hypotheses, models, principles, or paradigms as supportive elements that give insight into founder's syndrome behavior and its dynamic character. Our use of theory is not to prove its progenitor as being accurate in his or her role of predicting behavior or having the characteristics that enable the prediction of norms. We use theories as analytical concepts applied to complex behavior to enlighten our understanding of what occurs within organizations engaged in founder's syndrome behavior. Theories are used as a creative guide to gain insight into the observed behaviors that could help us in planned change efforts.

We often use more than one theory to gain broader perspectives and deeper understandings. Each approach is like looking at a framed picture and then changing the frame and its mat to a different color and style. The picture will look different, although in reality, it has not changed; our perception of the picture has changed. Similarly, examining a problem using multiple theories provides an opportunity to perceive the problem in alternative ways, which aids in our understanding and generating ideas for creating organizational change.

For this chapter, several theories were selected that we have previously used as lenses to expand our awareness of the human conditions in organizations that have perpetuated founder's syndrome. Depending on your professional discipline, some theories may be familiar, but likely have been applied differently than in your way of using them. Lastly, we selected some theories for their heuristic value. Among the theories that will be described include the following:

1. Attribution Theory
2. Change Theory
3. Upper Echelons Theory
4. Cognitive Dissonance Theory
5. Contingency Theory
6. Situational Leadership Theory
7. Personality Theory
8. Core Self-Evaluation Theory
9. Goal-Setting Theory

10. Punctual Equilibrium Theory
11. Relational-Cultural Theory
12. Rational Choice Theory (aka Decision Theory)

Attribution Theory

Founders, employees, and board members conduct themselves in a variety of ways within organizations regardless of mission or profit motives. They also search for and assign meaning or causality to their own behaviors as well as the behaviors of others. This exploration for meaning or 'soul-searching' is understood as Attribution Theory. On this point, the research of Choi, Chung, and Choi (2019) has a thought-provoking application for our interest in founder's syndrome. These researchers examined employees' perceptions and behaviors toward innovation in organizations. Understandably, innovation is an important development for organizational stability and growth. The key variables in Choi et al.'s study were constructive intentionality and deceptive intentionality. When employees attributed constructive intentionality to innovation, their attitudes were favorable and the employees' demonstrated greater dedication and responsibility to their work. On the flip side, when they attributed deceptive practices to the introduction of an innovation, employees considered the introduction to an innovative practice was for management's self-serving ends and intentions to manipulate and exploit employees. Choi et al.'s findings indicated that employees seek to avoid implementing innovations that they considered were deceptive in practice. To enforce the deceptive practice and circumvent the employee's avoidance, we can see through the lens of this theory, a founding CEO will place pressure on his or her employees. The researchers state, "As a core driver of sensemaking, attributions of intentionality underlying the adoption of an innovation play a crucial role in labeling the situation and determining subsequent behavioral reactions" (Choi et al., 2019, p. 2). The behavioral reaction of founder's syndrome becomes particularly evident when employees determine that they are being used for the sole benefit of the founder and not necessarily for the mission of the company. If a founder wants the cooperation of the employees, he or she needs to discuss the value of the innovation for its products, services, and customers. It would be advantageous if the founder could also demonstrate how the innovation provides benefits for the employees to balance the benefits that accrue to the founder and other senior managers or board members.

Heider (1958) is credited with the development of Attribution Theory and examining the concepts of responsibility, intention, and causality. Developing the attribution model further, Weiner (2006), as summarized by Sahar (2014), "argues that life is metaphorically like a courtroom in which we act as judges of others; he suggests that we often initiate causal analyses in order to inform these moral judgments" (p. 230). In view of this reasoning, Weiner's model can be used to provide insight into the motives of a founder. The founder renders a judgment on the ability of staff and board members to assist him or her in achieving the organizational mission and objectives. The founder's judgment will either lead him or her to dispense praise for the hard work of staff and/or board members or the founder will adjudicate punishment in the form of founder's syndrome behaviors.

Change Theory

Returning to Watzlawick et al.'s Change Theory, if we were to attempt to change the behavior of the founder, we would fail with a first-order change attempt of pointing out how his or her behaviors are detrimental to the employees. We might have a better chance of facilitating change by creating a second-order change strategy with the cooperation of the founder, which is as follows: *The objective is to explain to the founder that his or her founder's syndrome behavior has clearly been a punishment to the staff and that we understand that his or her behavior is no doubt the result of finding the staff guilty of some egregious acts. However, discharging justice within the organization is only morally correct if the employee understands their judgment before a punishment can be rendered. Also, each judgment should be time limited to a day or at the most a week in length. The founder would be required to personally inform the pronouncement of guilty before engaging in founder's syndrome behavior. The type of behavior would be selected from a prepared list of founder syndrome behaviors such as micromanaging, bullying, avoidance, etc.*

According to the researchers that have studied second-order manipulations for change, the target, in this case, it would be the founder, would change his or her deleterious impulsive behaviors as a result of taking the behaviors from the realm of spontaneity to consciously deciding to engage in detrimental behaviors with a set of pronounced rules. With this change, the founder is likely to see that his or her behaviors are injurious to others and to act on those harmful behaviors with pronouncements and rules creates a level of absurdity and embarrassment that becomes difficult to enact. We offer this approach as an example of the application of a second-order change methodology but caution our readers to first study the psychology and logic that is foundational to this mode of Change Theory before using such tactics. Watzlawick and his associates originally developed their theory and application in their work with individuals with psychiatric issues and in family therapy. If applied correctly, its application can be fruitful in other problem-solving situations, such as founder's syndrome. However, we recommend a careful reading of the writings of Bateson (2000), Watzlawick, Beavin Bavelas, and Jackson (1967), Ruesch and Bateson (2017), Haley (1993), and Watzlawick et al. (1974), and Watzlawick and Weakland (1977).

Upper Echelons Theory

There is no shortage of theories that focus on organizational leaders. Among them, one stands out for its recognition of various factors that influence behavior, that is, Upper Echelons Theory. In this theory, strategic decisions and implementation are influenced by the CEO's personality, values, and experiences. The theory also holds a place for the organization's upper echelons, which is the CEO and his or her executive management team that is customarily handpicked based on loyalty and support of the founder's vision.

It may seem obvious that a founding CEO will significantly affect what takes place in his or her organization. However, the founder's personality consisting of several cognitive factors may explain individual choices, decisions, as well as approaches to decision-making and its result on corporate performance. Mazzotta and Santella (2017) state that "Scholars have recognized core self-evaluation as the possible overall construct since it represents a unique latent psychological variable which causally influences a set of superficial qualitative traits: self-confidence, self-worth, self-potency and emotional stability" (p. 251). Furthermore, Wang, Holmes, Oh, and Zhu (2016) conducted meta-analytic research on over 300 studies with empirical findings that relied on Upper Echelons Theory to study CEO characteristics on organization strategic actions. They concluded that "firms tend to perform better when their CEOs are older, longer tenured, better educated, have more prior career experience, and score high on extraversion and charisma" (p. 827). On a more granular level, they did find that longer tenured CEOs are more averse to taking risks and appear to be more resistant to change. Also, in line with Mazzotta and Santella (2017), Wang et al. (2016) found that a CEO with a positive self-concept is more likely to be ambitious, confident, and willing to engage in the strategic activity (p. 821). However, the more grandiose the CEO is in his or her self-concept, the more frequent and audacious are the strategic actions. As risk-takers in starting an organization, founders are more likely to have a higher self-concept and therefore have a greater propensity to make riskier decisions based on emotionality and bounded rationality. Upper Echelon Theory and Wang et al.'s analyses may explain one finding in Block and Rosenberg's study (2002) that found that financial growth was more limited with founders with longer durations at the helm of their organizations. CEOs who were not founders were more likely to have more experience and success in revenue development and hired because of prior success in areas that are most important to financial growth and organizational stability.

Cognitive Dissonance Theory

In 1957, Leon Festinger published *A Theory of Cognitive Dissonance*. In it, he explains that people seek consistency in their cognitive beliefs. When a person has cognitions and behaviors that are at odds, then the individual experiences dissonance, a state of psychological discomfort. Once the tension is experienced, the individual seeks to reduce it. McGrath (2017) informs us of several studies that examined methods for dissonance reduction including Festinger's three original proposals: Changing one's cognition, creating new consonant cognitions, or minimizing the importance of the dissonant cognition. In examining dissonance reduction strategies, researchers have mostly investigated attitude change because it was an original construct put forth by Festinger and Carlsmith in 1959 (McGrath, 2017, p. 4). Harmon-Jones and Mills (2019) summarize how dissonance can be reduced "by removing dissonant cognitions, adding new consonant cognitions, reducing the importance of dissonant cognitions, or increasing the importance of consonant cognitions" (p. 4). Interestingly, the reduction of dissonance is also subject to resisting a change in cognition. According to Harmon-Jones and Mills (2019),

> Resistance to change is based on the responsiveness of the cognition to reality and on the extent to which the cognition is consonant with many other cognitions. Resistance to change of a behavioral cognitive element depends on the extent of pain or loss that must be endured and the satisfaction obtained from the behavior. (p. 4)

Several researchers (Kitayama, Snibbe, Markus, & Suzuki, 2004; Harmon-Jones & Mills, 2019; Hoshino-Brown et al., 2005) including Festinger (1957) have also determined that the extent of dissonance may be regulated based on cultural background such as individuals coming from collectivistic cultures versus individualistic cultures.

Unless a founder has a history of launching organizations, it is reasonable to assume that a founder will start his or her organization without an indication of the abundant decision items and conflicting choices he or she will face as a new CEO. Making decisions that have fiscal impacts comes with lingering doubts and second-guessing as to whether correct decisions were made. The greater the fiscal consequence of the decision, the greater will be the discomfort, tension, and stress experienced and the desire to achieve a psychological balance.

Some research suggests that as soon as cognitive dissonance occurs after decision-making, there is an attempt to reduce it through attitude change (Jarcho, Berkman, & Lieberman, 2011). In an earlier study, Pallak and Pittmann (1972) demonstrated that dissonance reduction is a result of a drive satisfied by specific behavior among eligible alternatives. Among the alternative behaviors for a founder inclined toward founder's syndrome include those actions that would satisfy his or her need to exercise power. Elaborating further on this idea, we think it is reasonable to deduce the hypothesis that the exercise of power by a founder can cause dissonance reduction. Our argument is supported by Smith, Jost, and Vijay (2008), who note, "Those with power are less inhibited in their behavior than are those without power. Power leads to increased action and approach behavior, even if it is socially inappropriate" (p. 360).

Another area of cognitive dissonance that is worthy of study with respect to founder's syndrome is the concept of belonging or ownership as we discussed in Chapter 1. In a 1987 study by Nuttin Jr., a hypothesis was advanced that suggested that the mere ownership of an object would enhance its attractiveness to the owner. Similarities to Heider's (1958) Balance Theory and Kahneman, Knetsch, and Thaler's (1990)' instant endowment effect' were cited by Watson and Winkleman (2005, p. 403) to support their view that cognitive dissonance is a possible means for explaining a perceived ownership effect in which people evaluate what they own more positively than nonowners of the same object. The interesting aspect of Kahneman et al.'s approach was based on aversion to loss, which is as follows:

> The generalization that losses are weighted substantially more than subjectively commensurate gains in the evaluation of prospects and trades. An implication of this asymmetry is that if a good is evaluated as a loss when it is given up and as a gain when it is acquired, loss aversion will, on average, induce a higher value for owners (pp. 1326–1328)

For our purposes, the application for this economic loss principle concerns the circumstances when a founder is engaged in a battle with a board of directors who are threatening to remove him or her for engaging in deplorable founder's syndrome behaviors. The consequences of loss of one's role and ownership will theoretically increase the founder's belief in the organization's value. Additionally, in those cases where there is forced separation, the theory of cognitive dissonance is applicable because the founding CEO will be seeking cognitive homeostasis to balance the losses of identity, status, job, and benefits. The founder may be more accepting of the outcome if the financial terms of separation are more than what he or she anticipated, plus if the departing CEO is able to leave with a sense of integrity by a public statement of appreciation for what he or she accomplished. However, if terms for a settlement do not rise to an acceptable level and/or the CEO departs with a publicly tainted reputation, the loss of job can be demoralizing and feelings of depression and accompanied by self-identifying as a failure (Langlais, 2010).

Based on our experience interviewing founders who were terminated, we found that the ability to reach dissonance reduction can be a multi-year phenomenon. Consequently, we find it necessary to offer an obligatory rebuke of the dissonance reduction literature that typically describes reduction strategies based on experiments that are limited to shorter term events. On the brighter side, there exists an opportunity for an enterprising researcher to investigate dissonance reduction among founders who were forcibly separated from the organization they founded.

Contingency Theory and Situational Leadership Theory

There is no shortage of theories on leadership and articles on the various types of leadership styles ranging from autocratic on one end of the continuum to laissez-faire on the opposite end. Fiedler's (1967) thesis about a contingency model of leadership is among the first to focus on a leader's effectiveness being contingent upon the specific demands of a situation. Accordingly, there is no one size-fits-all type of leadership style.

Prior to Fiedler's contingency theory, his earlier research on Assumed Similarity (1953) investigated individuals' perception of how similar or different they are in comparison to other individuals. Although it may seem obvious or predictable that individuals would prefer other persons that are similar to them, Fiedler found that task groups preferred to work with individuals and leaders who may be different from themselves, especially if the leaders are task-oriented and psychologically distant (p. 148). Perhaps this finding was foundational thinking for Fiedler's later development of contingency theory in which leaders are perceived as effective because of their ability to focus and help others succeed at their tasks. The ability to succeed is situational and contingent on a good match between the task to be accomplished and the style of the leader. Fiedler's approach should be distinguished with another model developed by Hersey and Blanchard (Hersey, Blanchard, & Johnson, 2012) known as Situational Leadership Theory, and formerly known as the Life-Cycle Theory of Leadership.

The key to Hersey and Blanchard's approach is the understanding of the leader to the task to be performed and his or her knowledge of the readiness of the staff to perform it. The leader-followership relationship is guided by the leader's interpersonal abilities to communicate and assess the willingness and confidence of each staff member, and in an assessment that staff will adapt to his or her leadership style that was determined to be a best fit with each follower. There are now two complementary models of leadership because Hersey (1985) and Blanchard (Blanchard, Zigarmi, & Zigarmi, 2013) decided to attend to their own independent work priorities in the late 1970s. The differences in their models are slight and follow their original work which described leadership styles as either fitting into one of four categories of styles. Table 4.1 lists the styles promoted by Hersey and Blanchard. The researchers also differentiate the followers by levels of psychological readiness or psychological development as identified in Table 4.2.

Table 4.1 Terminology differences between Hersey and Blanchard are identified in Hersey (1985) and Blanchard, Zigarmi, & Zigarmi (2013) and based on the original work of Hersey and Blanchard (Hersey, Blanchard & Johnson, 2012)

Hersey's Leadership Styles	*Blanchard's Leadership Styles*
S1-Telling	S1-Directing
S2-Selling	S2-Coaching
S3-Participating	S3-Supporting
S4-Delegating	S4-Delegating

Table 4.2 Terminology differences between Hersey and Blanchard are identified in Hersey (1985) and Blanchard, Zigarmi, and Zigarmi (2013) and based on the original work of Hersey and Blanchard (Hersey, Blanchard & Johnson, 2012)

Hersey's Psychological Readiness	*Blanchard's Psychological Development*
R1-Unable & Unwilling	D1-Unable & Willing
(Low Competence, Low Commitment)	(Low Competence, High Commitment)
R2-Unable & Willing	D2-Unable & Unwilling
(Low Competence, High Commitment)	(Low Competence, Low Commitment)
R3-Able & Unwilling	D3-Able & Unwilling
(High Competence, Low Commitment)	(High Competence, Low Commitment)
R4-Able & Willing	D4-Able & Willing
(High Competence, High Commitment)	(High Competence, High Commitment)

When staff members are lower in competence, the situational leadership style calls for a manager to be more directive. In some instances, staff may require step by step instruction. In other situations, the objective of the leader is to develop a staff member's confidence. The higher the level of a staff member's competence, the less the staff member needs to be told how to complete a task. A staff member may either need some support or can be autonomous.

Founders who exhibit founder's syndrome would benefit from understanding the situational leadership schema. When founder's syndrome is evident, we typically find a CEO who is clueless to the type of supervision and leadership style that would benefit individual staff members. Consider, for example, a highly knowledgeable and skillful employee being micromanaged. We can understand their feelings of resentment being told what to do and how to do it. However, take a new employee with minimal work experience not receiving any direction and then finding themselves being belittled by their CEO for their poor performance outcomes. Without the understanding of what would best motivate a staff member to complete their tasks, the CEO can create failing conditions. Moreover, if the CEO does not understand important aspects of supervision, they may hire or promote someone into a supervisory position who does not have the requisite knowledge and skills to guide their novice staff or how to give ample discretion to their highly experienced personnel. When supervisors cannot do an adequate job and staff members are also unhappy with the type of guidance they receive, the work environment becomes ripe for a founding CEO to become antagonistic, harsh, and intimidating, which adds the proverbial insult to injury.

The similarity between Contingency Theory and Situational Leadership Theory is that there is no one best way to lead and manage. Contingency theory is more reliant on organizational design and structure and its fit to the leader-manager (that is, roles, responsibilities, job design, organizational and departmental plans, type of hierarchy, and decision-making authority). The focus is on environment and task, whereas situational leadership is focused on task, readiness, and relationship. Fiedler believed some leaders are more prone to focus on tasks and others are inclined toward a focus on relationships. In either case, he suggests that it would be difficult for a leader with one style to change. Consequently, matching the right leader to the right type of situation is necessary for success. Assessing the favorability of a situation to the choice of leader is a difficult task if it requires an understanding of the leader's ideas about staffing, identifying the type of performance or task structure required, and how the leader uses his or her authority and power. In organizations with the presence of founder's syndrome, all the ingredients that go into a successful match between leader and staff are just a hit or miss occurrence, because there are no options in selecting the organizational leader.

Personality Theory

The inclusion of Personality Theory in this chapter was a given. Also, although it seems everyone has one time or another discussed the personality of some individual, the task of defining its meaning and its application to a founder engaged in founder's syndrome is not as simple as one might expect. One reason for its complexity is that each person (as in the word personality) is unique and yet some share similarities as a *personality type*. Additionally, there are as many different personality theorists as there are personality types and our choice of which theory to write about may also say something about our own personality!

Some of the most important or historically popular personality theorists include Freud (2018, 1966a, 1966b, 1966c), Freud (2018), Jung (2003), Adler (2010), Erikson (1993), Eysenck (2017), Maslow (1954, 1943), Rogers (1995), Skinner (2006), Horney (1937), and Bowlby (1983). Among the viewpoints about personality, there exists a split between personality theories based on clinical observation versus experimental research and the traditional theoretical approach versus contemporary ideas (McCrae, 2011). The traditional approach is also known as the structural approach, which is based on traits and characteristics. Although the structural approach dominates the personality literature, there has been evidence of alternative ideas underway by researchers such as Giordano (2014, 2015, 2017) and Uher (2015). Giordano argues that the structural approach has its place if attempting to make individual or group comparisons. However, he asserts that traits are not materially real. They are a cognitive construct. Giordano (2017) advocates for a process approach for understanding the individual *as an individual* and borrows from Eastern philosophy to differentiate process from structure. Unlike the Western approach of conceptualizing the idea of self as independent of others, Giordano (2014) explains that Eastern thought believes in a relational self, whereby the self always exists in relationship to others (p. 115). Giordano goes on to present a Confucian theory of personality stating,

> The relational self anchors personal identity in the ever-changing landscape of interpersonal contexts. It therefore obviates the role of traits as relevant in understanding intraindividual functioning because important aspects of personality do not reside 'inside' the person; the relevant dimensions of personality inhere 'between' persons as they interact and as they move from one interpersonal context into another. This suggests that personality transforms in concert with relational situations. Personality, therefore, is a process, not an entity or set of 'structures.' (p. 123)

In this Eastern philosophy, there is a recognition that an individual's personality shifts according to one's role. When a founder interacts with his or her managers, the founder might engage in micromanagement and provide harsh feedback when he or she hears unwanted advice. However, when this same founder is at home with a spouse, he or she may honor distinct roles and not direct or comment on how the spouse could improve on tasks that would satisfy his or her way of thinking. When the founder is among friends, he or she may remain quiet rather than comment on a statement he or she believes to be inappropriate. The differences in the founder's behavior are a result of how his or her personality transforms into a relational situation.

Core Self-Evaluation Theory

In their 1997 article where they introduced the concept of core evaluations, Judge, Locke, and Durham reasoned that,

> people's appraisals of the external world are affected not just by the attributes of objects and people's desires with respect to those objects (e.g., pay in relation to desired pay) but also by the deepest (e.g., metaphysical) assumptions people hold about themselves, other people, and the world. (Judge et al., 1998, p. 18)

Consequently, individuals who think highly of their job and professional capabilities represent a personality trait with high core self-evaluations. Consistent with that logic, individuals who have a lower opinion of their abilities have low core self-evaluations. The researchers theorize that a person's self-assessment stems from the subconscious and subjective appraisal of one's work factoring four dimensions of personality: Self-esteem, generalized self-efficacy, locus of control, and neuroticism.

In their explanation of the four dimensions of personality, the researchers assert that self-esteem is the most fundamental of self-assessments because of how one values themselves. They also consider self-esteem to be a predictor of job satisfaction (Judge, Locke, Durham, & Kluger, 1998, p. 19). They describe generalized self-efficacy as a component of self-esteem and also an estimate "of one's capabilities to mobilize the motivation, cognitive resources, and courses of action needed to exercise general control over events in one's life" (Judge et al., 1998, p. 19). Although self-efficacy refers to the level of confidence an individual believes about their actions and behaviors, locus of control "concerns the degree to which individuals believe that they control events in their lives (internal locus of control) or believe that the environment or fate controls events (external locus of control)" (Judge et al., 1998, p. 19). Because individuals with an internal locus of control believe they are in control of their work situations, they are more likely to feel satisfaction in their jobs and work environment. Lastly, individuals with negative affectivity or neuroticism view their world pessimistically. They are more likely to feel depressed, helpless, and anxious. In the workplace, they "rate peers less favorably, view themselves as victims, and tend to be dissatisfied with themselves, with their jobs, and with their lives in general" (Judge et al., 1998, p. 19). The founder who engages in founder's syndrome behaviors is more likely to adhere to a worldview of an external locus of control and is personally subjected to negative affectivity by not experiencing an internal locus of control.

Focusing their research on personality and the workplace, Farčić et al.'s (2020) application of Core Self-Evaluation (CSE) Theory is relevant to our interest in founder's syndrome. These researchers pay particular attention to the relationship between a CEO's decision-making abilities and the four dimensions of the CSE theory (i.e., locus of control, neuroticism, generalized self-efficacy, and self-esteem). It is given that CEOs make numerous decisions that impact staff and operations. When CEOs have a broad base of experience and training or higher education in management and strategic decision-making, the likelihood is that their decisions will include reasonable risk-taking. However, if their decisions result in problematic outcomes, the founding CEO may have a greater tendency to forego using appropriate information resources such as experienced members of the board of directors, internal staff, or the expertise available by engaging consultants. When the founder loses decisional focus and relies on his or her emotions and not rational logic, the tendency is to drift into founder's syndrome.

We think it is a fair hypothesis that when applying Core Self-Evaluation Theory to founding CEOs actively engaged in founder's syndrome, they will have a skewed view of their personality and will report a high core self-evaluation of self-esteem, self-efficacy, and executive competencies that do not match their lesser abilities. If the founding CEOs core-self-evaluations were genuinely high, their guidance and trust in their managers would likely mean they were open to sharing in decision-making and less likely to engage in micromanagement or other undesirable behaviors.

Goal-Setting Theory

As we continue to distinguish founders who engage in founder's syndrome from those who do not, we found it helpful to include an examination of Goal-Setting Theory (Locke & Latham, 1984) to the personality mix. Su and Zhang's (2020) contribution to personality research includes an examination of the proactive behavior of individuals in the workplace as well as graduate students who are goal setters and active to achieve their goals. They describe individuals with this personality as positive champions of environmental change in the workplace. This personality type not only welcomes feedback, they actively seek it to improve their performance. This pursuit for constructive advice does not fit the profile of a founder with a penchant to dismiss ideas from a board of directors or from his or her senior managers. Individuals who are dismissive of advice and ideas from staff have more difficulty adapting to organizational change (p. 2). Because founders who are more likely to engage in founder's syndrome have an aversion to hear advice and learn about their errors, then the Goal-Setting Theory can be used for diagnostic purposes to narrow the field of individuals who are more likely to have a false sense of their cognitive strengths and their judgment in executing a course of action (Bandura, 1997).

Another way of thinking about Goal-Setting Theory in an organization with founder's syndrome is to consider the likelihood of lost opportunities for increasing profits resulting from poor employee engagement. Shoaib and Kohli (2017) writing on performance outcomes related to goal setting and employee engagement state, "The importance of engagement has increased after its recognition in organizational efficacy and organizational profit" (p. 877). Engaged employees are those that focus on producing goals and objectives that further the organization's success. As part of their literature review on employee engagement, Shoaib and Kohli conclude that there is definitional agreement among researchers on two important characteristics of employee engagement: "(i) a positive and energized work-related motivational state and (ii) a genuine willingness to contribute to work role and organizational success" (p. 877). Of course, they are describing healthy organizations in which employees feel satisfaction, have opportunities for professional growth and experience success in meeting work challenges. Of importance to the issues of founder's syndrome, Chandani et al. (2016) assert that a high level of employee engagement is contingent on recognition and praise directly from an organization's leader. Another key driver of employee engagement is to include the employee in the leader's organizational vision (p. 2). Consequently, the quality of the exchanges between the CEO and employees is critical to the performance outcomes of the company. To the extent that founder's syndrome has created an undesirable work atmosphere, employee engagement will be unenthusiastic leading to diminished profits and lost opportunities for organizational growth.

Punctuated Equilibrium Theory

According to Punctuated Equilibrium Theory (PET), changes to organizational structures and policy are typically slow-moving processes, and major and more rapid changes are known as punctuations (Flink, 2017, p. 104). As witnessed in the case example of Gary in Chapter 3, it took several months for Gary to become aware of his role as a target of founder's syndrome and his willingness to undergo a personal transition to change his mindset and behaviors. Recall that Gary's transition after psychological treatment led him to deliver an ultimatum to the board of directors that they needed to intervene, which would create a punctuated change to the organization by dismissing the founding CEO or from the resignation of three department directors.

When organizations go from a state of stability to a strained environment due to founder's syndrome behavior, we can use PET to help explain radical or sudden organizational changes. When managers or board members purposely sabotage the founding CEO to force him or her out of the organization, punctuated organizational change is likely. The plotting against the CEO is hard to hide. When the subterfuge becomes known to the CEO, the reaction is usually explosive. The feelings of betrayal lead the founder to seek revenge against managers and disruption among board members. The outcome can only lead to a punctuated change in the organization. Either staff members are fired, and board members resign, or the CEO's behavior is met with the board hardening its stance leading to the termination or resignation of the founder.

Relational-Cultural Theory

In an interesting article tracing the historical development of Relational-Cultural Theory (RCT), Jordan (2017) first discusses the traditional psychological approach that is based on the concept of 'self.' This long-held idea includes a goal of achieving the separate self as a key to independence, success, health, self-esteem, and to be an individual. Lenz (2016) describes this viewpoint as a Western approach "to personal growth, which assume that autonomy and independence from others contribute to a sense of competence and esteem" (p. 415). The characterization of relying on self or not needing to rely on others is reminiscent of the alone status that we find founding CEOs engaged in founder's syndrome. A founder can choose an alone or separate-self status or become isolated as a result of engaging in repugnant behavior. Jordan writes, "Our social worlds are built to support the story of a dog-eat-dog, competitive,, individualistic, independent way of being" (p. 230). In this context, the winners are the personality types who are independent, self-determining, and perhaps prefer to stand alone than rely on relationships.

Jordan and others (Banks, 2016; Jordan, Kaplan, Miller, Stiver, & Surrey, 1991; Jordan, Walker, & Hartling, 2004) reject the psychology that promotes self-interest and the separate self. They understand the desire for separation as an attempt to have power over others. Specially, RCT advances the idea that social disconnections lead to power imbalances that marginalize others. We do see this in founder's syndrome.

The foundation of RCT stems from feminist ideology and promotes culture and connectivity as values of relationships that foster growth and healing. Consequently, founding CEOs who are empathic and demonstrate respect for their staff understand how working relationships are more likely to build loyalty and well-being which decidedly advances their organization's mission and objectives; accomplishing without the distrustful and guarded atmosphere that envelops organizations experiencing founder's syndrome.

Rational Choice Theory (also Referred to as Decision Theory)

Whether an organization is established as a for-profit entity or a nonprofit, the objective of acquiring money is critical for its success if not its survival. The lawful difference between the two types of organizations has to do with the distribution of profits. The nonprofit may not distribute the profits to its board members or organizational members, while the for-profit can share its profits with shareholders and provide payment for the advice giving and oversight of its board of directors. It would not be a rational decision for a nonprofit to share its revenues with its board of directors because it would decidedly lead to the loss of the organization's tax-exempt status. It would equally be an irrational act for the for-profit business to give its money away to everyone but its shareholders. Determining whether an act is rational, or illogical is the role of decision theorists, but few are ever consulted when it comes time for a CEO to make decisions.

With both nonprofits and for-profit organizations essentially resource dependent for their existence, then raising a critical question as to why a founding CEO would make decisions that would knowingly harm its revenue generation capabilities is more than a fair inquiry. The fundamental meaning of the last sentence presupposes that a founder knows that specific decisions will harm his or her organization's revenue potential. The fact is that when founders engage in destructive founder's syndrome behaviors, their actions are more than likely going to adversely impact resource development.

It may seem incredulous that an individual would have the intellectual capacity to incorporate and launch an organization, hire staff after raising finances and/or investing their own monies and then go about engaging in detrimental acts. By now, it should be obvious that the goal of generating financial profits and the aversion for financial loss are not mitigating factors to prevent founder's syndrome. Stanovich (2013) reminds us that "the model of rational judgment used by decision scientists is one in which a person chooses options based on which option has the largest expected utility" (p. 2). Therefore, when founders engage in founder's syndrome behaviors, we are witnessing an exception to the concept of the 'rational' person in economics. These founders deviate from the axioms of rational choice.

Perhaps we should not be surprised by such nonconforming behaviors. After all, Dietrich and List (2013) clarify that "Standard rational choice theory focuses exclusively on the rational pursuit of an agent's preferences, and is silent on how these preferences are formed and how they may be revised, for instance by deliberating about and responding to various reasons" (p. 104). In other words, we simply do not know the mechanics of the decision-making brain of a founder who damages organizational opportunities, although we have speculated and described both conscious and unconscious reasons throughout this book.

More to the point, Wajzer (2015) states,

> The adjective *rational* is usually defined as based on logical thinking, that is it is mind- and logic-driven. Is this the case indeed? Do we truly make decisions ... on the basis of reason only? Or are there other mechanisms that play a crucial role? Thus, how should we evaluate the usefulness of rational choice theory to explain the complex behaviors of the representatives of our species? (p. 66)

Wajzer presents a litany of reasons to demonstrate that rationality is compromised in decision-making. For his arguments, he relies on evolutionary biology, cognitive and social psychology, emotionality, unconscious prejudices, mono-logical belief systems, Neo-Darwinian ecology, and the entanglement of particles in quantum game theory. Among his conclusions, Wajzer states "we make decisions based on emotions and feelings, allowing our minds to alleviate inconveniences resulting from the fragmentation of perception" (p. 79). When it comes down to it, some people just make bad decisions!

On another line of thinking, Verbeek (2010) upholds the importance of Rational Choice Theory as though it were an arm of moral theories, arguing that agents who honor their commitments are upholding their end of cooperative virtues. Although Verbeek makes a Neo-Aristotelian argument about trustworthiness being multifunctional for meaningful relationships and mutual assistance, we are reminded of a less-theoretic argument that demonstrated the value of Rational Choice Theory as exemplified by the observations of Tocqueville (2006). Alexis de Tocqueville was a French diplomat and sociologist who came to America in the early 1830s to study the conditions of government in a relatively new republic, and penned his observations in a two-volume book translated into English entitled, *Democracy in America*. As he traveled the countryside of Pennsylvania, Tocqueville witnessed the voluntary exercise of democracy when farmers came together for a barn raising to help their neighbor whose barn had burned down. Tocqueville was surprised to see neighboring farmers who were engaged in agricultural commerce help a farmer-competitor get back into the business. Instead of feeling any sense of gratification to see a competitor go out of business as one might expect in a market economy, these farmers considered the barn raising a moral virtue to help a neighbor in need.

Viewing Rational Choice Theory, according to Verbeek's argument, we can conclude that all of the farmers that helped their neighbor in Tocqueville's barn raising example placed an unspoken trust that their neighbor's would also come to their aid if they experienced such a loss. Therefore, it was unnecessary for the farmers to have a written agreement to aid each other, it was a rational choice based on a belief of mutual expectation. Would our understanding and acceptance of the farmers' actions be as sympathetic in today's economic environment? What if Hewlett Packard was going under and Apple decided to give it all the resources necessary to get Hewlett Packard back into a competitive position, not by buying stock to infuse it with money, and not attempting to take it over, and not a loan, but simply a charitable act to make Hewlett Packard whole? Under that scenario would we expect *The Wall Street Journal* and *The Financial Times* and any other investment-oriented publication to editorialize Apple's actions as heroic or would it be seen as a violation of its fiduciary obligation to its shareholders? It would certainly be an irrational decision.

There are two factors in classical decision theory. One is response time and the other is the availability of alternative choices. According to Couto, van Maanen, and Lebreton (2020) "evidence suggests, however, that individuals' choices are biased towards default options, prompted by the framing of decisions" (p. 1). These researchers suggest that individuals are biased toward past choices and are naturally biased toward certain preferences that originate from an individual's internal state which they refer to as endogenous default options. If we accept that premise, we can hypothesize that founders who engage in founder's syndrome do so based on time pressures and one of two endogenous default options. First is a natural default option which is a general tendency that an individual would inherently prefer, and second is a learned default option based on a history of prior decisions (Druckman, 2001; Tversky & Kahneman, 1981).

We think that founder's syndrome behaviors can be used to disambiguate the choices of different types of endogenous default options to one specific choice, that is the natural default option. We reach this conclusion based on the belief that individuals who engage in founder's syndrome do not seek rational alternative decision options, they act on emotion or intuition which is intrinsic to the individual. We do not believe that founders consciously wrestle with their decision, selecting among alternative behaviors of acting inappropriately versus an appropriately suitable way. Peterson (2017) states that "Obviously, rival formalizations are troublesome if an act is judged to be rational in one optimal formalization of a decision problem, but irrational in another optimal formalization of the same decision problem" (p. 31).

One last thought about Decision Theory and founder's syndrome. Although selecting the appropriate behavior would be the best outcome for a wise decision, there is something missing in the analysis of choice making. The first step in rational decision-making is to determine the problem to be solved. For example, as an organization-based problem can we identify the likely cause of the problem: do we have competent staff, sufficient technology, adequate workspace, available capital and financial resources, or poor ratings and questionable reputation, or a terrific reputation but insufficient know-how on how to maximize the public's impression of the organization? To make a better decision, the founding CEO must be taught to question and examine the cause of his or her agitation before saying anything to his or her managers that cannot be easily forgiven. This one step can prevent a decision that is detrimental to the well-being of the staff and organization as a whole.

So, you ask, is it really possible to develop an organization that is free of founder's syndrome behaviors? We will answer this question in Chapter 8.

Discussion Questions

1. How do theories, paradigms, and models help us understand founder's syndrome? How do they expand our awareness of the human conditions and behaviors in organizations?

2. Name five theories from this chapter that you find helpful in enhancing your understanding of founder's syndrome. Explain why each theory is helpful.
3. Explain the differences between first-order change and second-order change in organizations.
4. What is the purpose of a theory?
5. How would you apply a theory to understand activities in an organization?
6. Which theory increased your understanding of founder's syndrome?
7. Why would a researcher state that a structural change requires a second-order type change?
8. In your own words, describe the Theory of Logical Types.
9. What experience have you had with an organization that can be described using one of the theories outlined in the chapter?
10. One of the leadership theories suggests that it is possible for a leader to change a supervisory style to fit the needs of a supervisee. Another theorist says that you must match the employee's task with a specific leader's style because it is not possible for leaders to change their styles. Which position do you agree with?
11. If a leader can change their style, why do you think is it so difficult for a founder engaged in founder's syndrome to change their behaviors?

References

Adler, A. (2010). *Understanding human nature.* Martino Fine Books. (Original work published 1927.)

Bandura, A. (1997). *Self-efficacy: The exercise of control.* Worth Publishers.

Banks, A. (2016). *Wired to connect: The surprising link between brain science and strong, healthy relationships.* Tarcher Perigee.

Bateson, G. (2000). *Steps to an ecology of mind.* University of Chicago Press.

Blanchard, K., Zigarmi, P., & Zigarmi, D. (2013). *Leadership and the one minute manager.* William Morrow Publishers. (Original work published 1985.)

Block, S. R. (2004). *Why nonprofits fail: Overcoming founder's syndrome, fundphobia, and other obstacles to success.* Jossey-Bass Publishers.

Block, S. R., & Rosenberg, S. (2002). Toward an understanding of founder's syndrome: An assessment of power and privilege among founders of nonprofit organizations. *Nonprofit Management & Leadership, 12*(4), 353–368.

Bowlby, J. (1983). *Attachment: Attachment and loss, Vol. 1* (2nd ed.). Basic Books. (Original work published 1969.)

Chandani, A., Mehta, M., Mall, A., & Khokhar, V. (2016). Employee engagement: A review paper on factors affecting employee engagement. *Indian Journal of Science and Technology, 9*(15), 1–7. doi: 10.17485/ijst/2016/v9i15/92145

Choi, S. Y., Chung, G. H., & Choi, J. N. (2019). Why are we having this innovation? Employee attributions of innovation and implementation behavior. *Social Behavior & Personality: An International Journal, 47*(7), 1–13.

Couto, J., van Maanen, L., & Lebreton, M. (2020). Investigating the origin and consequences of endogenous default options in repeated economic choices. *Public Library of Science One*, *15*(8), 1–19.

Dietrich, F., & List, C. (2013). A reason-based theory of rational choice. *Nous*, *47*(1), 104–134.

Druckman, J. N. (2001). Evaluating framing effects. *Journal of Economic Psychology*, *22*(1), 91–101.

Erikson, E. (1993). *Childhood and society*. W. W. Norton & Company. (Original work published 1950.)

Eysenck, H. J. (2017). *The biological basis of personality*. Routledge. (Original work published 1967.)

Farčić, N., Barać, I., Pluz, J., Iakovac, V., Pačarić, S., Gvozdanović, Z., & Lovrić, R. (2020). Personality traits of core self-evaluation as predictors on clinical decision-making in nursing profession. *Public Library of Science One*, *15*(5), 1–12. https://doi.org/ 10.1371/journal.pone.0233435

Festinger, L. (1957). *A theory of cognitive dissonance*. Row, Peterson and Company.

Festinger, L., & Carlsmith, J. M. (1959). Cognitive consequences of forced compliance. *Journal of Abnormal and Social Psychology*, *58*(2), 203–211. https://doi.org/10.1037/h0041593

Fiedler, F. E. (1953). The psychological-distance dimension in interpersonal relations. *Journal of Personality*, *22*(1), 142–150.

Fiedler, F. E. (1967). *A theory of leadership effectiveness*. McGraw-Hill.

Flink, C. M. (2017). Rethinking punctuated equilibrium theory: A public administration approach to budgetary changes. *Policy Studies Journal*, *45*(1), 101–120.

Freud, A. (2018). *The ego and the mechanisms of defense*. Routledge. (Original work published 1936.)

Freud, S. (1966a). Further remarks on the neuropsychoses of defense. In *The standard edition of the complete psychological works of Sigmund Freud* (Vol. 3, pp. 162–185). Hogarth Press. (Original work published 1896.)

Freud, S. (1966b). Repression. In *The standard edition of the complete psychological works of Sigmund Freud* (Vol. 14, pp. 141–158). Hogarth Press. (Original work published 1915.)

Freud, S. (1966c). The unconscious. In *The standard edition of the complete psychological works of Sigmund Freud* (Vol. 14, pp. 159–216). Hogarth Press. (Original work published 1915.)

Freud, S. (1977). *Inhibitions, symptoms and anxiety* (J. Strachey, Ed.). W.W. Norton. (Original work published 1926.)

Freud, S. (2018). *The ego and the id*. Dover Publications. (Original work published 1927.)

Giordano, P. J. (2014). Personality as continuous stochastic process: What Western personality theory can learn from classical Confucianism. *Integrative Psychological and Behavioral Science*, *48*(2), 111–128.

Giordano, P. J. (2015). Being or becoming: Toward an open-system, process-centric model of personality. *Integrative Psychological and Behavioral Science*, *49*(4), 757–771.

Giordano, P. J. (2017). Individual personality is best understood as process, not structure: A Confucian inspired perspective. *Culture and Psychology*, *23*(4), 502–518.

Haley, J. (1993). *Uncommon therapy: The psychiatric techniques of Milton Erikson, M. D.* W.W. Norton & Company.

Harmon-Jones, E., & Mills, J. (2019). An introduction to cognitive dissonance theory and an overview of current perspectives on the theory. In E. Harmon-Jones (Ed.), *Cognitive dissonance: Reexamining a pivotal theory in psychology* (2nd ed., pp. 3–24). American Psychological Association.

Heider, F. (1958). *The psychology of interpersonal relations.* Wiley.

Hersey, P. (1985). *The situational leader.* Warner Books.

Hersey, P., Blanchard, K., & Johnson D. E. (2012). *Management of organizational behavior: Leading human resources* (10th ed.). Prentice Hall

Horney, K. (1937). *The collected works of Karen Horney* (2 vols.) W.W. Norton & Company.

Hoshino-Browne, E., Zanna, A. S., Spencer, S. J., Zanna, M. P., Kitayama, S., & Lackenbauer, S. (2005). On the cultural guises of cognitive dissonance: The case of Easterners and Westerners. *Journal of Personality and Social Psychology, 89*(3), 294–310. https://doi.org/10.1037/0022-3514.89.3.294

Jarcho, J. M., Berkman, E. T., & Lieberman, M. D. (2011). The neural basis of rationalization: Cognitive dissonance reduction during decision-making. *Social Cognitive & Affective Neuroscience, 6*(4), 460–467.

Jordan, J., Kaplan, A., Miller, J., Stiver, I., & Surrey, J. (1991). *Women's growth in connection.* Guilford Press.

Jordan, J., Walker, M., & Hartling, L. (Eds.). (2004). *The complexity of connection: Writings from the Stone Center's Jean Baker Miller Training Institute.* Guilford Press.

Jordan, J. V. (2017). Relational–cultural theory: The power of connection to transform our lives. *Journal of Humanistic Counseling, 56*(3), 228–243.

Judge, T. A., Locke, E. A., & Durham, C. C. (1997). The dispositional causes of job satisfaction: A core evaluations approach. *Research in Organizational Behavior, 19*(1), 151–188.

Judge, T. A., Locke, E. A., Durham, C. C., & Kluger, A. N. (1998). Dispositional effects on job and life satisfaction: The role of core evaluations. *Journal of Applied Psychology, 83*(1), 17–34.

Jung, C. G. (2003). *Psychology of the unconscious.* Dover Publications. (Original work translated to the English language and published 1916. The original work in the German language was published 1912, as *Wandlugen und symbole der libido.*)

Kahneman, D., Knetsch, J. L., & Thaler, R. H. (1990). Experimental tests of the endowment effect and the course theorem. *Journal of Political Economy, 98*(6), 1325–1347.

Kitayama, S., Snibbe, A. C., Markus, H. R., & Suzuki, T. (2004). Is there any 'free' choice? Self and dissonance in two cultures. *Psychological Science, 15*(8), 527–533. http://dx.doi.org/10.1111/j.0956-7976.2004.00714.x

Kuhn, T. S. (1977). *The Essential Tension: Selected studies in scientific tradition and change.* University of Chicago Press.

Kuhn, T. S. (2012). *The structure of scientific revolutions: 50th anniversary edition* (4th ed.). University of Chicago Press. (Original work published 1962.)

Langlais, E. (2010). An analysis of bounded rationality in judicial litigations: The case with loss/disappointment averse plaintiffs. *Journal of Advanced Research in Law and Economics, 1*(1), 41–50.

Lenz, A. S. (2016). Relational-cultural theory: Fostering the growth of a paradigm through empirical research. *Journal of Counseling & Development*, *94*(4), 415–428.

Locke, E. A., & Latham G. P. (1984). *Goal setting: A motivational technique that works*. Prentice Hall.

Maslow, A. H. (1943). A theory of human motivation. *Psychological Review*, *50*(4), 370–396.

Maslow, A. H. (1954). *Motivation and personality*. Harper and Row.

Mazzotta, V., & Santella, R. (2017). CEO hubris: The impact of interpersonal effectiveness in the strategic decision-making activity. *Proceedings of the Multidisciplinary Academic Conference*. 250–257.

McCrae, R. R. (2011). Personality theories for the 21st century. *Teaching of Psychology*, *38*(3), 209–214.

McGrath, A. (2017). Dealing with dissonance: A review of cognitive dissonance reduction. *Social & Personality Psychology Compass*, *11*(12), 1–17. https://doi.org/10.1111/spc3.12362

Nuttin, J. M. Jr. (1987). Affective consequence of mere ownership: The name letter effect in twelve European languages. *European Journal of Social Psychology*, *17*(4), 381–402.

Pallak, M. S., & Pittmann, T. S. (1972). General motivational effects of dissonance arousal. *Journal of Personality & Social Psychology*, *21*(3), 349–358.

Peterson, M. (2017). *An introduction to decision theory* (2nd ed.). Cambridge University Press.

Reynolds, P. D. (1971). *A primer in theory construction*. Taylor & Francis.

Rogers, C. (1995). *On becoming a person: A therapist's view of psychotherapy*. Mariner Books. (Original work published 1961.)

Ruesch, J., & Bateson, G. (Eds.). (2017). *Communication, the social matrix of psychiatry*. Routledge. (original work published 1951.)

Sahar, G. (2014). On the importance of attribution theory in political psychology. *Social & Personality Psychology Compass*, *8*(5), 229–249.

Shoaib, F., & Kohli, N. (2017). Employee engagement and goal setting theory. *Indian Journal of Health and Well-being*, *8*(8), 877–880.

Skinner, B. F. (2006). *The behavior of organisms*. Copley Publishing Group. (Original work published 1938.)

Smith, P. K., Jost, J. T., & Vijay, R. (2008). Legitimacy crisis? Behavioral approach and inhibition when power differences are left unexplained. *Social Justice Research*, *21*(3), 358–376.

Stanovich, K. E. (2013). Why humans are (sometimes) less rational than other animals: Cognitive complexity and the axioms of rational choice. *Thinking & Reasoning*, *19*(1), 1–26. http://dx.doi.org/10.1080/13546783.2012.713178

Su, F., & Zhang, J. (2020). Proactive personality and innovative behavior: A moderated mediation model. *Social Behavior & Personality: An International Journal*, *48*(3), 1–12.

Tocqueville, A. (2006). *Democracy in America* (J. P. Mayer, Ed., G. Lawrence, Trans.) Harper Perennial Modern Classics. (Original work published 1835.)

Tversky, A., & Kahneman, D. (1981). The framing of decisions and the psychology of choice. *Science*, *211*(4481), 453–458.

Uher, J. (2015). Conceiving 'personality': Psychologists' challenges and basic fundamentals of the transdisciplinary philosophy-of-science paradigm for research on individuals. *Integrative Psychological and Behavioral Science*, 49(3), 398–458.

Verbeek, P. P. (2010). Designing the human condition: Reflections on technology and religion. *ET-Studies*, 1(1), 39–52.

Wajzer, M. (2015). The explanatory potential of rational choice theory: A critical assessment. *Social Evolution & History*, 14(1), 65–86.

Wang, G., Holmes Jr. R. M., Oh, I. S., Zhu, W. (2016). Do CEOs matter to firm strategic actions and firm performance? A meta-analytic investigation based on upper echelons theory. *Personnel Psychology*, 69(4), 775–862.

Watson, R. J., & Winkleman, J. H. (2005). Perceived ownership or cognitive dissonance? *Journal of Social Psychology*, 35(3), 403–411.

Watzlawick, P., Beavin Bavelas, J., & Jackson, D. D. (1967). *Pragmatics of human communication: A study of interactional patterns, pathologies, and paradoxes* (1st ed.). W. W. Norton & Company.

Watzlawick, P., & Weakland, J. H. (Eds.). (1977). *The interactional view: Studies at the Mental Research Institute, Palo Alto, 1965-1974*. W.W. Norton & Company.

Watzlawick, P., Weakland, J. H., & Fisch, R. (1974). *Change: Principles of problem formation and problem resolution*. W. W. Norton & Company.

Weiner, B. (2006). *Social motivation, justice, and the moral emotions: An attributional approach*. Erlbaum.

Whitehead, A. N., & Russell, B. (1910). *Principia mathematica* (Vol. 1). Cambridge University Press.

5 Theoretical Explanations of Stakeholder's Behaviors

Chapter Objectives

When you finish studying this chapter, you should be able to:

- Discuss theories that help us understand the motivations of organizational stakeholders to expel the founder of a company
- Explain how managers and board members might initiate activities that lead to ousting the founder
- Understand the psychological stress ousted founders might endure
- Identify theories that help to explain the experiences of staff or board members associated with organizations experiencing founder's syndrome
- Discuss reasons why managers might want to get rid of their founding CEO
- Describe some of the initial steps of consulting with an organization that complains of founder's syndrome behaviors
- Discuss the reason for internal stakeholders to be uncooperative and resistive to consultants brought in to help an organization

Introduction

In keeping with the aforementioned lessons from Lorenz (1966), Biddle (1979), and Thomas (1974), the objective for this chapter is to demonstrate how the use of theories facilitates our comprehension of other fundamental elements of founder's syndrome, that is, the reasoning and determination that motivates organizational stakeholders to expel the founding CEO. There are three conditions that motivate senior managers and/or board members to plan actions to remove the organization's founder. The most evident reason is the CEO engaging in founder's syndrome behaviors. Those senior management staff who are victims of the founder's unacceptable conduct become sympathetically aware of each other's delicate need for support. These co-participants will often gather and engage in discussion about their interactional episodes with the founder. As trust develops through these cathartic expressions of feelings and outrage, eventually the conversations shift to exploring their options to cause the downfall and removal of the founder.

The second reason organizational members conspire to ouster the founding CEO is because the 'ringleader' wants the CEO position for him or herself, or they have a friend or colleague they prefer to see in the executive role. As mentioned elsewhere in the book, once the founder becomes aware of the conspiracy to cause his or her termination, the founder will often feel betrayed and retaliate with founder's syndrome behavior. Although the founder's defensive reaction is understandable, it can be seen by the board of directors as inappropriate and move board members to support the managers, thus accelerating the founder's termination.

The third reason that management staff and/or board members seek the removal of the organizational founder is to relieve their pent-up frustration with the CEO's managerial style and a belief that the CEO does not possess the competencies that are necessary to successfully lead the corporation. Individuals seeking the removal of the CEO can often point to badly chosen decisions that have led to lost opportunities and organizational mediocrity. Similar to the second of the three situations, once the founder discovers the efforts to purge him or her from their position, it is not uncommon for the CEO to become enraged from feeling betrayed and such feelings manifest into founder's syndrome behavior aimed at the board of directors and senior management staff.

There is no single theory that can adequately explain the complexities of a group or individual who strives to get rid of an organizational founder because of the founder's deplorable behavior. In the case of undermining the founding CEO to suit someone's personal agenda, there are certain words that can be pinned on such a person, even explanations about a personality type or personality disorder but there is no theory that can comprehensively explain the motives and attributes of the individual. Consequently, over the years, we have been able to piece together organizational theories that have helped us conceptualize a framework for systematic understanding of the characteristics and dynamics of the schemers and plotters and the founder's reactions.

Although the theories that we include in this chapter have stood the test of rigid inquiry for deciphering the analytical problems of human intentions, we continue to study the organizational literature in search of additional coherent theories, models, and paradigms that will enhance our writing, teaching, and consulting on founder's syndrome. We believe that it is important to remain alert to the possibilities that other theories can be fruitful especially as new theories or recasting older theories find homes in the professional literature. Currently, the most meaningful configuration of theories applicable to dissecting the stakeholders' objectives to depose the founder include the following:

Conflict Theory
Conservation of Resources Theory
Ecological Theory
Role Theory
Social Interaction Theory
Theory of the Id, Ego, and Superego

In the early days of providing organizational development consultation with organizations experiencing founder's syndrome, we received a phone call from a board member of a medium-sized corporation on the southeast coast requesting help. He described the primary problem as an upset management team uniting with the aim to convince the board of directors to remove their founding CEO. Up until this latest development, the founding CEO did not have a history of founder's syndrome behavior but of late was displaying anger, bullying, and short temperedness after finding out his management team did not have confidence in his leadership. The board of directors was at a stalemate as to how to handle the organizational crises. Some board members were siding with the CEO and others expressed support with the management staff.

Because of their quandary of positions, their inclination was to involve their corporate attorney who met separately with the board, the CEO, and the management team. Their lawyer's approach included a less than humanistic approach with threats and lectures about legal exposure and other impediments. The approach proved incompatible with the nature of the organizational issues and only exacerbated feelings of frustration that further fueled the internal organizational conflicts.

Preparing for our visit included a brainstorming session of what data would be collected. The game plan for the first visit was not to present an intervention. To do so would have been premature. The first step was to draft a set of questions that would be used during our introductions and interviews with the key players. The primary purpose was to fact gather for the purpose of diagnosing the organizational dysfunction and to determine what the stakeholders' would be satisfied with as an outcome – beyond the managers wanting to get rid of the founder and the founder now wanting to fire all of the managers, and the board of directors wanting harmony and to refocus on their corporation's products, services, and profits. The diagnostic approach is a critical component for defining and describing an organization's current condition and simply parallels the scientific method of observation, fact gathering, hypothesis formation, feedback, and testing by an approved intervention, followed by evaluation of the results.

The importance of observation and determining patterns of communication should be emphasized during the diagnostic period. We needed to see firsthand the interactions between the stakeholders, including the social emotional behaviors during their meetings. We were interested in identifying the frequency of interactions, when someone became silent, who dominated the discussion, who agreed with each other and who disagreed. We used a sociogram to graphically plot the interactions to determine the alliances between the participants.

Because we were dealing with real problems and not test subjects, there were important considerations to weigh. After collecting and deciphering the information, a key question was whether this dysfunctional organization would be able to survive critical changes to its environment? Would it be possible to create a change to its organizational structure and the behaviors of its key stakeholders? The answers depended on knowing the type of communications, control, and information mechanisms that were in place. What were the unwritten rules of behavior? How did the organization members and the CEO attempt to problem-solve? What patterns of novel behavior supported the activities of the management team? What were the location and function of negative feedback loops in the organization? Could the board and its CEO clarify its direction and develop a compatible organizational culture?

After interviewing the management staff, CEO, and board members and listening to the varied accounts of their organization's issues, it was not surprising to find their descriptions amounted to a mélange of blame and finger-pointing. After a few days onsite, we were able to determine one of the root causes of the problem that led to the management team's wish to ouster the founding CEO. There was a history of participative inequality. Some members of the management team were able to gain the CEO's acceptance for their ideas and actions which also created an assumed ranking of favorites. The CEO's tendency to accept suggestions from some but not all eventually led to arousing negative reactions by managers who felt slighted. Managers vying for status created a competition for position. During the periods that a manager seemed to be on top of the ranking, also seemed to create internal hostility by some managers toward that temporary leader. This oscillation of rank among managers caused consternation instead of an appreciation for each other's specializations, knowledge, and skills. In her book on territorial games, Simmons (1998) captured the dynamics:

> Once people start wrangling for a territorial advantage, pushing their hidden agendas, and undercutting their peers, no one is focused on organizational goals. The turf war mentality lowers our sights, and we waste valuable time and effort crushing an enemy who could be, and should be, on our side. (p. 1)

The managers' reactions suggested that the organization was missing shared values and norms. Overall, there was an absence of a shared organizational culture.

The one area where the managers were able to coalesce was their dislike of the founder's management style and what they perceived as his lacking in leadership with the CEO's minimal emphasis on strategic direction. Additionally, from their parochial viewpoint, some managers concluded they were being pitted against each other which kept them all in a subordinate position and the CEO in a comfortable position of superiority. Hence, they preferred that the board of directors hire a capable CEO who would be respectful of their varied talents and who would create opportunities for professional growth. They wanted an experienced CEO who had the know-how to achieve strategic goals and objectives and capable of sizing up staff's talents for selective assignments.

In small group discussions, some of the managers were realistic and recognized their own contributions to a hostile and competitive environment with their self-confessed shark-like behavior to gain the top manager spot. Some also confessed to an unwillingness to forego their competitive behaviors out of fear that other managers would not acquiesce. These sentiments of distrust among the managers signaled that they felt threatened and anomic. Sherman, Brookfield, and Ortosky (2017) point out that "conflict-supporting beliefs are sustained by selective, biased, and distorted processing of conflict-related information" (p. 5).

Although all the stakeholders contributed to the organization's dysfunction, the founding CEO had not understood how he played a role in the organization's instability and management team's distress. We discovered that he had not communicated his purpose for holding management team meetings, did not have meeting agendas nor convey his current vision for the corporation, nor had he required progress reports from division managers. However, those managers with more management savvy gave reports on their division's progress and identified barriers to success. The CEO's positive recognition to the substantive details signaled that a manager said something of transcendent importance. Some managers mistakenly interpreted the CEO's expressed affirmation of a manager's report as signaling favoritism. Instead of concentrating on the report of a division manager's significant contribution to the organization, some managers were comparatively focused on the presumed footing and reputation of their colleagues. According to Hudak (2000),

> Envy is a complex phenomenon. When we talk about it in the workplace we should recognize that we're really talking about a specific sort of relationship between people: the relationship between the envied and the envier ... [T]he envying person often feels 'consumed' by an intense hunger for what is perceived as missing in their lives, but rather located in someone else's life. The envying person will turn the other into an object of desire, but an object where 'envy aims to spoil the object, to empty it of its good stuff, whether or not we can acquire it. ... [I]t sees only the part of an object, never that whole. (p. 609)

Our assessments of the dysfunctional behaviors were aided by our theoretical understanding that an organization's social structure is a product of the stakeholders' interdependence. In this regard, conflict theory was a useful tool for analyzing the exchanges among the stakeholders because conflict theorists place emphasis on interactional behaviors being motivated by self-interest that lead to competition for personal gain and advantages over others. In this case, managers' attitudes about competition had some bearing on team member's well-being and raised concerns about one's positionality in the workplace. Grasseni and Origo (2018) raise an interesting point about the potential impact of competition on a work-team, stating "since competition emphasizes personal success, it shifts attention from the well-being of the group to that of the individual, thus lessening social cohesion" (p. 1984).

We agree with the predominant theoretical viewpoint that conflict is an inevitable occurrence in the workplace when thinking individuals interact (Blank, 2019). In fact, the topic of conflict and its conceptual explanations has been ubiquitous in the writing of theorists from the classical periods and into contemporary professional literature. Rahim (2015) provided an informed review of scholarly interpretations of conflict and conflict theory starting with Plato and Aristotle's belief that conflict is a threat to social order (p. 3). Much of the historical thinking about the subject of conflict were produced by philosophers with their macro focus on society. However, some of their key points can be translated into the domain of present-day organizations, such as Hegel's (2015) often cited statement, "Contradiction is the root of all movement and vitality; it is only in so far as something has a contradiction within it that it moves, has an urge and activity" (Hegel, p. 382). Hence, the conflicts within an organization struggling with founder's syndrome are prime for some corrective reaction, otherwise the entity will suffer and possibly not survive.

Social psychologists have contributed to the study of conflict theory in the twentieth and twenty-first centuries (Heider, 1958; Jones & Davis, 1965; Sherif, Harvey, Hood, Sherif, & White, 1988) in addition to neo-Freudian theories that build from Freud's contribution to unconscious drives to resolve aggressive tendencies (Adler, 2010; Erikson, 1993; Horney, 1937). In their insightful article on intergroup conflict and barriers to common ground, Sherman et al. (2017) state that a group's attitudes "become self-perpetuating by channeling motivated information processing that focuses attention on belief-confirming information, leading to even greater perceived polarization between and making it difficult to acknowledge ingroup wrongdoing." We found this last statement resonated true. Although the managers, CEO, and board of directors claim they wanted to resolve the organizational difficulties, they initially held to their conflict-oriented beliefs, thus creating an initial challenge for problem-solving (see, Condor & Brown, 1988). Writing about Realistic Conflict Theory, Thomson, Outram, Gilligan, and Levett-Jones (2015) state that "Superordinate goals require intergroup cooperation (interdependence) in order for goals to be achieved" (p. 635). Consequently, if we were to be engaged to intervene following our organizational assessment, we would need some form of stratagem to accommodate a plan for conflict resolution and planned change.

The stakeholders' entrenched positions were anticipated. One of the important lessons we share with our students about organizational development consultation with organizations involved with founder's syndrome is to be prepared to encounter conflict and hardened positions when being invited into a troubled organization. Internal conflict may carry over from between the participants to encompass hostility toward the consultants. A breakdown of organizational civility is related to resistance and initial distrust by organizational members toward 'the so-called' experts. Even when informing the participants of the purpose of our presence, it is not uncommon for some to mistakenly believe that we hold some power over them and have been assigned an arbiter and decision-making role. This view becomes a strong myth with several individuals feeling trepidation over the ultimate outcome of our rulings and potential verdicts, which in reality we will not be making. However, it is not altogether surprising that organizational members may hold this belief. Peate, Platow, and Eggins (2008) remind us that "In formal theories of procedural fairness, fair process control occurs when all parties involved in a conflict can argue their cases to an arbitrating decision-making authority in an attempt to influence that authority's final decision" (p. 175). However, activities with the intent to expel a founding CEO are not categorized as simple disagreements. They parallel the intensity of marital divorce proceedings that are unreceptive to interventions using the tools of mediation or negotiation. But as Gawerc (2013) states,

> all of these represent tools and strategies for managing or resolving conflict focused on the disagreement rather than a broader, more transformative, and more preventative focus on strengthening the relationships, which could allow withstanding more disagreements and minimizing their potential destructiveness. (p. 220)

In the interest of understanding the stakeholder relationships, we make use of role theory because "roles are not only about perceived behaviors or position, but just as important, roles are about a person's perception of a given situation" and his or her "self-conception within that situation." Additionally, Biddle (1986) states,

> role theory concerns one of the most important features of social life, characteristic behavior patterns or roles. It explains roles by presuming that persons are members of social position and hold expectations for their own behaviors and for those of other persons. (p. 67; see also Lemay, 1999, p. 225)

The management team's reactions and activities were fixated on changing the structure of the organization's social system. Although their intentions were understandable, their use of work time and energy to accomplish that end were not consistent with their hired roles as managers. In other words, an attempt to rid the organization of the founding CEO does not come close to resembling any expectations of the managers' job responsibilities. Instead, their actions promoted substantial work role conflicts and undermined the norms of the corporation. Jensen (2016) offers a clear definition of work role conflict being "simultaneous contradictory expectations from colleagues that interfere with one another and make it difficult to complete work tasks" (p. 591). Another way of looking at this issue is the recognition that a person's role in an organization creates patterns of predictable behavior. Co-workers count on this predictability to function effectively within their own roles. When an individual steps out of their role and introduces role variance, they are sacrificing predictability in exchange for conflict and strain in the system. Because of the managers and the CEO disengaging from their roles and responsibilities, the employees who are supervised by the various managers also experience job challenges. Lynch (2007) explains that "persons affect situations and situations affect persons such that the unfolding of time produces continuous changes in role identification dynamics" (p. 380).

After an adequate period of being onsite and having gained a handle on the organizational dynamics and troublesome interactions, we believe it was important to require all participants to adhere to certain ground rules. Specifically, all participants were to agree that while in the workplace, they were to communicate only on matters of organizational tasks related to one's job role and responsibilities and forego the additional encounters that fall outside of what would be considered a stable social organization. By limiting the work-day communications to goal-directed activities, we placed a Band-Aid on the off-putting conversations in the workplace and created a temporary social system that intentionally obligated the participants to a schema of etiquette (see, Li, Li, Fu, & Ullah, 2019). Theoretically, we were attempting to protect what Thompson (2017) called the technical core of an organization, that is, the processes that carry out the primary purposes for which the organization was created.

We operated with no illusion that this temporary truce was fragile with precarious points of weakness such as the participants remaining in a stressed condition while the system issues remained unresolved. However, as participants scaled down their voice in the workplace and returned to productivity, we had an opportunity to complete our interviews, examine survey results, and prepare a written and verbal report of our findings that we would share with all of the employees. In our role as informants, we include our professional opinions based on a comprehensive assessment. This task requires a review of all analyses of individual and group interviews, written surveys, interactional observations, examination of metacommunications, and our assessment of the management strengths and weaknesses of the organization, appraisal of the clarity of the mission, vision, and organizational values and culture. Ecological theory provided a basis for our analytical thinking.

The rationale for using ecological theory is its framework which places an emphasis on examining individuals in their environment. In this case, the workplace setting is the environment. Social and developmental psychologist Bronfenbrenner (1979) is credited with developing ecological theory after initially recognizing the many influences that affect a child's developmental growth into adulthood. His approach took on an application of examining how individuals adapt and change according to the events within their social environment.

According to ecological theory, an individual's perception of their own experiences and transactions shapes how they react and how they cope. For this reason, we observe each person in the work setting and attempt to determine how their interactions under the stressors and conflict of founder's syndrome impact their work and attitudes. Furthermore, according to Shelton (2019), the interconnectedness of individuals who construct an understanding of their experiences within a system influences changes to the system. He writes, "the development of the person changes the system. The system changes because as a person develops, his or her actions change, and other people in the system therefore respond differently to the developing person" (p. 10).

We also find useful the reconceptualization of Bronfenbrenner's ecological systems theory proposed by Neal and Neal (2013), who "defines ecological systems in terms of patterns of social interaction" (p. 735). Their model provides a theoretically informed application for clarifying the relational approach and how it intersects or overlaps between the three major participant microsystem groups in the troubled organization, that is, the management staff, the founding CEO, and the board of directors. Ecological theory and social interaction theory highlight the patterns of the management team members' responses to each other as well as to the attitudes and behaviors of the CEO and board of directors. Although the management staff had some trust issues within their own group and suspended some aspects of their managerial role, their collective patterns of behavior all pointed to a concern that corporate goals needed emphasis, their CEO was not competent, he was weakening the company and placing it in jeopardy. Moreover, their coalescing to expel the founding CEO reinforced their alliance. Interviews with this group did not reveal issues with wages, work hours, building conditions, or other extrinsic factors.

For further insight, we examined the research literature on work-related stress and burnout because these conditions are known outcomes of founder's syndrome. During the meta-analysis, we were introduced to a process-oriented Conservation of Resources (COR) Theory that was developed by social psychologist Hobfoll (1998) and is germane for understanding the reasons that management staff and/or board members would initiate activities to expel the founding CEO. The theory was described by Vinokur-Kaplan (2009) as one that can be refocused for a "strengths-based perspective regarding organizations and their employees" (p. 228). According to Rogers (2013), a strengths perspective incorporates an individual's "skills, goals, talents, abilities and resources, as well as the strengths and resources found in their environments" that can be used for assessment and intervention (p. 49). Thus, we can examine each organizational player alone, in tandem, or combined to assess attitudes, objectives, and results of their organizational participation.

According to Hobfoll (1998), the central tenet of COR theory is that "people strive to obtain, retain, and protect that which they value" (p. 55). He further states that "people work to obtain resources they do not have, retain those resources they possess, protect resources when threatened, and foster resources by positioning themselves so that their resources can be put to best use" (p. 55). An essential component of COR theory is the classification of resources. In the taxonomy of the theory there are four different types of resources:

1. Object resources have physical qualities such as a home, a car, or other acquired valuables that affect social status, self-esteem or to gain social dominance and self-worth. These also include what Maslow referred to as basic needs, such as food, clothing, and shelter.
2. Personal resources can include occupational skills, leadership aptitude, and other learned resources through work experience, role adaptation, or education. Personal resources also include certain traits such as self-efficacy and self-esteem.
3. Conditioned resources are foundational because they can lead to other resources. Among conditioned resources include one's health, employment, seniority at work, and social networks.
4. Energy resources can also lead to other resources. They include money, knowledge, and credit.

COR theory provides an effective framework for elucidating the reasons that managers and board members would initiate activities to oust a founding CEO. These actions come about when the CEO is unreceptive to examining conflicts and ignores efforts or requests to establish environmental work conditions to build trust, and does not devote time to problem-solving issues that exist throughout the organization. When management staff express their concerns to their CEO, COR theory would explain that the managers' interactional process is an attempt to invest resources to improve organizational conditions. Consider Buchwald and Schwarzer's (2003) statement, according to COR theory, human beings' primary motivation is to build, protect and foster their resource pool in order to protect the self and the social bonds that support the self. Moreover, coping is not only an individual but also a communal process. (p. 281)

However, if after explaining their concerns to their CEO and not receiving a satisfactory reaction, the theory would conclude that the managers had depleted a portion of their resources. The theory also states that continued attempts that fail will yield additional secondary losses of resources. When resource loss becomes protracted, it becomes less likely that the resources can be replenished. With substantial resource depletion, the likely outcome is the imminent loss of employment. Thus, feeling threatened that their employment is in jeopardy because of a CEO they believe is uncaring and not competent, a management team becomes motivated to undertake activities to oust the CEO and attempt to preserve what is left of their personal and conditioned resources. An additional motivating factor is the belief that if a new CEO is hired who possesses considerable executive management expertise, then work conditions will be restored and managers and staff will regain and expand individualized resources.

On the other hand, if the founding CEO demonstrates a willingness to listen to the management team's complaints and actively explores their concerns, COR theory explains this response as a positive development and it prevents the powerful downward spiraling of resource losses which would lead to an organizational crash. To prevent a complete organizational loss, the CEO must take critical action, according to Hobfoll, Halbesleben, Neveu, and Westman (2018),

to counteract loss and to build engagement. One caveat to this principle is that resource gain spirals do gain in saliency in high-loss settings and conditions, which means that the motivation to build a resource gain cycle will increase when losses occur and will have higher payoff under high stress conditions. (p. 107)

COR theory's framework can be useful to understand the retaliatory behavior of the founding CEO after learning of plans to expel him or her. As stated earlier, COR theory's basic tenet is that "people strive to obtain, retain, protect, and foster that which they value" (Hobfoll, 1998, p. 55). The struggle between the management staff and the founding CEO, as in this case study, hindered morale and organizational productivity and created a demanding milieu for the board of directors, thus creating limitations on their resource investment. Also, the fact that the board of directors were split on how to proceed and did not altogether support their CEO left the CEO in the stance of defending himself. As a result, the founding CEO experienced a diminishment of his own personal resources. COR theory states that when an individual "loses resources, they are decreasingly capable of withstanding further threats to resource loss. These loss cycles are more momentous and move more quickly than gain cycles" (Vinokur-Kaplan, 2009, p. 231). Furthermore, "Conservation of Resources (COR) theory predicts that resource loss is the principal ingredient in the stress process" (Hobfoll, 2001, p. 337). While under a great deal of stress and with the potential of losing his position, (and without any outside intervention) we can anticipate the founding CEO will take extreme action by way of founder's syndrome behaviors as an attempt to hold onto his job and resources.

In this example, the loss of staff resources was slowed by the board of directors' actions to bring in our consulting group for the purpose of assessing the organizational issues related to founder's syndrome and to help the board determine what to do about the management team's efforts to expel the founding CEO. Although we determined that the CEO was limited in his ability as a hands-on manager, ultimately the board of directors did not want to replace him. Instead, the board of directors selected a compromised set of objectives. They recast the CEO's position to take advantage of his entrepreneurial spirit that was essential in founding the company. They believed his strengths were better suited to developing relationships important to the organization such as with civic leaders, potential investors, and government regulators with an eye toward expansion. In addition, by focusing on the external environment and meeting with staff, not to supervise them, but to stay abreast of their ideas, the CEO would be able to share information with the board of directors and offer judgmental forecasts.

To offset the CEO's managerial weaknesses, the board promoted one of the members of the management team to the position of Chief Operating Officer (COO), responsible for the daily operations of the company. Two of the division directors opted to resign and were replaced with outside candidates. Over the next several months, we facilitated the development of a revised strategic plan with quantifiable objectives for the CEO and COO that were tied to the organizations' vision, mission, and primary products and services. Working with the COO and management team, an action plan was developed that identified the specific activities required to achieve the objectives with assignments to appropriate personnel. Team members developed Gantt charts for their specific activities and tracking the resources that would be needed to accomplish their tasks. Strategic control systems were designed with channels to report on progress and problems. With an agreement and a commitment to the unity of direction of the organization, there appeared to be a reawakening of an esprit de corps. We stressed the importance of developing and reinforcing a supportive work culture and making certain that leadership behavior and messaging were congruent.

Although we attempt to remain neutral, nonjudgmental, and objective when engaged to help organizations struggling with founder's syndrome, it is difficult to avoid feelings of consternation in those instances when we discover a manager or board member conspiring against the CEO because they want the job and will strive to unseat the CEO and manipulate their way into the CEO role. When we discuss such findings with our students, we express our opinions as a response to what we consider to be an individual's ethical breach of professional behavior and our serious concerns about the moral character of the person scheming to oust the CEO or had schemed and was either successful or failed in causing the ouster of the CEO.

To understand the underlying motivation of the individual seeking to remove the founding CEO for their own gain, it seems reasonable to begin with one of the earliest personality theories for an explanation. Without delving into all the psychoanalytic details of Freud's work, we only need to discuss the theory of the id, ego, and superego as a starting point. Freud described the Self as consisting of a triparte interacting system beginning with the id. This part of a person's personality exists since birth and operates on an unconscious level. The theory describes the id as the center of psychic energy that drives impulses and the need for gratification.

The ego develops from the id and mitigates the id impulses relying on a reality principle to achieve the id desires in socially acceptable ways. The superego is the internalized standards that we learn through family and other social networks. Ideally, the three components of the personality operate together to prevent wanton and impulsive behavior and seek solutions that are consistent with the standards of society. The ego and superego can operate at the level of consciousness. Consequently, a person who has a less developed ego and superego can make socially acceptable allowances for plotting the removal of the founding CEO and seek the position for themselves or for a friend. Although their impulses are strong and their motives may cast doubt on their ethics or morals, an individual who plots and conspires likely has enough self-control not to act in an extreme unorthodox manner such as securing their objective through murder or kidnapping. Instead, they are likely to engage in deceptive tactics and give the appearance of acting in acceptable ways as they manipulate others to achieve their goals.

It is common knowledge that successful organizations rely on a culture that includes trust between managers and the staff they supervise as well as between managers and their CEO. Because plotting to remove the CEO for one's own gain is a breach of trust, a comprehensive understanding of the dynamics requires an examination of the theories of trust and mistrust. When considering trust in the workplace, our theoretical understanding is that trust is a psychological and dyadic process in which a social exchange takes place and is influenced by everyone being a trustworthy collaborator. Korsgaard (2018) refers to this cooperative and "bidirectional phenomenon" as "reciprocal trust" (p. 14). Consequently, an individual who is planning to sabotage the CEO's standing must act and disguise their deviancy to maintain a facade of trustworthiness.

The masking of aberrant behavior is known as sociopathy. Because of the seriousness of the behavior, the term sociopath or sociopathy is often mistaken as a psychiatric diagnosis. It is not, but it is mentioned as a diagnostic feature of antisocial personality disorder in the *Diagnostic and Statistical Manual of Mental Disorders* (American Psychiatric Association, 2013). Both antisocial personality disorder and narcissistic personality disorder have features that have become common idiomatic terms as a person being narcissistic or referring to someone as a sociopath. Those terms are often used to describe an individual who has proven to be untrustworthy and self-centered. The term sociopath is a pejorative label that is applied to a person who shows no remorse for their unsavory activities. Individuals with sociopathy have no qualms in betraying friends or coworkers. They will use previously confided information to gain an upper hand. Among the behaviors of a person diagnosed as having an antisocial personality disorder includes a total disregard for the feelings of other persons, they are manipulative and deceitful and lack empathy, plus they may have a history of engaging in crimes and using aliases. They may use superficial charm and tend to be verbally facile in addition to having an inflated self-appraisal. Although we can point to the descriptors that are used to diagnose an individual as being someone with an antisocial personality disorder, we are not in a position to state that all individuals who plot against their founding CEO are personality disordered. But to actively devise a plot against another person so that they lose their job for the benefit of someone else's personal gain is in our opinion sinister, manipulative, and selfish.

There is also a growing theoretical and empirical-based literature on distrust as separate from that of the trust literature. This expansion is helpful for acquiring information on the motives of individuals seeking to expel the founding CEO for their own gain. Moreover, the distrust literature offers a theoretical lens to understand the reactions of the founder when suspicious feelings of distrust emerge. For example, a founder may get an inkling that they are a target of someone on their management staff and hold a belief that the staff member's "conduct involves a malicious intent" (Korsgaard, 2018, p. 14). Furthermore, Sitkin and Bijlsma-Frankema (2018) refer to Lewicki, McAllister, and Bies's (1998) definition that we can use as a framework to ground the reaction of the founder who suspects betrayal among a manager or board member: "Confident negative expectations and perception about the intentions and beliefs of another" (p. 50), as well as assuming a defensive posture as stated by Rousseau, Sitkin, Burt, and Camera (1998), distinguishing distrust as "A psychological state, comprising the unwillingness to accept vulnerability, based on pervasive perceptions and expectations of ... motives, intentions, or behaviors" (p. 50).

Knowing or suspecting that someone close is engaged in betrayal can cause the target psychological harm. Goldsmith, Chesney, Heath, and Barlow (2013) state,

> Betrayal trauma, or trauma perpetrated by someone to whom the victim was close is more strongly related to anxiety, depression, and posttraumatic stress than is trauma perpetrated by someone to whom the victim was not close ... [P]sychological outcomes vary as a function of the victim–perpetrator relationship may reflect several emotional processes and contextual features related to betrayal." (p. 376)

Betrayal is a serious breach within an organization and its impact can be felt beyond the targeted individual. On this point, Frey (2018) reveals,

> in intentional betrayal the goal is to violate fundamental trust expectations in order to cause harm to a specific individual(s). Because the affective consequences of both incidental and intentional betrayals can be intense, however, the organizational climate is impacted ... such breaches in trust decrease employee openness, productivity, and innovation, and drain employee resources. (p. 90)

Besides wanting the position of CEO, the increased salary, benefits, and positional authority and public attention the role may hold, the reason a manager moves forward with their plans to unseat a founding CEO is theoretically the result of not being able to regulate self-control. According to Fan, Ren, Zhang, Xiao, and Zhong (2020),

> Research has indicated that exercising self-control requires using cognitive resources that may become temporarily exhausted, causing an individual to underperform ...
>
> Humans must maintain self-control to inhibit traits such as hedonism, selfishness, and vested interests ... Individuals with high self-control ability are more successful in restraining selfish motives and behaving prosocially compared with individuals with low self-control. (pp. 228–229)

Researchers attribute social shortcomings to individuals with low self-control epitomized by engaging in more deceptive behaviors (Kouchaki & Smith, 2014) as well as antisocial behaviors (Righetti & Finkenauer, 2011). In addition, Fan et al.'s (2020) research found "that individuals with strong self-control ability can better suppress selfish motives, consider long-term interests, and are less likely to deceive on the basis of their own interests" (p. 238).

What options does a founding CEO take when they are accused by a manager in the manager's pursuit to discredit the CEO to get them fired? A similar question was posed by Vaillancourt (2013) writing in the *Chronicle of Higher Education*,

> At some point in your career ... you may struggle to make sense of something that makes no sense at all – perhaps called to defend yourself for taking actions that you never took, accused of failing ... or charged with uttering words that would never come out of your mouth. ... If you look closely, you will find yourself covered with marks that could have come only from the wheels of a very large bus. ... To 'throw (someone) under the bus' as an idiomatic phrase meaning 'to sacrifice another person (often a friend or ally), who is usually not deserving of such treatment, out of malice or for personal gain.' None of us appreciate being sacrificed for someone else's greater glory, but it is especially painful and disorienting when we discover that we have been played as a pawn by someone we counted as a colleague or confidant. (p. 39)

The jolt of being 'thrown under the bus' eventually subsides, but not the scars. We are reminded of the classic statement in the film The Godfather explaining to the protagonist that the murder of his brother could be explained away because 'it was only business.' Similarly, should the attempt to sabotage the CEO to get him or her fired be simply accepted because 'it's only business?' The typical founding CEO reaction is an aggressive campaign of revenge.

We posed this question to two former founding CEOs who were terminated by their Boards of Directors following a betrayal of their management staff. The interview with Mark took place eight years after his termination and the interview with Helen took place three years after her termination.

After completing his MBA and 10 years working in the field of eldercare, Mark founded a successful business of Memory Care Homes for persons with dementia and Alzheimer's. After 15 years of directing and growing the business into 16 Memory Care Homes in two gulf coast states, the business went public and was demonstrating favorable interest as a small-cap stock. Three years after going public, Mark had a heart attack in his office and was found by the janitorial crew just as the attack started. Fortunately, his office was within a mile of a firehouse station and paramedics were minutes away. His cardiologist referred him to a rehabilitation program and warned Mark that he needed to change his lifestyle and diet. According to Mark, "life was looking up until this heart ailment and then I started thinking about how fragile life can be." Mark made three important decisions. One was that he would take the next two years of work decreasing his hours and taking time off. He planned to live more frugally, invest wisely, and have enough money to comfortably retire. Two, he would take a long-awaited vacation and take his wife on a European River Cruise. Three, he would name his likely company successor, Brad.

Mark told Brad of his plans and his interest in seeing Brad step into his shoes when he retired. He promised Brad that when he returned from his trip, he would begin the steps of meeting with board members to inform them of his plans and who he thought his successor should be. Mark told Brad that he would mentor him on an area he thought needed strengthening for the betterment of the company and Brad's future.

During our interview, Mark said, "I should have seen the warning signs, but dismissed them. Instead of expressing appreciation for what I wanted to do for Brad, he acted as though it was no big deal that I wanted to appoint him as my successor. Brad told me that he was ready to lead and didn't need the mentoring!" Mark told us that he dismissed Brad's remarks as being "overconfident, a bit full of himself, and not wanting to admit that he had any weaknesses."

During the three-week holiday that Mark was away, Brad and another company division director met with key members of the board of directors. The two division directors expressed concerns about Mark's ability to continue to run the company. Aside from Marks's recent health issues, Brad told board members that Mark had missed many days of work and was unnecessarily spending company money on items that did not enhance the company's position. He said that when Mark would go to nearby states to meet with potential investors and determine the suitability to open a new memory care facility, he would spend extra days on the company's monies on the golf course without investors, and simply take minivacations. He accused Mark of fudging receipts to cover his expenses and wouldn't be surprised if some extra funds were taken, although he couldn't prove it.

Outraged by these accusations, the executive board members agreed to place Mark on paid leave while they investigated the accusations. The Vice Chair said he knew a forensic accountant and would engage him as a consultant to see if there was financial wrongdoing.

When Mark returned from his vacation, he was faced by the Board Chair waiting in his office to inform him of the allegations and what the Board decided. The Board Chair was careful not to accuse Mark of any wrongdoing and even said he was sure Mark would be back into his CEO role in no time. The Board Chair said the Executive Committee was being prudent because the allegations were coming from his senior management staff and believed they needed to take this action to ensure the shareholders were protected. Mark told us he "became dizzy and short of breath" when he heard these accusations. He wanted details and questioned why the Board would take any action without first waiting for his return and meet with him to discuss the allegations. Mark said he went home and called the company attorney to discuss the matter but was told he really could not discuss the Board's actions and he would need his own legal counsel. Mark said, "The company was 'my baby' and I felt so betrayed by the individuals that I trusted. I knew some of those board members for several years and just could not believe that they took action without even the courtesy of a discussion."

Mark had repeated himself several times out of frustration that he didn't do any of the things he was accused of doing and couldn't believe that his integrity was questioned. Mark said, "as soon as I engaged a personnel attorney to help me negotiate the issues with the Board, the Board terminated my employment contract. The accusations were egregious, and I felt like I had no choice but to sue the Board of Directors for damaging my reputation and breach of contract."

During the period of the lawsuit, the Board appointed Brad the acting CEO and then permanently hired him when the lawsuit concluded with the Board's insurance company negotiating a settlement out of court.

Helen started her nonprofit company after completing her Doctor of Speech-Language Pathology degree and having practiced as a speech therapist for five years with her Master's Degree in Communicative Disorders/Speech-Language Pathology.

Helen became interested in the field as a teenager when she learned that her older cousin's infant was being treated by a speech pathologist for swallowing and feeding problems. Her nonprofit provided a range of services including assessment, diagnosis, and treatment of speech, language, social communication, cognitive-communication, voice, fluency, and swallowing disorders in children and adults. The services were provided on a sliding scale based on an individual or family's income if they did not have insurance coverage. To cover all expenses of the business and services, Helen and board members held periodic fundraising events. Also, Helen met with foundations and businesses to raise grant funds and hired a development specialist to focus on resource development and writing grant proposals. In addition to Helen, the nonprofit had three speech therapists, the development specialist and two clerical staff who answered calls, made appointments, and filed reports. One of the clerical staff also functioned as the office manager and was responsible for billing insurance companies in those instances when insurance covered some of the costs. When possible, Helen would have an intern from a nearby university.

Unlike the accusations of financial wrongdoing that Mark experienced, Helen was accused of being disorganized and creating undue pressure on clerical staff and the speech therapists. She frequently reviewed the professional staff's written reports who resented Helen providing any feedback because they had more years of hands-on experience than she had, although she had advanced education and wanted the reports written in a certain format. Unfortunately for Helen, she was unaware that her behaviors were causing stress in the workplace or, at least, that was the complaint. During our interview, Helen said, "I was stunned to learn from the Board that staff had gone around me and complained about me. Had I known that I was causing a problem, I would have done whatever I could to alleviate the problems." The fact that staff never provided Helen with direct feedback appears to be a common occurrence, according to Lam and Xu (2019) who believe that in modern organizations there is widespread employee silence, "referring to employees' deliberate and conscious withholding of potentially important information, usually from leaders who are in positions to receive and address it" (p. 513).

Helen continued,

> I thought I was doing a great job, raising money, and ensuring children and adults received proper attention and got the services they needed. I asked, but the Board refused to tell me who or how many staff complained, but I suspect it was one of the speech therapists who led the get-rid-of-Helen campaign, since he was hired as the executive director after I left the organization.

We discussed whether Helen had received personnel evaluations. She said, "Yes, they were always good feedback from the Board, so I was shocked when they said I was not cut out to be an executive director and gave me a choice of giving up my position and becoming a staff therapist or they would fire me! I was so embarrassed and angry by their offer. I started the organization and now they wanted to demote me. I told them I would prefer to leave, and I resigned so that I wouldn't have a record of being fired."

When asked whether she thought of hiring an attorney to fight the board of directors, Helen said,

> I did think about it. My husband was so angry, he called a lawyer and wanted to sue the Board. But I just wanted to run away and hide. I was so despondent; I couldn't deal with the stress of fighting the Board with an attorney and it is not like we have lots of money to fund a lawsuit. I also thought about my future and did not want any bad publicity for me and for the organization. I mean it. I felt betrayed by the staff and no one coming forward to support me, but I didn't want the organization to fail. It was doing good work and I created it.

Questions about her health revealed the following:

> Yes, I was angry and became depressed and had to be treated for depression. I still take medication ... I have no contact with any of the

staff or board members ... there are occasions when I keep going over in my mind what the board told me and I guess you can say I obsess and start to feel all the old feelings of anger and resentment. I will never forget that none of the staff said anything on my behalf or afterwards. I thought they cared about me and I was wrong, so wrong.

Helen also informed us that she would never start another nonprofit and work directly for a board of directors or want to have to rely on raising money. She said her embarrassment turned into paranoia, and she felt uneasy and did not want to run into anyone associated with the organization or even old patients. She admitted to feeling uneasy when she would go to the grocery store out of fear of seeing someone from her former organization. Consequently, she and her husband relocated to another state and she went to work for a children's hospital (and her husband went to work as a physical therapist for a private rehabilitation clinic that had offices located in three health clubs).

Mark and Helen's experiences are representative of other founding CEOs who were targeted by a manager or board member for removal with the aim of securing the CEO position for themselves or another person. The betrayal by individuals close to the CEO becomes a scarring episode. The founding CEOs have ego investment in the organizations they created. Their persona and the identity of their organization meld together. Consequently, when they are forced to leave their organization they feel as though they have lost something of themselves, and the feelings of loss and betrayal can last a lifetime. The hurt lasts due to a breach of trust, as explained by Birrell and Freyd (2006), "traumas that occur in the context of interpersonal relationships can be particularly detrimental because of the betrayal involved in the violation of basic assumptions of interpersonal and social relationships" (p. 50). In their research study on involuntary job loss, Nuttman-Shwartz and Gadot (2012) state that job loss "undermines the individual's self-esteem, to the point of causing feelings of insecurity and helplessness vis-à-vis one's social surroundings and vis-à-vis the workplace that caused the harm. Job loss has also been associated with health problems such as depression" (p. 275).

Although Helen's loss triggered depression that required treatment, she was able to relocate and find employment. Mark finally went for counseling because he was thrust into retirement and felt helpless that he was not in control of his life plans. Mark experienced panic attacks and depression and received medication for his symptoms. His mental health issues were exacerbated by his belief that he needed two additional years of employment to comfortably retire. After his job loss, he thought he might be able to find work as a consultant to other organizations in the field of eldercare. Although he had some inquiries about his consultation services, he was unable to secure any clients. Mark was certain that when potential clients did a search of his name on the internet, they found a brief article that appeared in the local press about him suing the Board and information about the lawsuit referring to Mark as being terminated from employment. Mark was certain that his reputation was sullied, and no one wanted to engage a consultant who was tainted. Mark also gave up applying for full-time employment. He attributed his age as the reason he was turned down application after application in an industry in which he had substantial knowledge and experience. According to a longitudinal study conducted by Taris (2002), individuals who experienced psychological distress from job loss were less likely to find employment. Furthermore, Knabe and Ratzel's (2010) research found unemployment weakens a person's health and well-being especially when it proves difficult to find new employment. These findings do not bode well for someone like Mark who had an issue with his heart health just prior to being terminated.

Undermining the founding CEO for one's own personal gain is a moral and ethical decision. Theorems about personality, selfishness, self-regulation, self-control, self-esteem, egoism, sociopathy, and other situational factors and ethical ideologies help us understand the defiant workplace behaviors and motives of a manager or board member willing to sabotage the CEO. Individuals inclined to plot against the CEO are resistant to normative organizational culture and defy company values of respect. Although the harm these organizational saboteurs can cause toward the founding CEO is critical knowledge for our understanding of the dimensions of founder's syndrome, we do recognize that the perpetrators seem to lack a social consciousness and unconcerned about the hurt and potential damage their actions cause other persons. Instead, they are driven by status and personal rewards.

Discussion Questions

1. Explain how mistrust can lead to founder's syndrome and provide two examples from the readings. Name three other conditions that might lead the board or managers to pursue ousting the founder.
2. How can theory help us understand stakeholders' desires and motivations to oust a founder?
3. Think back to the cases of the founders Mark and Helen who were ousted from their organizations. How did each founder react to feelings of betrayal? What kinds of psychological stress did each founder endure after being ousted?
4. How is the use of theory helpful in explaining a staff member's desire to see their CEO fired?
5. Explain role theory.
6. In one of the cases, the founder was fired and hired an attorney to sue the board of directors. In another case, the founder decided to resign and not engage an attorney. Explain the different approaches these former founders took?

7. If you were a founder and were terminated would you engage an attorney or put the experiences behind you and just get on with life?
8. Have you ever been accused of doing something wrong that you did not do? How did that feel? What if anything did you do to resolve the allegations?
9. Imagine you are a manager in an organization and learn that a colleague is actively working to sabotage the founding CEO to get the CEO fired. What would you do with your information?

References

Adler, A. (2010). *Understanding human nature*. Martino Fine Books. (Original work published 1927.)

American Psychiatric Association (2013). *Diagnostic and statistical manual of mental disorders* (5th ed.). American Psychiatric Publishing.

Biddle, B. J. (1979). *Role theory: Expectations, identities, and behaviors*. Academic Press.

Biddle, B. J. (1986). Recent developments in role theory. *Annual Review of Sociology, 12*, 67–92.

Birrell, P. J., & Freyd, J. J. (2006). Betrayal trauma: Relational models of harm and healing. *Journal of Trauma Practice, 5*(1), 49–63.

Blank, S. (2019). *Managing organizational conflict*. McFarland Publishers.

Bronfenbrenner, U. (1979). *The ecology of human development*. Harvard University Press.

Buchwald, P., & Schwarzer, C. (2003). The exam-specific strategic approach to coping scale and interpersonal resources. *Anxiety, Stress, and Coping, 16*(3), 281–291.

Condor, S., & Brown, R. (1988). Psychological processes in intergroup conflict. In W. Stroebe, A. W. Kruglanski, D. Bar-Tal, & M. Hewstone, M. (Eds.), *The social psychology of intergroup conflict theory: Research and applications* (pp. 3–26). Springer Publishers.

Erikson, E. (1993). *Childhood and society*. W. W. Norton & Company. (Original work published 1950.)

Fan, W., Ren, M., Zhang, W., Xiao, P., & Zhong, P. (2020). Higher self-control, less deception: The effect of self-control on deception behaviors. *Advances in Cognitive Psychology, 16*(3), 228–241.

Frey, L. L., (2018). When it hurts to work: Organizational violations and betrayals. *New Directions for Teaching & Learning, 2018*(153), 87–98.

Gawerc, M. I. (2013). Research note: Integrative ties as an approach to managing organizational conflict. *Conflict Resolution Quarterly, 3*(2), 219–225.

Goldsmith, R. E., Chesney, S. A., Heath, N. M., & Barlow, M. R. (2013). Emotion regulation difficulties mediate associations between betrayal trauma and symptoms of posttraumatic stress, depression, and anxiety. *Journal of Traumatic Stress, 26*(3), 376–384.

Grasseni, M., & Origo, F. (2018). Competing for happiness: Attitudes to competition, positional concerns and wellbeing. *Journal of Happiness Studies, 19*(7), 1981–2008.

Hegel, G. W. F. (2015). *Georg Wilhelm Friedrich Hegel: The science of logic* (G. Di Giovanni, Trans.). Cambridge University Press. (Original work published 1812.)

Heider, F. (1958). *The psychology of interpersonal relations.* Wiley.

Hobfoll, S. E. (1998). *Stress, culture, and community: The psychology and philosophy of stress.* Plenum Press.

Hobfoll, S. E. (2001). The influence of culture, community, and the nested-self in the stress process: Advancing conservation of resources theory. *Applied Psychology: An International Review, 50*(3), 337–370. doi: 10.1111/1464-0597.00062

Hobfoll, S. E., Halbesleben, J., Neveu, J.-P., & Westman, M. (2018). Conservation of resources in the organizational context: The reality of resources and their consequences. *Annual Review of Organizational Psychology and Organizational Behavior, 5*, 103–128.

Horney, K. (1937). *The collected works of Karen Horney* (2 vols.). W.W. Norton & Company.

Hudak, G. M. (2000). Envy and goodness in academia. *Peace Review, 12*(4), 607–612.

Jensen, M. T. (2016). A two wave cross-lagged study of work-role conflict, work-family conflict and emotional exhaustion. *Scandinavian Journal of Psychology, 57*(6), 591–600.

Jones, E. E., & Davis, K. E. (1965). From acts to dispositions the attribution process in person perception. *Advances in Experimental Social Psychology, 2*, 219–266. doi: 10.1016/S0065-2601(08)60107-0

Knabe, A., & Ratzel, S. (2010). Better an insecure job than no job at all? Unemployment, job insecurity and subjective wellbeing. *Economics Bulletin, 30*(3), 2486–2494.

Korsgaard, M. A. (2018). Reciprocal trust: A self-reinforcing dynamic process. In R. H. Searle, A. I. Neinaber, & S. B. Sitkin (Eds.), *The Routledge companion to trust* (pp. 14–28). Routledge Publishers.

Kouchaki, M., & Smith, I. H. (2014). The morning morality effect: The influence of time of day on unethical behavior. *Psychological Science, 25*(1), 95–102. doi: 10.1177/0956797613498099

Lam, L. W., & Xu, A. J. (2019). Power imbalance and employee silence: The role of abusive leadership, power distance orientation, and perceived organizational politics. *Applied Psychology: An International Review, 68*(3), 513–546. doi: 10.1111/apps.12170

Lemay, R. A. (1999). 10 roles, identities, and expectancies: Positive contributions to normalization and social role valorization. In R. J. Flynn & R. A. Lemay (Eds.), *A quarter-century of normalization and social role valorization: Evolution and impact* (pp. 219–240). University of Ottawa Press.

Lewicki, R. J., McAllister, D. J., & Bies, R. J. (1998). Trust and distrust: New relationships and realities. *Academy of Management Review, 23*(3), 438–458.

Li, X., Li, M., Fu, J., & Ullah, A. (2019). Leader humility and employee voice: The role of employees' regulatory focus and voice-role conception. *Social Behavior and Personality: An International Journal, 47*(6), 1–12.

Lorenz, K. (1966). *On aggression.* Routledge Publishers.

Lynch, K. D. (2007). Modeling role enactment: Linking role theory and social cognition. *Journal for the Theory of Social Behavior, 37*(4), 379–399.

Neal, J. W., & Neal, Z. P. (2013). Nested or networked? Future directions for ecological systems theory. *Social Development, 22*(4), 722–737.

Nuttman-Shwartz, O., & Gadot, L. (2012). Social factors and mental health symptoms among women who have experienced involuntary job loss. *Anxiety, Stress, & Coping, 25*(3), 275–290.

Peate, V. G., Platow, M. J. & Eggins, R. A. (2008). Collective voice and support for social protest among Indigenous and non-Indigenous Australians: Considering the role of procedural fairness in an intergroup conflict of interest. *Australian Journal of Psychology, 60*(3), 175–185.

Rahim, M. A. (2015). *Managing conflict in organizations* (4th ed.). Transaction Publishers.

Righetti, F., & Finkenauer, C. (2011). If you are able to control yourself, I will trust you: The role of perceived self-control in interpersonal trust. *Journal of Personality and Social Psychology, 100*(5), 874–886. doi: 10.1037/a0021827

Rogers, A. T. (2013). *Human behavior in the social environment*. Routledge Publishers.

Rousseau, D., Sitkin, S., Burt. R., & Camera, C. (1998). Not so different after all: A cross-discipline view of trust. *Academy of Management Review, 23*(3), 393–404.

Shelton, L. G. (2019). *The Bronfenbrenner: A guide to develecology*. Routledge.

Sherif, M., Harvey, O. J., Hood, W. R., Sherif, C. W., & White, J. (1988). *The robbers cave experiment: Intergroup conflict and cooperation*. Wesleyan Publishers. (Original work published 1961.)

Sherman, D. K., Brookfield, J., & Ortosky, L. (2017). Intergroup conflict and barriers to common ground: A self-affirmation perspective. *Social & Personality Psychology Compass, 11*(12), 1–13. doi: 10.1111/spc3.12364

Simmons, A. (1998). Territorial games: Understanding and ending turf wars at work. American Management Association.

Sitkin, S. B., & Bijlsma-Frankema, K. M. (2018). Distrust. In R. H. Searle, A. I. Neinaber, & S. B. Sitkin (Eds.), *The Routledge companion to trust* (pp. 50–62). Routledge Publishers.

Taris, T. W. (2002). Unemployment and mental health: A longitudinal perspective. *International Journal of Stress Management, 9*(1), 43–57. doi: 10.1023/A:1013067101217

Thomas, L. (1974). *The lives of a cell: Notes of a biology watcher*. Viking Press.

Thompson, J. D. (2017). *Organizations in action: Social science bases of administrative theory*. Routledge Publishers. (Original work published 1967.)

Thomson, K., Outram, S., Gilligan, C., & Levett-Jones, T. (2015). Interprofessional experiences of recent healthcare graduates: A social psychology perspective on the barriers to effective communication, teamwork, and patient-centered care. *Journal of Interprofessional Care, 29*(6), 634–640.

Vaillancourt, A. M. (2013). The view from under the bus. *Chronicle of Higher Education, 59*(42), 39.

Van Dyne, L., & LePine, J. A. (1998). Helping and voice extra-role behavior: Evidence of construct and predictive validity. *Academy of Management Journal, 41*, 108–119. doi: 10.5465/256902

Vinokur-Kaplan, D. (2009). Motivating work performance in human service organizations. In R. J. Patti (Ed.), *The handbook of human services management* (2nd ed., pp. 209–238). Sage Publishers.

6 Founder's Syndrome in Public Companies

Chapter Objectives

When you finish studying this chapter, you should be able to:

- Identify prominent individual characteristics of founders who have experienced founder's syndrome
- Identify notable themes within organizations that have suffered from founder's syndrome
- Discuss multiple examples of founder's syndrome in public and private companies
- Discuss examples of founder's syndrome that occurred in well-known companies
- Explain that founder's syndrome can be triggered by different factors, such as power, external pressures, and other causes
- Identify any trends among founders or their high profiled organizations
- Discuss why some founding CEOs are fired and some resign

Introduction

As discussed in the previous chapters, there are many anecdotal and empirical illustrations explaining the reasons for founder's syndrome ranging from issues of power and control to incompetent leadership in an organization, to personality and behavioral conflicts, to feelings of ownership. We wondered, then, whether publicized and notable cases of founder's syndrome reflect the observations made in this volume. What characteristics are prevalent for founders of popular or widely known companies that have experienced founder's syndrome? Can any obvious themes be derived regarding the individuals and the companies they founded? To answer these questions, we reviewed 22 cases of founder's syndrome that occurred in familiar or popular public, nonprofit, and social enterprise organizations. Although we recognize that the type of organization matters in terms of developing organizational culture and relationships between founders and their boards of directors, in our initial review of the cases, we searched for common themes between the entire group of 22 founders who experienced founder's syndrome in their organizations.

In many cases where founder's syndrome has occurred, intrinsic motivators are the driver for the founder's need for power and control in an organization. Often, however, external forces or events such as stakeholder pressure to 'go public' can occur that also contribute to conflict between a founder and his or her board of directors. In short, there is no singular reason that causes founder's syndrome. The storylines differ greatly between each ousted or resigned founder, and in some cases, varying perspectives of the truth are given to the media and other sources. Thus, our discussion is one informed and gathered from both academic and news media sources, with an occasional interview or video offering supplemental information and insight.

We begin with a discussion and examples of the individual characteristics and notable themes that emerged from our review of the 22 founders and their companies that experienced founder's syndrome. These individual characteristics and other notable themes are as follows:

Individual characteristics:

Age
Gender
Attended college
Prior career experience
Notable behavior and personality characteristics

Other notable themes:

Partnered with co-founders
Moved the founder to another position in the company
Fired versus resigned
Founded another company after leaving
Replaced the founder from within the company

Before diving into the themes, it is important to look at an overview of the cases we reviewed where founder's syndrome occurred. Of the 22 companies in our study, 4 are private companies, 2 are private social enterprises, 2 are public companies, 11 are public social enterprises, and 3 are nonprofit organizations.

Private companies are privately owned. They may issue stock and have shareholders, but their shares do not trade on the public exchanges (Chen, 2020). In contrast, public companies are owned by shareholders through the free trade of shares or stock on the stock exchange or markets. In many cases, daily trading of shares or stock in the market determine the value of a public company, although only a small percentage of shares are initially offered to the public (Banton, 2020).

A more complex organization is the social enterprise. Social enterprises are defined as "an organization or venture that achieves its primary social or environmental mission using business methods" (Katz & Page, 2010, p. 1496). Social enterprises are also referred to as hybrid social ventures, social purpose business ventures, companies with a conscience, and fourth sector organizations. Social enterprises differ from nonprofit organizations in that they can use their surplus revenues as a personal incentive for the leadership or to benefit the company's shareholders. In contrast, nonprofit organizations are prohibited from distributing any earned profits to individuals who exercise control over the organization and instead put surplus revenues back into the organization to be used toward the organization's mission (Hansmann, 2000).

This study divides social enterprises into two categories. The first category is private social enterprises, which are privately owned companies that have a social or environmental mission or purpose. The social impact work does not need to be the primary purpose of the company but can be secondary. The second category is public social enterprises, which are public companies with a social or environmental aspect of the company that works to make an impact on a social or environmental issue.

The companies included in our review as social enterprises need to meet two criteria. First, the company must have a visible social impact statement on its website. Social impact statements are often couched under headings such as 'Our Impact' (Lululemon) or 'Impact Reporting' (Etsy), 'Giving Back' (Men's Wearhouse), 'Corporate Social Responsibility' (Research in Motion), 'Social Responsibility' (Groupon), or 'Global Citizenship' (Uber). Social impact statements specifically note the issue a company is trying to address either directly or indirectly through its business. For example, Cisco's Corporate Social Responsibility statement says "We empower social change agents with technology and expertise. Our goal: Accelerate global problem solving to benefit people, society, and the planet" (Cisco, 2020). Cisco's impact efforts are vast and include partnerships with other organizations that use technology to detect and end cholera or improve the sustainable management of water and sanitation. In another program, Cisco offers digital financial services and training to individuals around the globe with the goal of "empowering people living in poverty to transform their lives, their children's futures, and their communities" (Cisco, 2020, para 1). Another example, JetBlue, states on its JetBlue For Good web page that "You'll find JetBlue caring in the air and on the ground. Here are the meaningful ways we give back, from schools to relief efforts. Join us" (JetBlue, 2020, para 1). JetBlue partners with nonprofit organizations such as KaBoom! and the DREAM Project that support children and education opportunities, in addition to engaging in environmental impact programs that support clean energy and recycling.

The second criteria a company needs to meet in order to be categorized as a social enterprise is the clear discussion and use of a metric to measure the impact the company is making in the community or with the environment. Impact measurement varies greatly between companies given the wide degree of intended impacts the companies wish to make, and the different means used to achieve those goals. Regardless, most social enterprises share their impact accomplishments on their websites by providing either a measurement of intended impact or an impact the company has already made. On Best Buy's Corporate Responsibility and Sustainability website, the company says its goals by 2030 are to "reduce carbon emissions in [its] operations by 75%" and to "reduce carbon emissions for [its] customers by 20%" (Best Buy, 2020, para 2). These statements are followed by a video explaining how Best Buy intends to reach its goals. On the Groupon Community web page, the company lists the impacts it made in 2019 including highlights such as launching a food recovery program in Chicago where 1,300 pounds of excess food was given to individuals without access to nutritious food (Groupon Community, 2020).

The nonprofit organizations in our review of founder's syndrome are classified as 501(c)3 organizations by the Internal Revenue Service and are approved tax-exempt, charitable organizations. These organizations are established for charitable purposes and use revenues to benefit the mission of the organization (Foundation Group, 2020). Nonprofit organizations do not have shareholders, but they are accountable to the public at large. Nonprofit organizations will be discussed in much more detail in the next chapter, but the founders of the three nonprofit organizations are included in our initial review of themes across the 22 companies that have experienced founder's syndrome.

The list given below includes 22 companies that have experienced founder's syndrome as defined in this volume. The organizations are listed by type: Private companies, private social enterprises, public companies, public social enterprises, and nonprofit organizations. It should be noted, however, that some companies have moved between categories at some point in time.

Private companies:

Zenefits
Miramax, LLC
WeWork Companies Inc. (WeWork)
Craigslist Inc. (Craigslist)

Private social enterprises:

Research in Motion Ltd.
American Apparel Inc.

Public companies:

Yahoo Inc.
Alphabet Inc.

Public social enterprises:

Lululemon Athletica Inc.
Etsy Inc.
Uber Technologies Inc. (Uber)
JetBlue Airways Corp. (JetBlue)
Cisco Systems Inc. (Cisco)
Twitter Inc.
Groupon Inc.
Papa John's International Inc. (Papa John's)
Tesla Inc. (formerly Tesla Motors)
Best Buy Inc.
The Men's Wearhouse, Inc.

Nonprofit organizations:

Mothers Against Drunk Driving
The Southern Poverty Law Center
Livestrong Foundation

With this basic understanding of the five types of companies we reviewed that have experienced founder's syndrome, we turn to a discussion of the characteristics of the founders and then move to the more nuanced themes found across the companies. Each theme is discussed from a broad perspective across the 22 cases we reviewed, followed by examples from one of the companies listed previously.

Individual Characteristics

When analyzing the group of 22 founders from the companies noted previously, a number of individual characteristics begin to emerge including the age of the individual founding the organization, the gender of the founder, whether the founder attended college, prior career experience of the founder, and notable behavior and personality characteristics. Each characteristic is discussed in subsequent paragraphs.

Age

All of the founders we reviewed were under the age of 50 when his or her organization was founded. Two of the founders were in their 40s, 8 in their 30s, and 11 in their 20s. This trend is consistent with many studies that find the average age of founders to be 31, 29, or 42 depending on the study (Azoulay, Jones, Kim, & Miranda, 2018). The youngest founder in our review is Dov Charney. At the age of 20 years, Charney founded his first company, American Apparel. He served as CEO from 1989 until 2014 when he was fired by his board of directors for alleged misconduct and violations of company policy (Li, 2014). The oldest founder in our review is Martin Eberhard, who at 43 co-founded Tesla Motors. Martin Eberhard's tenure as CEO at Tesla Motors lasted five years, at which time he was asked to leave his role of CEO and instead serve on the advisory board to the company (Reed, 2020). Although age may not be a significant indicator of whether founder's syndrome occurs in an organization, it is still worth noting that founders of the most successful startups who are "among the top 0.1% of startups based on growth in the first five years" are on average 45 years old concurring with empirical evidence showing the most successful firms are often founded by the middle-aged, not the younger adult (Azoulay et al., 2018, para 4).

Gender

Only two of the 22 founders in our sample are women. In general, female entrepreneurs are underrepresented and the number of female founders is small (Spiegel, Abbassi, Schlagwein, & Fischbach, 2013; Zisser, Johnson, Freeman, & Staudenmaier, 2019). Women often enter the role of entrepreneur with the challenge of fighting the myth that female-owned businesses underperform given the expectations of female weakness in the context of 'male normativity and superiority' (Marlow & McAdam, 2013). It is assumed and supported by gender stereotypes that entrepreneurs are men and that females are less interested or likely to found their own company. However, female entrepreneurs are shown to perform equally as well as their male counterparts, and in some cases, they perform better (Robb & Watson, 2012; Solesvik, Iakovleva, & Trifilova, 2019; Watson, 2002). Notably, the two women in our sample both founded organizations that are deeply committed to helping others, including Candy Lightner who founded Mothers Against Drunk Driving and Sandy Lerner who co-founded Cisco. Candy Lightner's story is discussed in detail in Chapter 7 on founder's syndrome in nonprofit companies.

Attended College

All but one of the founders we reviewed attended college for some duration of time. College attendance is not a surprising characteristic because education has been shown to be a factor that increases entrepreneurial intention (Florin, Karri, & Rossiter, 2007; Kuratko, 2005).

Only one of the founders, Parker Conrad of Zenefits, attended an Ivy League School (Harvard) where he graduated in 2003 with an undergraduate degree in Chemistry (Bort, 2015). Other founders attended highly ranked colleges or universities including Stanford, the Massachusetts Institute of Technology (MIT), and the University of California Los Angeles (UCLA). Jerry Yang of Yahoo attended Stanford where he received a Bachelor of Science and Master of Science in electrical engineering. Yang accomplished both degrees in only four years (Schlender, 2000). Sergey Brin of Alphabet, Inc., also a Stanford graduate, received a Master's degree in computer science (Stanford Engineering, 2020). In an interesting run at school, Rob Kalin of Etsy dropped out of high school but then won admission to a studio program at Boston's Museum of Fine Arts. In total, Kalin attended five different colleges and eventually graduated in 2004 with a Classics degree from New York University (Muniz, 2013).

As discussed in Chapter 4, college education is considered a resource the founder has to offer. A college degree, experience, or training – especially if it is in management and strategic decision-making – may increase the likelihood that a founder's decisions will include reasonable risk-taking rather than becoming distracted by emotions that are not logical and can lead to founder's syndrome. A college education may also lead to feelings of legitimate power by the founder. Legitimate power can work in the organization's favor if the person with that power creates networks to prestigious and wealthy individuals who then serve on the board of directors or donate to the company. However, legitimate power can also lead to cultural or hierarchy conflicts with the board of directors or employees of the organization when the founder is distracted by control and being the 'boss' in charge.

Prior Career Experience

Thirteen of the 22 founders had a career of some kind prior to founding their business. In a study comparing entrepreneurs with no prior career experience to entrepreneurs with career experience, those with prior career experience were more confident in their abilities to found a new firm (Shane & Khurana, 2003). Prior career experience of the founders in this discussion varied by type. For example, Craig Newmark, founder of Craigslist, was an IBM programmer for 17 years and a computer engineer for Charles Schwab. Richard Schulze, the founder of Best Buy, spent time in the United States Air Force with the Minnesota Air National Guard (Richard M. Schulze Family Foundation, 2020).

Other founders had a history of starting prior companies, and a few started multiple companies before they founded the company in our review. Eleven years prior to starting Uber, Travis Kalanick co-founded Scour, Inc., a search engine and file-sharing service. In 1998, Scour, Inc.

was a pioneer in offering online shared movies and music. The company filed for bankruptcy in 2000 after being sued for copyright infringement by the recording and motion picture industries. In 2001, Kalanick started Red Swoosh, a peer-to-peer file-sharing company that was acquired by another company in 2007 (Hollar, 2020).

Another example of prior experience starting a company is Chip Wilson of Lululemon. Wilson founded the clothing retail company Westbeach Snowboard Limited in 1979, which he brags as being "an important part of Canadian snowboard history" (Howland, 2015, para 4). The company was known as the world's first manufacturer of snowboard clothing and its colorful and edgy designs stood out to the young 'hip' crowd (Wright, 2007, para 5). Twenty years later, Wilson sold the surf and skateboard company to the United States skateboard maker Morrow S.B. Inc. (Howland, 2015).

As noted in Chapter 4, Mazzotta and Santella (2017) find that companies tend to perform better when the founder has prior career experience. This conclusion seems logical given that founders will learn from past mistakes and successes. Prior career experience may also contribute to a founder's financial and emotional stake in the success of their creation because the experienced founder has a better grounding of entrepreneurial decision-making and risk-taking. This foresight, however, may work against the founder and contribute to founder's syndrome because the individual may believe their experience means they 'know all,' thus making it difficult to acquiesce to others.

Notable Behavior and Personality Characteristics

In the first three chapters, behavior and personality characteristics are discussed at length. Notable behavior can include actions that express power "even if [the behavior] is socially inappropriate" or destructive behaviors that eventually lead to the dismissal of a founder (Smith, Jost, & Vijay, 2008). Notable personality characteristics can be described as self-centered, narcissistic, unreasonable, or unwilling. A founder's personality characteristics are often a significant driver of both conflict and performance of a new firm (de Jong, Song, & Song, 2013).

Many of the founders we reviewed have notable behavior or personality characteristics. Craig Newmark of Craigslist has been referred to as arrogant and insensitive and describes himself as a "self-proclaimed nerd and reformed jerk" (Dolcourt, 2019, para 1). Rob Kalin, founder of Etsy, is noted as being "socially awkward, reticent, and given to eccentricities that can seem downright crazy" (Dooley, 2020, para 1). The founder of WeWork, Adam Neumann, has been discussed in many media forums for his odd-seeming behavior such as walking barefoot through New York City, jumping on desks to yell at employees, and banning his employees from eating meat during the workday (Maida, 2019). Andrew Mason, the founder of Groupon, posted online videos of himself wearing underwear and dancing or doing yoga. When asked if he was mature enough to be the CEO of a multi-billion-dollar company, he responded,

> I got the company this far. To the degree I was weird, I was weird before we were a public company and managed to get it worth whatever it's worth. I'm going to continue doing my thing and work my butt off to add value for shareholders and as long as they and the board see fit to keep me in this role, I feel enormously privileged to serve. (Raice, 2012, para 7)

Narcissistic behavior is discussed in many of the cases we reviewed for this book. The next chapter goes into detail regarding one very relevant case of narcissism as it relates to founder's syndrome, that of Lance Armstrong and the Livestrong Foundation.

Other Notable Themes

Although the themes so far have focused on traits and characteristics across the sample of 22 founders, other notable themes are worth addressing. These themes include whether the founder partnered with a co-founder, if the founder was moved to another position in his or her company before being ousted, whether the founder was fired or resigned from his or her company, whether he or she founded another company after leaving, and if the company replaced the founder with someone from within the company.

Partnered with Co-Founder(s)

Fourteen of the 22 founders we reviewed started his or her company in collaboration with another person, and in some cases with more than two co-founders. A co-founding model is not uncommon with entrepreneurs and is often desired because two individuals can offer diversity in knowledge and complementary skills (Burton, Sørensen, & Beckman, 2002). In one study of 91 startup organizations, seventy-one percent of the companies had co-founders (Spiegel et al., 2013).

Sibling 'copreneurship' and family collaboration are also found among entrepreneurs who found companies (Madichie, 2013). For example, George Zimmer founded The Men's Wearhouse in 1973 with his father Robert Zimmer who had previously founded two other retail companies (Greenwichfreepress, 2017). Harvey Weinstein founded Miramax with his brother Bob Weinstein in 1979. Together, the two started multiple companies including Lantern Entertainment, Dimension Films, and The Weinstein Company (Carvell, 2000).

Although the co-founder model is appealing, it also creates challenges and conflict if the team is not cohesive (Ensley, Pearson, & Amason, 2002).

Co-founders may find themselves in conflicts of power over the organization where they question the number of board seats each founder has control over, or how the shares of equity in the company will be divided (Wasserman, 2008). In some cases, co-founders are pushed out by the other founder when conflict cannot be mitigated, or when one founder positions himself or herself so that the power balance is uneven (Kim, 2015).

Twitter's co-founder Noah Glass is one example of a founder who was pushed out after a falling out with his partners. According to one source, Glass had become unpredictable, distracted, and increasingly anxious because of his divorce and also paranoia that his co-founders wanted him to leave the company (Boorstein, 2013; Mohsenin, 2013). His paranoid thoughts came to fruition and Glass was ousted from Twitter in 2006. After his termination Glass noted that his firing from the company he co-founded was "difficult to deal with in the beginning, since it was a massive labor of love and a massive labor to get it created" (Kim, 2015, para 17). Clearly, working with a partner is a decision that involves risk and can have either positive or negative results for the founder.

Moved the Founder to Another Position in the Company

When reflecting on the feelings a founder endures after being demoted or fired, Strauss (2013) notes, "It must be a surreal moment to be cast aside by a company you've founded. At best it must be like being dunked on by your own son, at worst like being shot in the knee by him" (para 2). He follows by saying, "A number of founding company leaders have been dressed down by their own companies, some are stories of betrayal, some failure and some of redemption" (para 3). In the cases we reviewed, it was common for the CEO or founder who was removed from his or her position to be moved to another role in the company. For example, Jerry Yang of Yahoo took on a corporate strategy role after he stepped down as CEO. He also remained on the board of directors for some time (Stone & Miller, 2008).

After resigning from his position as CEO, Martin Eberhard of Tesla took on the new title of President of Technology and joined the Advisory Board. However, this only lasted for one year (Baer, 2014; Schreiber, 2009). Eberhard remarked of the demotion,

> I am not at all happy with the way I was treated, and I do not think this was the very best way to handle a transition – not the best for Tesla Motors, not the best for Tesla's customers (to whom I still feel a strong sense of responsibility), and not for Tesla's investors. (Miller, 2007, para 1)

WeWork's founder Adam Neumann arranged perhaps the most lucrative deal at the time of his termination of all the founders in our review.

As part of the former startup chief's exit package, SoftBank agreed to buy about $1 billion of stock from Mr. Neumann, refinance a $500 million debt, and pay him $185 million to consult. WeWork employees and others criticized the payments as a sweetheart deal for the co-founder. (Winkler, 2020, para 1)

One year later, the agreement was no longer in place with the new WeWork Executive Chairman Marcelo Claure noting "I think Adam may have violated some of the parts of the consulting agreement, so that's no longer in effect" (Winkler, 2020, para 2).

Moving a founder to another position in the company can be interpreted as a sign of respect for the individual who started the company, or perhaps one of fear of retaliation from the founder. Regardless, many of the boards of directors of the companies in our review tried to give the founder an easy exit out of the company before ousting them as a last resort.

Fired versus Resigned

Most of the founders in our review either resigned or were asked to resign, but a few were fired. According to Murphy (2005), CEO's are outright fired for three vital reasons: 'Soft' issues that are unrelated to the 'hard' issues like finance, strategy, and operations; lack of execution; and not getting 'into the field.' For example, David Neeleman was fired from JetBlue after his tenure of seven years due to poor company performance and a series of missteps brought on by weather issues and operation failures. In response to his firing, Neeleman said,

> It was not only devastating, but it was just absolutely the wrong decision … My office was just off the boardroom and two of the board members came in and said, this is what we're going to do. And then they all got up and left. (Murphy, 2019, para 19)

The founder of Cisco, Sandy Lerner, was fired for making poor decisions regarding a deal with a venture capital firm that her board of directors did not support. After her termination, she remarked,

> I always thought that if someone invested in your business, that meant he or she believed in it. I assumed our investor supported us, because his money was tied up in our success. I did not realize he had decoupled the success of the company from that of the founders. (Quittner, 2020, para 4)

Lerner and her husband learned a hard lesson believing "a company and its founder are the same. They absolutely are not" (Quittner, 2020, para 6).

Founded Another Company after Leaving

Of the 22 founders in our review, 10 moved on to start another company. These founders are referred to as serial entrepreneurs. "A serial entrepreneur is someone who started and ran multiple businesses throughout their career" (Finerva, 2020, para 2). For example, George Zimmer of Men's Wearhouse founded zTailors and Generation Tux in 2015, only two years after he was asked to leave Men's Wearhouse (Gelles, 2015).

Some founders in our review shifted their work to a philanthropic focus by starting a nonprofit organization or foundation. Rob Kalin of Etsy created Parachute, Inc. to help Etsy sellers run their businesses better. His nonprofit organization did not survive (Gobry, 2011). Fifteen years after leaving Craigslist, Craig Newmark founded Craig Newmark Philanthropies, a foundation aimed to

> support and connect people and drive broad civic engagement, working to advance grassroots organizations that are effective and getting stuff done in the areas that include: trustworthy journalism & the information ecosystem, voter protection, women in tech, and veterans & military families. (Craig Newmark Philanthropies, 2020, para 2).

Although founder's syndrome can end with the founder resigning or being asked to resign, the trauma from this experience does not stop him or her from founding another company. The question, then, is whether the founder learns from past mistakes and perhaps becomes a better leader. Ousting a founder is by no means a panacea, but one hopes the individual learns and improves from the experience. However, this hope may be ill-founded because as discussed in the first three chapters, founders who are more likely to engage in founder's syndrome have an aversion to heeding advice and learning from their errors.

Replaced the Founder from within the Company

Thirteen of the companies in our review replaced the ousted founder with someone from within the company.

> Whether an organization has planned a relay succession (e.g., identified one heir apparent) or a horse race (e.g., identified a few possible contenders), or is seeking leadership from outside, there is typically a set of executives which are viewed, by both the organization and the external labor market, as possible future chief executive officers (CEOs). (Mooney, 2005, p. xiv)

For example, in the case of JetBlue, David Neeleman was replaced with the then-President of the company Dave Barger. The two had worked together for nine years prior to Neeleman leaving the company (Reiter, 2007). In another example, Papa John's founder John Schattner was replaced by the company's Chief Operating Officer Steve Ritchie. Schattner stepped down as a result of receiving pressure from the board of directors to resign as CEO after he criticized the national anthem protests in the National Football League (NFL) (Eltagouri, 2017).

In some cases, interim CEOs were chosen while the board of directors searched for a permanent replacement. After losing a quarter of its market value resulting from an underwhelming earnings report, Andrew Mason of Groupon was replaced with Executive Chairman Eric Lefkofsky and Vice Chairman Ted Leonsis, who served as interim co-CEOs until a permanent CEO was chosen (Crook, 2013).

Appointing a new or interim CEO from within is important to recognize because it is often the case that this individual was initially a handpicked hire by the ousted CEO. This individual was most likely chosen based on loyalty and support of the founder's vision, and in many cases will continue to advance the company's mission and objectives in the founder's place. In other cases, however, the newly appointed CEO may have been part of the conflict or the ousting of the founder, in which case feelings of anger and resentment may accompany this individual in his or her new role.

Summary

At the beginning of this chapter, we asked the following questions: What characteristics are prevalent for founders of popular or widely known companies that have experienced founder's syndrome? Can any obvious themes be derived regarding the individuals and the companies they founded? From the discussion above, it is clear a few notable characteristics and themes stand out, many of which are in line with discussions in previous chapters. Age, gender, college education, and prior career experience appear to be possible antecedents of whether an individual starts a new company. Once this company is founded, behavior and personality traits seem to influence the outcome of the company, or at least the trajectory of the company's founder. After the CEO or founder is removed from his or her position, this person may move or be assigned to a different role in the company and their former role may be filled from within. Although our sample of founders who experienced founder's syndrome is limited, the themes are evident. With these individual characteristics and themes in mind, we now turn to a discussion of individual cases where founder's syndrome occurred in public and private companies.

Cases of Founder's Syndrome in Public and Private Companies

In the previous chapters, we have explored the reasons founders are ousted from their own companies. Keeping those chapters in mind, we provide examples from our review of 22 cases of founder's syndrome that illustrate the most common reasons the situation occurs. As indicated in the title of this chapter, the examples discussed below focus on public companies, including public social enterprises. This chapter also includes a few examples of private companies. As noted previously, a discussion of cases of founder's syndrome in nonprofit companies is included in the next chapter.

To frame our discussion, we focus on examples illustrating the primary reasons founders experience founder's syndrome, which include conflict over the direction of the company, unsatisfactory performance of the CEO or company, and a leadership style that is no longer a good fit.

Conflict over the Direction of the Company: Men's Wearhouse

In a discussion of why founders are fired from their own companies, an unnamed author at Global Founders London (2015) notes, "The number one reason: Founders who have a disagreement in vision and management with the board of directors and their investors are fired. There is a tenuous balance between diplomacy, integrity and standing up for what Founders believe in vs. making shareholders and investors happy" (para 2). As noted prior in the volume, conflict theory analyzes exchanges among stakeholders with an emphasis on interactional behavior being motivated by self-interest. This self-interest often leads to competition for personal gain and advantages over others. Conflict theory is useful in dissecting disagreements or conflicts between the CEO and board of directors and helps us understand that perceived roles in an organization can be a source of conflict (Lemay, 1999).

The conflict of perceived roles versus actual roles is evident in the story of George Zimmer of Men's Wearhouse. Founded in 1973, Zimmer marketed his men's retail store as an "alternative to stuffy department stores and chichi boutiques – a comforting setting where buying men's clothes is painless and maybe a little fun, too" (Lee, 2004, para 2). In the mid-1990s, the company quickly grew with 17 new stores in 1990 and 19 additional stores the following year. In 1992, Men's Wearhouse went public selling 2.25 million shares at $8.67 per share in addition to opening another 31 stores (Funding Universe, 2003). Between 1991 and 1993, the company doubled its net earnings. In the following years, Men's Wearhouse acquired or purchased multiple smaller companies, expanding its retail offerings and by the early 2000s, there were nearly 1,400 stores across the United States (Bhasin, 2013; Lee, 2004).

For the next three decades, Zimmer served as CEO of Men's Wearhouse until 2011 when he was asked to step down from the position. At this point, the role of CEO was given to his chosen successor Doug Ewert who had worked in management positions at the company since 1995. Despite not being the CEO of the company he founded, Zimmer continued to hold the position of Executive Chairman on the board of directors (Bhasin, 2013). Although Zimmer intended to have a smaller role in the company after stepping down as CEO, he had difficulty letting others lead the business and he often clashed with board members on the strategic direction of the company (Bhasin, 2013; D'Innocenzio, 2013). His inability to 'relinquish the reins,' in addition to his disagreements with the board of directors over the future of the company, eventually led to the termination of the founder from his board role (Stewart, 2015; Wilson, 2013). In 2013, Zimmer was suddenly fired from any involvement with Men's Wearhouse after serving as CEO from 1974 to 2010 and as a chairman and spokesperson for the company from 2010 to 2013. On the day he was fired, Zimmer owned 1.8 million shares of Men's Wearhouse stock with a value of $67.45 million (D'Innocenzio, 2013).

In response to his termination, Zimmer issued a statement saying,

> Over the last 40 years, I have built The Men's Wearhouse into a multi-billion-dollar company with amazing employees and loyal customers who value the products and service they receive at The Men's Wearhouse. Over the past several months I have expressed my concerns to the Board about the direction the company is currently heading. Instead of fostering the kind of dialogue in the Boardroom that has, in part, contributed to our success, the Board has inappropriately chosen to silence my concerns by terminating me as an executive officer. (Business Wire, 2013)

The board of directors released its own statement saying, "Mr. Zimmer had difficulty accepting the fact that Men's Wearhouse is a public company with an independent board of directors and that he has not been the chief executive officer for two years" (Wilson, 2013, para 3). In another statement the board of directors said,

> He [Zimmer] advocated for significant changes that would enable him to regain control, but ultimately he was unable to convince any of the board members or senior executives that his positions were in the best interests of employees, shareholders and the company's future. (Wilson, 2013, para 4)

Another board member said he was "thrilled with the direction the retailer is heading and throws his [the board member's] full support behind the current management team" (Bhasin, 2013, para 4), implying that it was time for Zimmer to exit the company.

Zimmer took his firing personally because many of the board members were his friends, one of whom was a close friend since childhood (D'Innocenzio, 2013). The feelings of betrayal from close friends who are board members illustrate the error discussed in Chapter 1 of stacking a board of directors with friends and relatives who, it is believed, will support the founder's ideas and governing policies.

Once Zimmer realized the intentions of his board of directors, his feelings of betrayal led to actions that ultimately resulted in his termination. As discussed in the first few chapters, the founder's defensive reaction to feeling betrayed is understandable, but board members often interpret this type of reaction as inappropriate thus accelerating the founder's termination. Since Zimmer's ousting, Men's Wearhouse has struggled, their stock decreasing in value after the acquisition of their rival company Joseph A. Bank and as they compete with online shopping (Stewart, 2015).

This case is an illustration of the difficulties a founder may encounter when trying to 'hand over the reins' to another executive, or when working with the board of directors on the future of the company. Zimmer seemed unable to come to terms with the fact that being the founder and Executive Chairman of the board, as opposed to founder and CEO, relieved him not only of his previous responsibilities but also his power and control over the future of the company. Once he realized this loss of control, he tried to regain it, but to no avail. In many ways, he had created a patriarchal style of managing the company he founded, one for which he eventually faced scorn from the board of directors. This type of supervisory style is difficult to come back from once a change in leadership has been made, and thus a termination or resignation becomes permanent.

Unsatisfactory Performance of the CEO or Company: Yahoo and Groupon

The two examples below, Yahoo and Groupon, illustrate founder's syndrome that results from a CEO or founder's poor performance and decision-making, which may manifest as inadequate performance of the company. In both cases, the founder exhibited poor decision-making, whether from stress or other cognitive distractions. In a discussion of organizational development and talent management presented in Chapter 1, Church (2013) notes that if the company's performance begins to decrease, or shareholders are negatively impacted by poor management decisions, then "there is not much that can be done short of changing leaders to impact the overall level of engagement of high potentials" (p. 46). In many cases, the board of directors is tasked with either terminating the CEO or founder or convincing him or her to voluntarily resign.

Our first example, Yahoo, is an illustration of poor decision-making from a founder and CEO who was ill-prepared to take on the role of CEO, and whose decisions cost the company a potentially lucrative deal. Jerry Yang co-founded Yahoo in 1994 with his college friend David Filo, and at this time the startup's website was called 'Jerry and David's Guide to the World Wide Web.' After gaining a considerable amount of traction, they renamed it Yahoo. The company secured venture capital in 1995 and in 1996 went public (Pickert, 2008). After the dot-com bubble crash, Yang was named as interim CEO from 2007 to 2009. Prior to being named CEO, he had the self-proclaimed title of 'Chief Yahoo,' which essentially meant 'innovator.' As an innovator, Yang was successful in the company, but as interim CEO he did not perform as well (Oreskovic, 2012).

In 2008, Yang declined a $47 billion buyout bid from Microsoft and instead preferred to seek a minority investment in Yahoo from private equity firms. This decision enraged the shareholders of the company. The board of directors viewed Yang's business decisions as weak and faulted him for "pursuing an ineffective personal vision and impeding investment deals that could have transformed the struggling company" (Oreskovic, 2012, para 1). One analyst noted, "The perception among shareholders was Jerry was more focused on trying to rebuild Yahoo than necessarily on maximizing near-term shareholder value" (Oreskovic, 2012, para 5). It was widely believed that Yang let his feelings for Yahoo impair his decision-making, and that he was clouded by pursuing a direction for the company that would benefit himself. Yang denied the accusations, saying he was acting with the approval of the board of directors (Efrati, Lublin, & Letzing, 2012).

Pressure from dissatisfied stakeholders and the board of directors eventually led to Yang's voluntary resignation from all positions at Yahoo. Yang had been described as flip-flopping with the direction of the future of the company, and the company was mired by competing interests (Oreskovic, 2012). After the announcement of his resignation, Yahoo chairman Roy Bostock referred to Yang as a "visionary and a pioneer" who had "always remained focused on the best interests of Yahoo's stakeholders, including shareholders, employees, and more than 700 million users" (Waters, 2012, para 4).

For numerous reasons, Yang's time at Yahoo is an interesting case study of founder's syndrome. Yang admitted he started his company with no experience or background, not even a business plan. In an interview with The Startups Team (2018), Yang says "we didn't have the expertise [to found a company] and we certainly didn't have our own ability to run the company" (para 27). Thus, the co-founders hired another person to fill the role of CEO. When Yang moved into the CEO position many years later, he approached the position from a rational standpoint, noting that "I think as CEO, you really have to make decisions. [COEs] get all the input but at the end of the day, you have to work with your board and you have to make the decisions" (para 38). Despite his rational approach to the CEO position, Yang's board of directors was unhappy with his performance.

When reflecting on his resignation, Yang said,

> Being founder, it's a little different. It's also your company. I really felt like you do the best you can and you make the best decision you can, and how it shakes out it shakes out. It's probably hard to believe, but I never really paid attention to what people said, because at the end of the day, in some respect, they don't know what's really going on. (The Startups Team, 2018, para 47)

Although Yang's departure from Yahoo was voluntary, he left with the understanding that his co-founder would continue the vision they started together. This understanding made the transition easier for Yang to accept.

Another example of unsatisfactory performance of a CEO is the case of Andrew Mason and Groupon. Mason started Groupon in 2008, and in 2010 the company was considered by Forbes as "the fastest-growing company" of all time (Steiner, 2010, para 1). In this same year, Yahoo offered to buy Groupon for $2–$3 billion, and another offer was received by Google, but Mason and the board of directors declined both offers. In an interview asking about his decline of the Yahoo offer, Mason noted he perceived Yahoo as a "graveyard for cool companies" (Blumberg, 2018, para 39). Instead, Mason and the board of directors preferred to take the route of an independent company. As an alternative to being acquired by Google or Yahoo, Groupon decided to go public in the fall of 2011 (Blumberg, 2018).

After the company went public, Groupon started to receive negative publicity as the United States Securities and Exchange Commission (SEC) scrutinized the company's accounting methods. As a result of this scrutiny and statements made by Mason that were not well thought-out to please shareholders, the stock price decreased (Greenberg, 2012). Employees at the company started to worry about their jobs, and Mason and his team were faced with various degrees of fallout from the decision to go public (Blumberg, 2018). In 2012, members of the board of directors wanted Mason to be fired and replaced. According to Mason, the board said,

> Okay, Andrew, you get one more chance here. Deliver a great Q4 and let's take it from there. But we still believe in you … . Two weeks later, me and my CFO were in Barcelona meeting with some

investors when we get a call from our controller in France. They had forgotten to accrue a profit-sharing tax, and we had just lost $10 million. So that was it. We missed our numbers. That was the end. I called the executive recruiter and said I wanted to recruit a great CEO. (Blumberg, 2018, para 50)

Although Mason's intent was to assist in finding a new CEO for the company, at which time he would step aside, the board of directors wanted him to leave immediately. Mason denied their request to resign, resulting in the board firing him from the CEO position of the company he founded. In December 2013, CNBC's Herb Greenberg named Andrew Mason the worst CEO of the year with an $81 million loss in the fourth quarter of that year (Greenberg, 2012).

Mason's experience is another illustration of the board of directors' dissatisfaction of the CEO's decision-making and management style. When negative publicity started to highlight Mason's poor decision-making and management of the company, the board of directors challenged him to prove his worth as CEO. When the fourth quarter of 2013 showed a negative loss, the board of directors sought quick action to remove Mason from the organization, although Mason wanted to remain with the company during the hiring process of a new CEO (Blumberg, 2018). One can posit that Mason's desire to remain as CEO during the hiring process resulted in part from his feelings of ownership of the organization he founded and his desire to help find the 'perfect' replacement to take over and continue his vision.

Leadership Style Is No Longer a Good Fit: Lululemon

As discussed in Chapter 4, there is no one-size-fits-all leadership style. Different leadership styles suit different companies, and some leadership styles are more likely to experience founder's syndrome. One case illustrating the intersection of leadership style and founder's syndrome is that of Chip Wilson, the founder of Lululemon. Wilson was an integral part of his company at one time, but eventually realized his leadership style no longer fit the direction the company was heading.

Chip Wilson founded the workout apparel store Lululemon in 1998. In 2012, he stepped down from his role in management to take a leave in Australia, but then returned as chair of the board of directors one year later to help with a public relations debacle related to 'too sheer' yoga pants (Howland, 2015; O'Connor, 2015). Instead of improving the situation, Wilson made it worse by saying in a 2013 interview with Bloomberg TV, "Quite frankly, some women's bodies just actually don't work. It's about the rubbing through the thighs," and "how much pressure is there" (Memmott, 2013, para 2–3). The fallout from the interview was severe, and individuals over social media did not respond kindly to Wilson's remarks. In response to public scrutiny, Wilson recorded and released an apology on YouTube that said,

> I'd like to talk to you today about the last few days of media that's occurred around the Bloomberg interview. I'm sad. I'm really sad. I'm sad for the repercussions of my actions. I'm sad for the people of Lululemon who I care so much about, that have really had to face the brunt of, of my actions. I take responsibility for all that has occurred and the impact it has had on you. I'm sorry to have put you all through this. For all of you that have made Lululemon what it is today, I ask you to stay in the conversation that is above the fray. I ask you to prove that the culture that you have built cannot be chipped away. Thank you. (Petri, 2013)

Wilson was subsequently criticized for his apology, and media outlets described his statement as child-like in that he did not express regret for making Lululemon's customers upset. Rather, he apologized for upsetting his employees (Petri, 2013). With such public criticism, Wilson stepped down as chair of the board of directors at the end of 2013 but remained a board member. The following year, tensions rose again with the board arguing that innovation in the company had 'dried up,' although Wilson had presented multiple new product ideas that the board rejected (Howland, 2015; O'Connor, 2015).

In late 2014, tensions between Wilson and the board were eased when Wilson sold half of his stock to a private equity firm and that firm was granted two of Wilson's board seats. In early 2015, Wilson acknowledged his vision for the future of the company differed from the board of directors. He stepped down from his role on the board noting "I have achieved the goals I set when I came back, and after careful thought, I believe that now is the right time to step away from the board" ... . I leave behind a new and talented management team and new board construct" (O'Connor, 2015, para 14).

As the founder of Lululemon, Wilson believed he could return to the company and save the brand he created when the public relations debacle over sheer yoga pants emerged (Memmott, 2013). His handling of this situation, however, revealed he lacked the management skills and approach the company needed at that point in time. Rather than acting as the apologizer to his aggrieved customers, Wilson offended them even more with his emotional reaction that seemed misguided toward his employees and his company instead of the people purchasing the company's product. The apology was interpreted as egotistical and short-sided.

Despite Wilson's attempts to 'reinvent' Lululemon with his innovative ideas, the board decided to move in a different direction. This created a negative and stressful relationship and power struggle between the founder and the board of directors (Howland, 2015; O'Connor, 2015).

Wilson can be credited with having the foresight, however, to leave the company he started before being forced out. As noted previously in Chapter 2, negative behavior and power struggles can lead to damaged morale, lack of innovation, defensiveness, and may ultimately destroy an organization. Wilson did not want to destroy Lululemon and therefore chose to leave altogether.

Conclusions

At the outset of this chapter, we questioned whether the publicized and notable cases of founder's syndrome explored above would reflect our previous observations regarding why founder's syndrome occurs. It is clear there are myriad reasons as to why founders and their companies undergo this experience, and from the cases presented here we can see that no two stories are alike. Thus, we hope to have shed some light on these founders who, because of the nature of their companies, are often under the scrutiny of the news media.

In the next chapter, we provide a description and analysis of founder's syndrome in nonprofit companies that have led to the ousting of their founders.

Discussion Questions

1. How might individual traits and characteristics shape the success, or lack of success, of a founder?
2. Do you think it was fair and justified for the board of directors to fire George Zimmer after he had founded and worked at the Men's Wearhouse for nearly four decades?
3. If you were Jerry Yang of Yahoo or Chip Wilson of Lululemon, would you have voluntarily resigned from the company you founded? Do you think voluntary resignation is easier on the founder than getting fired by the board of directors? Explain your answer.
4. Of the list of companies that terminated their founding CEO (or the CEO was pressured to resign), which two on the list were a surprise to you. Explain.
5. We learn in the chapter that some founders are relieved of their role as CEO but are given other jobs in the company. Does that surprise you?
6. Imagine you were fired from your role as the founding CEO and were offered another job in the company. Would you take it or leave the company? Explain your reasoning.
7. We stated in an earlier chapter that we stress to our students there is a difference in skill sets between being an entrepreneur versus being a manager. In the example of Chip Wilson of Lululemon, explain his organizational strengths and weaknesses as an entrepreneur and/or a manager.

References

Azoulay, P., Jones, B. F., Kim, D. J., & Miranda, J. (2018). Research: The average age of a successful startup founder is 45. *Harvard Business Review*. Retrieved September 2, 2020 from https://hbr.org/2018/07/research-the-average-age-of-a-successful-startup-founder-is-45

Baer, D. (2014, November 19). Tesla's original CEO reveals what it's like to get fired by Elon musk. *Business Insider*. Retrieved July 2, 2020 from https://www.businessinsider.in/teslas-original-ceo-reveals-what-its-like-to-get-fired-by-elon-musk/articleshow/45197252.cms

Banton, C. (2020, March 19). Public company. *Investopedia*. Retrieved September 30, 2020 from https://www.investopedia.com/terms/p/publiccompany.asp

Best Buy (2020). Corporate responsibility and sustainability. Retrieved September 30, 2020 from https://corporate.bestbuy.com/sustainability/

Bhasin, K. (2013, June 19). George Zimmer: Men's Wearhouse has 'chosen to silence my concerns by terminating me'. *Huff Post*. Retrieved July 14, 2020 from https://www.huffpost.com/entry/george-zimmer-mens-wearhouse_n_3466654

Blumberg, A. (2018, October 10). The super-quick rise and even faster fall of Groupon. *Intelligencer*. Retrieved August 14, 2020 from https://nymag.com/intelligencer/2018/10/andrew-mason-on-groupon.html

Boorstein, J. (2013, November 5). Twitter's power players and ousted leaders. *CNBC*. Retrieved July 16, 2020 from https://www.cnbc.com/2013/11/05/-and-ousted-leaders.html

Bort, J. (2015, February 22). How a series of humiliating events led to one of the fastest-growing startups EVER. *Business Insider*. Retrieved August 31, 2020 from https://www.businessinsider.com/the-incredible-story-of-zenefits-founder-parker-conrad-2015-2

Burton, M. D., Sørensen, J. B., & Beckman, C. M. (2002). Coming from good stock: Career histories and new venture formation. *Research in the Sociology of Organizations*, *19*, 229–262.

Business Wire (2013, June 19). George Zimmer issues statement regarding announcement by the board of directors of the Men's Wearhouse. *Business Wire*. Retrieved August 4, 2020 from https://www.businesswire.com/news/home/20130619006226/en/George-Zimmer-Issues-Statement-Announcement-Board-Directors

Carvell, T. (2000, March 6). The talented Messrs. Weinstein. They built Miramax films into a movie powerhouse. But how big can the company get and still be the Bob and Harvey show? Retrieved June 13, 2020 from https://money.cnn.com/magazines/fortune/fortune_archive/2000/03/06/275241/index.htm

Chen, J. (2020, August 8). Private company. *Investopedia*. Retrieved September 30, 2020 from https://www.investopedia.com/terms/p/privatecompany.asp

Church, A. H. (2013). Engagement is in the eye of the beholder: Understanding differences in the OD vs. talent management mindset. *OD Practitioner*, *45*(2), 42–48.

Cisco (2020). Corporate social responsibility. Retrieved September 30, 2020 from https://www.cisco.com/c/en/us/about/csr.html

Craig Newmark Philanthropies (2020). About Craig Newmark Philanthropies. Retrieved September 30, 2020 from https://craignewmarkphilanthropies.org/about-us/

Crook, J. (2013, February 28). CEO Andrew Mason replaced by Eric Lefkofsky and Vice Chairman Ted Leonsis at Groupon. *TechCrunch*. Retrieved August 15, 2020 from https://techcrunch.com/2013/02/28/ceo-andrew-mason-replaced-by-eric-lefkofsky-and-vice-chairman-ted-leonsis-at-groupon/

de Jong, A., Song, M., & Song, L. Z. (2013). How lead founder personality affects new venture performance: The mediating role of team conflict. *Journal of Management*, *39*(7), 1825–1854. doi: 10.1177/0149206311407509

D'Innocenzio, A. (2013). Men's Wearhouse ousts founder, pitchman Zimmer. *Associated Press DBA Press Association*. Retrieved July 17, 2020 from https://apnews.com/article/aeecc9465a1e4626982f789615acbaaa

Dolcourt, J. (2019, July 25). Nerdy Craigslist founder wants to change the world – Starting with your news. *CNET*. Retrieved September 15, 2020 from https://www.cnet.com/features/nerdy-craigslist-founder-wants-to-change-the-world-starting-with-your-news/

Dooley, R. (2020). Why Etsy's Rob Kalin is like Steve Jobs. *Neuromarketing*. Retrieved September 30, 2020 from https://www.neurosciencemarketing.com/blog/articles/etsy-rob-kalin-steve-jobs.htm#:~:text=magazine's%20Max%20Chafkin%20describes%20Kalin,knife%20at%20me%20for%20emphasis

Efrati, A., Lublin, J. S., & Letzing, J. (2012). Founder severs ties to yahoo. *Wall Street Journal*. September 14, 2020. Retrieved from https://www.wsj.com/articles/SB10001424052970204555904577167251792053494

Eltagouri, M. (2017, December 21). Papa John's founder will step down as CEO after criticizing national anthem protests in the NFL. *The Washington Post*. Retrieved July 15, 2020 from https://www.washingtonpost.com/news/business/wp/2017/12/21/papa-johns-founder-replaced-as-ceo-weeks-after-blaming-the-nfl-for-sagging-pizza-sales/

Ensley, M. D., Pearson, A. W., & Amason, A. C. (2002). Understanding the dynamics of new venture top management teams: Cohesion, conflict, and new venture performance. *Journal of Business Venturing*, *17*(4), 365–386. doi: 10.1016/S0883-9026(00)00065-3

Finerva (2020). *Serial entrepreneurs explained: The data liking experience to success*. Retrieved September 30, 2020 from https://finerva.com/report/serial-entrepreneurs-explained/

Florin, J., Karri, R., & Rossiter, N. (2007). Fostering entrepreneurial drive in business education: An attitudinal approach. *Journal of Management Education*, *31*(1), 17–42.

Foundation Group (2020). What is a 501(c)(3)? Retrieved September 30, 2020, from https://www.501c3.org/what-is-a-501c3/

Funding Universe (2003). The Men's Wearhouse, Inc. history. Retrieved July 15, 2020, from http://www.fundinguniverse.com/company-histories/the-men-s-wearhouse-inc-history/

Gelles, D. (2015, May 31). George Zimmer starts an 'Uber for tailors'. *New York Times*. Retrieved June 16, 2020, from https://www.nytimes.com/2015/06/01/business/dealbook/george-zimmer-starts-an-uber-for-tailors.html?_r=0

Global Founders London (2015). Why founders get fired from their own companies. Retrieved August 13, 2020, from https://www.globalfounders.london/blog/why-founders-get-fired-from-their-own-companies

Gobry, P. (2011, April 5). Holy moly did Inc. just publish a brutal profile of Etsy CEO Rob Kalin. *Business Insider*. Retrieved June 17, 2020, from https://www.businessinsider.com/etsy-rob-kalin-2011-4

Greenberg, H. (2012, December 17). Greenberg: Worst CEO of 2012. *CNBC*. Retrieved August 17, 2020, from https://www.cnbc.com/id/100320782

Greenwichfreepress (2017, September 7). Robert 'Bob' Elkin Zimmer, 93, co-founded the Men's Wearhouse. *Greenwich Free Press*. Retrieved July 18, 2020, from https://greenwichfreepress.com/news/obituaries/robert-bob-elkin-zimmer-93-co-founded-the-mens-wearhouse-94076/

Groupon Community (2020). Community involvement. Retrieved September 30, 2020, from https://community.groupon.com/community-involvement/

Hansmann, H. (2000). *The ownership of enterprise*. Harvard University Press.

Hollar, S. (2020). Travis Kalanick. *Britannica*. Retrieved September 30, 2020, from https://www.britannica.com/biography/Travis-Kalanick

Howland, D. (2015, February 5). Lululemon founder Chip Wilson moves on. *Retail Dive*. Retrieved June 14, 2020, from https://www.retaildive.com/news/lululemon-founder-chip-wilson-moves-on/360672/#:~:text=Dennis%20%E2%80%9CChip%E2%80%9D%20Wilson%20started%20up,a%20year%20before%20;founding%20Lululemon

JetBlue (2020). JetBlue for good. Retrieved September 30, 2020, from https://www.jetblue.com/jetblue-for-good

Katz, R. A., & Page, A. (2010). The role of social enterprise. *Vermont Law Review*, 35(1), 59–104.

Kim, E. (2015, April 27). Here's what getting fired from their own companies taught these famous founders. *Business Insider Australia*. Retrieved July 18, 2020, from https://www.businessinsider.com.au/what-5-founders-learned-from-getting-pushed-out-of-their-own-companies-2015-4

Kuratko, D. F. (2005). The emergence of entrepreneurship education: Development, trends, and challenges. *Entrepreneurship: Theory & Practice*, 29(5), 577–597. doi: 10.1111/j.1540-6520.2005.00099.x

Lee, L. (2004, November 1). Spiffing up Men's Wearhouse. *Business Week*. Retrieved June 19, 2020 from https://www.bloomberg.com/news/articles/2004-10-31/spiffing-up-mens-wearhouse

Lemay, R. A. (1999). 10 roles, identities, and expectancies: Positive contributions to normalization and social role valorization. In R. J. Flynn & R. A. Lemay (Eds.), *A quarter-century of normalization and social role valorization: Evolution and impact* (pp. 219–240). University of Ottawa Press.

Li, S. (2014, December 16). American apparel fires founder Dov Charney after internal. *Los Angeles Times*. Retrieved August 19, 2020, from https://www.latimes.com/business/la-fi-dov-charney-american-apparel-fired-20141216-story.html#:~:text=Charney%20was%20suspended%20as%20president,internal%20investigation%20into%20the%20allegations

Madichie, N. O. (2013). Copreneurship is sibling rivalry in family business research: Building or stumbling block? *Institute for Small Business and Entrepreneurship Conference*, 1–6.

Maida, S. (2019, September 30). The weirdest habits of disgraced WeWork CEO Adam Neumann. *Guest of a Guest*. Retrieved June 30, 2020, from https://guestofaguest.com/new-york/nyc-society/the-weirdest-habits-of-disgraced-wework-ceo-adam-neumann

Marlow, S. and McAdam, M. (2013). Gender and entrepreneurship: Advancing debate and challenging myths; exploring the mystery of the under-performing female entrepreneur. *International Journal of Entrepreneurial Behavior & Research*, 19(1), 114–124.

Mazzotta, V., & Santella, R. (2017). CEO hubris: The impact of interpersonal effectiveness in the strategic decision-making activity. *Proceedings of the Multidisciplinary Academic Conference, 250–257.*

Memmott, M. (2013, November 7). Lululemon founder: Our pants won't work for some women. *NPR*. Retrieved July 15, 2020, from https://www.npr.org/sections/thetwo-way/2013/11/07/243706174/lululemon-founder-our-pants-wont-work-for-some-women

Miller, P. (2007, December 7). Tesla co-founder gets the boot, 'not at all happy' about it. *Engadget*. Retrieved July 21, 2020, from https://www.engadget.com/2007-12-07-tesla-co-founder-gets-the-boot-not-at-all-happy-about-it.html

Mohsenin, J. (2013). How did Noah Glass get forced out of Twitter? *Quora*. Retrieved August 13, 2020, from https://www.quora.com/How-did-Noah-Glass-get-forced-out-of-Twitter#:~:text=After%20conferring%20with%20the%20Odeo,he%20would%20be%20publicly%20fired

Mooney, C. H. (2005). *Moving up or out? An examination of non-CEO inside directors becoming CEO* (Doctoral dissertation). Indiana University.

Muniz, K. (2013, August 8). 9 entrepreneur dropouts now worth millions. *Business Insider*. Retrieved July 20, 2020, from https://www.businessinsider.com/9-entrepreneur-dropouts-worth-millions-2013-8

Murphy, M. (2005). Why CEOs get fired. *Leadership Confidence*, 22(9), 14.

Murphy Jr., B. (2019). Southwest airlines and JetBlue both fired him. Then this entrepreneur made an eye-opening decision. *Inc*. Retrieved September 14, 2020, from https://www.inc.com/bill-murphy-jr/fired-by-southwest-airlines-fired-by-jetblue-heres-how-this-inspiring-entrepreneur-keeps-coming-back.html

O'Connor, C. (2015, February 2). Lululemon billionaire Chip Wilson quits board, moves into performance cashmere. *Forbes*. Retrieved July 20, 2020, from https://www.forbes.com/sites/clareoconnor/2015/02/02/lululemon-billionaire-chip-wilson-quits-board-moves-into-performance-cashmere/?sh=613391705edf

Oreskovic, A. (2012, January 17). Yahoo co-founder Jerry Yang resigns. *Reuters*. Retrieved August 5, 2020, from https://www.reuters.com/article/us-yahoo/yahoo-co-founder-jerry-yang-resigns-idUSTRE80G28120120118

Petri, A. (2013, November 16) You call this an apology? *The Washington Post*, Winter, 11AD.

Pickert, K. (2008, November 19). Yahoo! CEO Jerry Yang. *Time*. Retrieved June 13, 2020, from http://content.time.com/time/business/article/0,8599,1860424,00.html

Quittner, J. (2020). Sandy Lerner: The investor is not your friend. *Inc*. Retrieved September 30, 2020, from https://www.inc.com/magazine/201303/how-i-got-started/sandy-lerner.html

Raice, S. (2012, January 31). Groupon and its 'weird' CEO. *The Wall Street Journal*. Retrieved July 23, 2020, from https://www.wsj.com/articles/SB10001424052970203920204577193181377853716

Reed, E. (2020, February 4). History of Tesla: Timeline and facts. Retrieved September 30, 2020, from https://www.thestreet.com/technology/history-of-tesla-15088992

Reiter, C. (2007, May 10). JetBlue removes Neeleman as CEO. *Reuters*. Retrieved August 13, 2020, from https://www.reuters.com/article/us-jetblue-ceo/jetblue-removes-neeleman-as-ceo-idUSN1040438220070510

Richard M. Schulze Family Foundation. (2020). Our founder. Retrieved September 30, 2020, from https://www.schulzefamilyfoundation.org/our_founder/

Robb, A. M., & Watson, J. (2012). Gender differences in firm performance: Evidence from new ventures in the united states. *Journal of Business Venturing, 27*(5), 544–558. doi: 10.1016/j.jbusvent.2011.10.002

Schlender, B. (2000, March 6). How a virtuoso plays the web eclectic, inquisitive, and academic, Yahoo's Jerry Yang reinvents the role of the entrepreneur. *CNN Money*. Retrieved June 15, 2020, from https://money.cnn.com/magazines/fortune/fortune_archive/2000/03/06/275253/index.htm

Schreiber, B. A. (2009, January 28). Martin Eberhard and Marc Tarpenning. Retrieved September 20, 2020, from https://www.britannica.com/biography/Martin-Eberhard-and-Marc-Tarpenning

Shane, S., & Khurana, R. (2003). Bringing individuals back in: The effects of career experience on new firm founding. *Industrial & Corporate Change, 12*(3), 519–543. doi: 10.1093/icc/12.3.519

Smith, P. K., Jost, J. T., & Vijay, R. (2008). Legitimacy crisis? Behavioral approach and inhibition when power differences are left unexplained. *Social Justice Research, 21*(3), 358–376. doi: 10.1007/s11211-008-0077-9

Solesvik, M., Iakovleva, T., & Trifilova, A. (2019). Motivation of female entrepreneurs: a cross-national study. *Journal of Small Business and Enterprise Development, 26*(1), 684–705.

Spiegel, O., Abbassi, P., Schlagwein, D., & Fischbach, K. (2013). Going it all alone in web entrepreneurship? A comparison of single founders vs. co-founders. *Special Interest Group on Computer Personnel Research Annual Conference, Association for Computing Machinery,* 21–32. doi: 10.1145/2487294.2487301

Stanford Engineering (2020). Sergey Brin – Google co-founder. Retrieved September 30, 2020, from https://engineering.stanford.edu/about/heroes/2014-heroes/sergey-brin#:~:text=Brin%20earned%20his%20master's%20degree,pages%20that%20linked%20to%20it

Steiner, C. (2010, August 12). Meet the fastest growing company ever. *Forbes*. Retrieved June 17, 2020, from https://www.forbes.com/forbes/2010/0830/entrepreneurs-groupon-facebook-twitter-next-web-phenom.html?sh=57031ee64c2e

Stewart, J. B. (2015, November 25). Ousted founder of Men's Wearhouse watches his old company struggle. *New York Times*. Retrieved August 15, 2020, from https://www.nytimes.com/2015/11/27/business/george-zimmer-former-face-of-mens-wearhouse-watches-his-old-company-struggle.html

Stone, B., & Miller, C. C. (2008, November 17). Jerry Yang, Yahoo chief, steps down. *New York Times*. Retrieved July 13, 2020, from https://www.nytimes.com/2008/11/18/technology/companies/18yahoo.html

Strauss, K. (2013, March 28). When CEOs get demoted (by companies they founded). *Forbes*. Retrieved September 4, 2020, from https://www.forbes.com/sites/karstenstrauss/2013/03/28/when-ceos-get-terminated-by-companies-they-founded/?sh=4ecb1e701800

The Startups Team (2018). It's complicated. Retrieved July 17, 2020, from https://www.startups.com/library/founder-stories/jerry-yang

Wasserman, N. (2008). The founder's dilemma. Retrieved September 5, 2020, from https://hbr.org/2008/02/the-founders-dilemma

Waters, R. (2012). Founder Yang leaves Yahoo. *Financial Times*, Jan 18, 15.

Watson, J. (2002). Comparing the performance of male and female-controlled businesses: Relating outputs to inputs. *Entrepreneurship: Theory & Practice, 26*(3), 91–100. doi: 10.1177/104225870202600306

Wilson, J. (2013). Finding lessons in Men's Wearhouse founder's firing. *Charlotte Business Journal*. Retrieved June 14, 2020, from https://www.bizjournals.com/charlotte/news/2013/06/26/finding-lessons-in-mens-wearhouse.html

Winkler, R. (2020, October 19). WeWork chairman says consulting deal with Adam Neumann no longer in place. *The Wall Street Journal*. Retrieved September 30, 2020, from https://www.wsj.com/articles/softbank-backs-out-of-consulting-deal-with-wework-co-founder-adam-neumann-11603136659

Wright, R. (2007, April 12). Return of the underdog. *Canadian Business*. Retrieved June 15, 2020, from https://www.canadianbusiness.com/innovation/return-of-the-underdog/#:~:text=In%201997%2C%20Westbeach%20was%20sold,%2Dbased%20Wyndcrest%20Partners%20Ltd

Zisser, M. R., Johnson, S. L., Freeman, M. A., & Staudenmaier, P. J. (2019). The relationship between entrepreneurial intent, gender and personality. *Gender in Management, 34*(8), 665–684.

7 Founder's Syndrome in Nonprofit Companies

Chapter Objectives

When you finish studying this chapter, you should be able to:

- Identify how a nonprofit organization differs from a private-sector company
- Understand how the founder and mission of the nonprofit organization are bound together
- Discuss multiple examples of founder's syndrome in nonprofit companies
- Discuss the reasons that individuals are motivated to start nonprofit organizations
- Identify how founder's syndrome can develop in nonprofit organizations
- Discuss how a nonprofit's mission can be the antecedent to trigger founder's syndrome
- Discuss the role of power between a founding CEO of a nonprofit and a board of directors
- Explain similarities between founder's syndrome in nonprofit organizations compared to for-profit organizations

Introduction

When contemplating the reasons an individual or individuals would want to start a company, our initial speculations might be 'to make money' or 'to prove they can do it.' Founders of nonprofit organizations, however, might respond differently saying, 'to make a difference' or 'to give back to my community.' In Chapter 1, we began with a discussion of the motivations of individuals who start their own company, with the reasons including having had an unpleasant work experience and not wanting to repeat that experience, a desire to be the person in charge, or creating their own lifetime work security, among others. When starting a nonprofit organization, however, the intentions slightly shift. Individuals interested in starting a nonprofit organization contemplate the reasons just mentioned, but they also want to be community problem solvers. In some cases, an individual has had a family member or friend who experienced an illness or trauma, and this will be the driving factor to start a nonprofit organization with a mission related to that particular issue. In other cases, the founders of a nonprofit organization might be inspired by religion or other ideological reasons. In short, Chapter 1 surmises that founders are not only satisfied with being the boss, but instead have a motivational drive to create their own organization.

In one study of 31 nonprofit founders, Carman and Nesbit (2012) asked the founders why they decided to start a nonprofit organization. One respondent said he or she started the nonprofit because it 'felt like there was a need,' and others 'just knew' based on personal or work experiences. A third founder responded he or she was inspired by stories in the media, and he or she wanted to address that particular issue. Others noted they started their nonprofit because of a personal calling or personal interest, and some said they wanted to make a living doing something they 'love.'

Often, individuals are drawn to the nonprofit sector because of the underlying values that shape their personal behavior and decision-making. Acting in the public interest is a commitment, as is improving the lives of others (Haque, 2001; Ventriss, 1997). Philanthropic behaviors, like giving and volunteering, are commonplace for these individuals, along with an innate desire to give back. Bold ambitions and strong desires to fulfill a mission often drive these nascent entrepreneurs to found a nonprofit organization (Van Slyke & Lecy, 2012). In general, nonprofit founders are characterized as being ideologically motivated, personable, charismatic, and inspirational (Carman & Nesbit, 2012; James, 2003; Stevens, 2001).

Nonprofit founders are also drawn to the sector itself. The nonprofit sector provides goods and services to fill a demand that cannot, or will not, be met by the government and the private sector (Weisbrod, 1977). The nonprofit sector is often a champion of the underserved or underprivileged, and with this comes a responsibility to address, and in many cases attempt to solve, public problems (LeRoux & Feeney, 2014). Nonprofit organizations are viewed as both service provider and advocate in that "many nonprofit organizations simultaneously provide public goods and services, supported by both charitable giving and government contracts, as well as advocat[ing] for changes in public policy and practice" (Miller-Stevens, Taylor, & Morris, 2015, p. 2428).

An important characteristic of a nonprofit organization is that it is prohibited from distributing any earned profits to individuals who exercise control over the organization. Instead, profits are distributed internally within the organization to improve the programs and work environment (Hansmann, 2000). Without the incentive to increase profits for shareholders, nonprofit organizations and the people who run them are often viewed as more trustworthy and accountable than their private-sector counterparts (Glaeser & Shleifer, 2001).

Nonprofit organizations are categorized as tax-exempt organizations with the Internal Revenue Service (IRS). The IRS identifies more than 25 501(c) categories of nonprofit organizations that are exempt from paying federal corporate income tax on income generated from activities related to the mission of the organization (National Center for Charitable Statistics, 2020b). One of these categories, 501(c)3 organizations, makes up seventy-five percent of the sector. This category includes charitable organizations such as churches, animal welfare nonprofits, and educational organizations to name a few, in addition to private foundations (Internal Revenue Service, 2020). Today, there are approximately 1.6 million 501(c) organizations in the United States. The sector makes up ten percent of the workforce totaling 11.4 million jobs (Independent Sector, 2020).

Each year, approximately 45,000 nonprofit startups receive tax-exempt status from the IRS (National Center for Charitable Statistics, 2020a). Of the 45,000, some only exist on paper and never transform into an operating business, whereas others are small family-run nonprofit organizations with small revenues. Only a small number of nonprofit startups enter the market with solid financial grounding (Van Slyke & Lecy, 2012). The founders who start these mission-driven organizations are referred to as nonprofit entrepreneurs or nonprofit founders, but Van Slyke and Lecy (2012) note that "caution should be taken to avoid calling all startup organizations and their leaders entrepreneurial. Many new nonprofit organizations start small, lack formal staff structures, and rely heavily on private contributions – and they continue to function this way through their lifespan" (p. 9).

Despite the fact that roughly sixteen percent of all nonprofit startups fail in the first five years (National Center for Charitable Statistics, 2020b), individuals are still driven to found nonprofit organizations. In a survey of 1,106 nonprofit founders who recently incorporated a nonprofit startup, Van Slyke and Lecy (2012) characterize the makeup of the typical 'nonprofit founder' as most likely female (a slight majority of the sample were women), an average age of 53, and white (seventy-five percent of the sample responded with a race of 'white'). Fifty-six percent of the sample had over 15 years of work experience with thirty-two percent of the sample having founded another nonprofit organization. Only nine percent reported hundred percent of their work experience in the nonprofit sector. Fifty-seven percent had served as board members at another nonprofit prior to founding their own nonprofit startup. Finally, eighty-nine percent of respondents had a bachelor's degree or higher.

The Mission

The mission and mission statement of a nonprofit organization represent the personal stake in, and interest of, the founder's goals and vision for the organization in addition to stating why the organization exists. Writing the mission statement is one of the first tasks of the founder, and this is done at the onset when the articles of incorporation and bylaws are created. Thus, the mission in the form of the mission statement and the founder are linked and bound together from the beginning stages of the organization's creation.

The mission and mission statement of a nonprofit organization are also the motivator of most employees in their daily work, in addition to being the bedrock of the organization's programs and services. But, as discussed in Chapter 1, the mission can also be an antecedent to founder's syndrome in that over time board members and staff may find the CEO is running the nonprofit in a way that does not align with the mission, or the CEO is so closely tied to the mission that he or she is unwilling to shift when the nature of the work changes. This tension may result in a strained work environment leading to founder's syndrome. Often, when the board of directors questions the founder's intentions or vision, a conflict ensues, and the only solution is to initiate change at the leadership level. What follows is a description of three case studies of founder's syndrome occurring in 501(c)3 nonprofit organizations. The first two cases illustrate tension between the CEO and board of directors, and the third illustrates the impact of a scandal on the founder of a nonprofit organization.

Nonprofit Organizations

Mothers Against Drunk Driving

The story of Candy Lightner is one of heartbreak, emotion, and inspiration. Born in 1946, Lightner grew up in California with a father who served in the United States Air Force and mother who worked as a civilian for the Air Force. She attended college at American River College in Sacramento and married Steve Lightner with whom she had three children; twin daughters and a son (Biography, 2020; Wade, 2014). In 1980, Lightner lost her 13-year-old daughter to an impaired driver who had multiple drunk driving incidents on his record. Only two days earlier, the man who hit Lightner's daughter had been released from jail on bail where he was held for another hit and run drunk driving incident, adding to his three previous impaired driving arrests and two convictions (Fell & Voas, 2006; Weed, 1993). At the time, drunk driving incidents were increasing in the United States and there was a real and legitimate public fear of being hit by a person under the influence of alcohol (Warr & Stafford, 1983). In one recount of the period, "traffic safety experts and alcohol researchers had already created the public image of the 'killer drunk,' a socially irresponsible drunk driver who injures or kills innocent people" (Gusfield, 1981).

After her daughter's death, Lightner was told by police and the courts that the driver would receive little punishment, which at that time was common for drunk driving convictions. Her emotional turmoil and anger regarding the justice system's response motivated Lightner to found Mothers Against Drunk Driving (MADD) (Reinarman, 1988). In an article, she wrote for *The Judges Journal* in 1984, Lightner commented that she knew nothing about the criminal justice system when she started MADD, but she and her colleagues felt strongly that drunk drivers should no longer be on the roads.

The emotions that drove Lightner to start MADD were further explained in this statement regarding the man who killed her daughter,

> In my case there was anger at the man, but more than that I was angry with his wife and the system because she had bailed him out of jail two days before and let him drive her car when he was drunk, and the system allowed him back out on the streets. The anger was then directed at the public for not having done anything about this problem and for being so apathetic. All of that was channeled into MADD. (Perkins, 1986, p. 15)

Within one year of starting MADD, Lightner's nonprofit had become a national organization registered with the IRS as a 501(c)3 organization. The increased revenue from national status and tax-deductible contributions from donors quickly resulted in a large organization with chapters throughout the country. Lightner and her dedicated employees and volunteers visited legislators and talked with newspapers, radio, and television to inform others of drunk driving statistics, 'appalling' courtroom facts, and the victims' sides of drunk driving tragedies (Fell & Voas, 2006; Lightner, 1984). In her own words, Lightner (1984) summarized the advocacy work of MADD as the following:

> When judges informed us of their concern for the drunk driver's family's plight if he were thrown into jail, we countered with the victim family's emotional and financial plight when a loved one is killed or maimed. When we learned that many judges were being too lenient, we proposed legislation that provided for mandatory sentences. When our bills were introduced, we lobbied – probably not very professionally, but from our hearts. (p. 37–38)

In the first two years of MADD, Lightner's organization, the data it collected, and the heartfelt stories it represented gained enough recognition to change national legislation on impaired driving. In 1982, President Reagan signed into law the Howard-Barnes Alcohol Traffic Safety Law that provided three-year incentive grants from the Highway Trust Fund for states to increase their drunk driving prevention programs and pass laws lowering the legal levels for impaired driving (American Addiction Centers, 2020). By the end of 1982, thirty-nine "states ha[d] passed more than 700 new laws aimed at curbing drunk driving" (Lightner, 1984, p. 38). Her organization's efforts also helped create governors' task forces on drunk driving in 41 states, and at the national level a National Commission Against Drunk Driving (Fell & Voas, 2006). As the movement gained momentum, people associated with MADD started speaking in schools and with community groups, and increased funding was received to conduct research on drunk driving statistics to inform public policy decisions on the topic. When addressing the complex policy issues related to alcoholism, MADD's stance was that "we favor punishment for the crime of drunk driving and treatment of alcoholics, but not treatment in lieu of the punishment" (Lightner, 1984, p. 38).

Conflict between Lightner and the board of directors was evident early in the organization, much of it stemming from Lightner's charismatic leadership style and her inability to work with the administrative structures of the board (Fell & Voas, 2006; Weed, 1993). In 1983, disagreements between Lightner and the board of directors began to emerge when board members expressed discontent over Lightner's excessive use of funding for operations and fundraising activities at MADD. Board members questioned how donations and other funding were being spent, and whether the expenses were in line with the mission of the organization. Although Lightner was not fired during this first episode with the board of directors, the conflict led to an overhaul of the governance structure of the organization (Perkins, 1986). With this new board came a stipulation that 17 of its members needed to be from the local chapters, rather than from the business community, and a new executive director had to replace Lightner to oversee operations. With the new executive director came a relocation of the organization's headquarters and a new approach to operations, each of which shifted the grassroots-oriented nonprofit organization into a more business-like company. The new executive director was fired from MADD within a few years, and with no executive director in place, Lightner now held the positions of President, Founder, Chairman of the Board, and Chief Executive Officer (Weed, 1993).

As a leader, Lightner was described as adaptable in that she learned how to influence people and implement strategies at all levels of the organization. She was notably charismatic with her strong drive and willingness to be the voice of the victim (Fell & Voas, 2006; Lightner, 1984). In 1983, she was named one of the top 100 American women by the *Ladies Home Journal* (McCarthy, Wolfson, Baker, & Mosakowski, 1988).

Externally, she was described as an "emotionally expressive, self-confident leader with a moral mission" (Weed, 1993, p. 337). Internally, however, staff interviews revealed that Lightner had an autocratic style that manifested in her need for power. She was viewed as insensitive to others and unaware of the work and time commitments and capacity of employees working with and around her. Lightner was also inconsistent regarding internal policies and operations and was described as being unpredictable with no focus. She ran the organization with centralized leadership and an 'egocentric nature' where all criticisms or oppositions were taken personally (Weed, 1993, p. 339–340).

In 1984, Lightner and her board of directors decided to expand the organization's network by recruiting new board members with important contacts in business and government, regardless of whether the individual had a personal connection with MADD or the drunk driving issue. With the addition of five new board members, including some new board members with skills in finance and corporate law (Fell & Voas, 2006), the bylaws were amended to reduce the number of chapter representatives on the board from seventeen to four giving the chapter representatives much less power than in prior years. In the same year, the Better Business Bureau criticized MADD for spending an excessive percentage of its income on administration and fundraising expenses (McCarthy, Britt, & Wolfson, 1991). This public criticism was soon followed by an audit of MADD's finances by the California Attorney General for the years 1983–1984. Despite no wrongdoing being found, the negative public criticism from the two incidents put pressure on MADD's board to implement changes at the leadership level (Madigan, 1985).

As a result of Lightner's new board and recent public attention by the Better Business Bureau and California Attorney General's audit, she again found herself engrained in conflict with her board of directors. New members of the board were not as taken with Lightner's charismatic leadership and authoritarian management style. Her board of directors questioned her financial management practices when at the end of 1984, MADD had a net deficit of over $100,000 (Sant'Anna & Weiss, 1986). In 1985, the board of directors also raised its displeasure over Lightner's rising salary, benefits, and bonuses that had increased with the fundraising success of the organization. Aside from questioning the appropriateness of a nonprofit executive receiving a bonus, the board was also concerned with the personal expenses she charged to the organization including "child care in the home – babysitting – clothing, carpet and drapery cleaning services, and a limousine service" (Weed, 1993, p. 341).

Lightner's decision to accept funding from the alcohol industry was also in question. In an interview with the *Chicago Tribune*, Lightner said,

> I assume some people will say, 'Gee, what's she doing working for the industry, the other side … . I don't see it as the other side. They're

just as affected by drunk driving as anyone else. Drunk driving certainly doesn't enhance their business. They have friends, neighbors and relatives hurt by drunk driving. (Adams, 1994, para 5)

Given the board of director's concerns over her management, financial, and fundraising practices, Lightner hired a new controller and central office manager to help run the organization, and at this point a critical fight for power between Lightner and the board of directors ensued. The conflict came to a head when Lightner's contract expired at the end of June 1985, at which time the board of directors appointed an executive committee made up of newer board members who were interested in restructuring the organization and creating a limited role for Lightner (Sant'Anna & Weiss, 1986, p. 5; Weed, 1993). In this new limited role she was to act as spokesperson for the organization, a change Lightner did not adapt to easily. The conflicts between Lightner and her board of directors over the role she should fill in the organization, and the compensation associated with that role, continued until October 1985 when Lightner was "relegated to a position as a consultant under a two-year contract with a reduced salary" (Weed, p. 342). At this time, a new National President of MADD was appointed (Fell & Voas, 2006).

Despite her success as the head of a national organization, Lightner was fired by the board after five years in her role as President and Executive Director for unsatisfactory performance as a leader and financial manager. At the time of her departure, MADD's annual budget was approximately $13 million (Montague, 1989). In his review of Lightner's departure, Weed (1993) notes "the organization became dominated by specialists who held the expectation that MADD should be operated like any other complex organization and not function as an organization that was responsible to a single charismatic leader," and these changes led to the departure of the MADD's founder (p. 330). Lightner denied allegations that she mishandled funds and attributed her ousting to disagreements with the board of directors over communication with the chapters and differences over where the mission was heading (Hughes, 1985). Lightner wanted MADD to continue focusing on drunk driving and the board wanted to widen its focus to the broader impacts of alcohol. Lightner's response to being fired was to say "After five years of being the heroine one day and the devil the next, it will be nice to say to people: 'It ain't my fault'" (Hughes, 1985, para 2).

The case of Cindy Lightner and MADD is a classic tale of founder's syndrome. Lightner's motivation to found MADD was based on the emotional turmoil and energy she felt from the death of her daughter and her realization and life experience that impaired drivers were not being held accountable by the court system. This realization inspired Lightner to found MADD with the mission to change drunk driving legislation and the way impaired driving incidents were being handled by police and the courts. Lightner's passion for the mission and her charismatic personality catapulted her organization into the national spotlight. With the growth of her organization came a need for power and control leading to board members questioning her financial management, leadership, and fundraising practices. Over time, the conflict between Lightner and her board of directors grew, lending to a dysfunctional workplace. Ultimately, Lightner was forced out of the organization. Her firing supports the notion mentioned earlier in this volume that an organization struggling with founder's syndrome is prime for some corrective reaction; otherwise, the entity will suffer and possibly not survive.

The Southern Poverty Law Center

In 1971, Morris Dees and Joe Levin co-founded the nonprofit organization Southern Poverty Law Center (SPLC) after witnessing the consequences of racial injustice in the deep south (O'Brien, 2019). The nonprofit organization was founded "to ensure that the promise of the civil rights movement became a reality for all" (Southern Poverty Law Center, 2020b, para 1). Two of Dees' life experiences acted as drivers to the founding of the SPLC: One being his maternal grandfather's involvement and membership in the Ku Klux Klan, and the second being the guilt Dees felt as a result of working as legal counsel for a Ku Klux Klan member who physically beat 'freedom riders' in the 1960s, a job he said he only took for the money (Dees & Fiffer, 1991, p. 56). Prior to founding SPLC, Dees earned his law degree from the Alabama School of Law and was a successful entrepreneur in the direct-mail publishing business (Dees & Fiffer, 1991).

Dees lamented his close ties with racism. After reading the story of another famous lawyer who worked in defense of the underrepresented, Dees vowed to make an impact on racial issues, using his law degree to start a civil rights law practice that would work and provide a voice for the disenfranchised (Southern Poverty Law Center, 2020a). When reflecting on his decision to found the SPLC, Dees notes in his autobiography that he

> would sell [his] company as soon as possible and specialize in civil rights law. All the things in my life that brought me to this point, all the pulls and tugs of my conscience, found a singular peace. It did not matter what my neighbors would think, or the judges, the bankers, or even my relatives. (Dees & Fiffer, 1991, p. 97)

In the early years of the organization, Dees and his colleagues took on cases that desegregated all-white institutions and defended the rights of black men who were wrongly accused of a crime and were on death row (Silverstein, 2000). In its long history, the SPLC has tackled many difficult issues and has been the trusted source for identifying hate groups such as the Ku Klux Klan (O'Neil, 2020), in addition to dismantling laws that negatively impact "women, children, the LGBT community and the disabled" as well as "protect[ing] low-wage immigrant workers from exploitation, and more" (Southern Poverty Law Center, 2020b, para 8).

In 2019, 48 years after co-founding the SPLC, serving as its chief legal counsel, and being the face of the organization, Dees was fired. The SPLC's decision was based on accusations that Dees misled the public with his fundraising practices, frequent sexual harassment of women in the workplace, and his promotion of racial inequality with hiring practices (O'Neil, 2020). At the time, the newly hired President Richard Cohen released a statement saying "as a civil rights organization, the SPLC is committed to ensuring that the conduct of our staff reflects the mission of the organization and the values we hope to instill in the world" (O'Brien, 2019, para 3). Concurrently, the organization removed Dees' biography from its website. Cohen also said, "When one of our own fails to meet those standards, no matter his or her role in the organization, we take it seriously and must take appropriate action" (National Public Radio, 2019).

Although the organization did not make a public statement as to why Dees was fired, stories and allegations of misconduct emerged from within and outside of the organization dating back to the 1980s. Three notable themes were evident including accusations of misguided fundraising practices, sexual exploits, and racial discrimination. As the SPLC started to ramp up in the 1970s and 1980s, Dees' fundraising practices were viewed in a positive way as a strategy to support legal cases assisting wrongly accused people of color in clearing their names. The strategy emphasized finding liberal donors who cared about wrongdoings to people of color in the South. Through this approach, Dees and the SPLC quickly raised more funding than anticipated. The organization grew exponentially in the first seven years with more than adequate funding. Instead of being comfortable with the organization and its size, however, Dees continued to fundraise at a level beyond the organization's needs (Silverstein, 2000). The amount of time and energy Dees and the organization's employees put in to fundraising created internal and external questions of Dees' priorities – that is, whether the organization needed the funding he was raising for the amount of services the organization provided, whether the organization's fundraising efforts were excessive, and whether Dees enjoyed too much publicity and attention resulting from the organization's fundraising campaigns, which some argued capitalized on fear and hate (Morabito, 2017; O'Neil, 2020).

Dees had been accused by multiple media sources and his own employees of being a fraud and conman given the large amount of money the organization raised compared to the impact it made. Dees and the SPLC had also been criticized for creating a "malleable definition of hate that applies to its political enemies" and for using hate accusations against others as a con and "deceptive scheme" to raise money (O'Neil, 2020, p. 7). One media outlet referred to the SPLC as a 'propaganda smear machine' (Morabito, 2017, para 6) and another said Dees was 'fundraising on the blood of innocents' (PA Pundits – International, 2019). It was well-founded that Dees thrived on notoriety and he used controversial political or social issues that would heighten emotions and publicity of the organization, thus bringing in more donations (O'Neil, 2020).

The second long-running criticism of Dees centered on his sexual exploits. Dees had been accused of inappropriate behavior in the workplace such as hugging his employees and behaving inappropriately with women at fundraising events. In one of his divorce trials, he admitted to sleeping with coworkers at SPLC and a woman who was interviewing for a job at his organization (O'Neil, 2020). During his tenure at the SPLC, multiple complaints from women had been filed against the founder for various acts of inappropriate behavior with women (O'Neil, 2020; Satija, Lowery, & Reinhard, 2019).

The third reason Dees was purported to be fired relates to racially insensitive comments he made in the workplace, including insensitive comments about young black voters and black political candidates. Another cited incident involved a lunch in 2015 where Dees made a racial comment regarding black teenagers and their driving. Internal emails at the SPLC also illustrate racial biases in the promotion and hierarchy of the organizations, which had been an issue for decades (Brown & Edwards, 2019a; Coombs, 2019). In an interview with *the Washington Post*, employees of SPLC "suggest that the celebrated civil rights organization had been bitterly at odds with its founder for several years. Those battle have centered on his refusal to retire, his behavior towards women, and his comments regarding race" (Satija et al., 2019, para 8).

Following multiple allegations of questionable or inappropriate conduct, members of the board of directors met with Dees to convince him to retire. With no success, board members and other leadership strategized to force Dees out of the organization, at which time the board cut his pay by $100,000 and placed him on 'board emeritus status' (For Purpose Law Group, 2019). Dees was no longer involved in the day-to-day activities of the organization, and was no longer part of the legal counsel, yet he continued to maintain a desk in the office (Brown & Edwards, 2019a).

In March 2019, the interim CEO offered to let Dees voluntarily resign, informing him that if he refused he would be terminated. Dees did not accept the offer, and the interim CEO fired him the next day. Afterward, "more than a dozen staff members signed an email to senior executives that applauded Dees' firing and demanded accountability from 'those individuals in leadership and on the board of directors who, for years, were aware of and covered up or ignored' allegations of misconduct by

Dees" (Satija et al., 2019, para 37). Soon after Dees left the organization, the co-founder announced an outside investigation of the internal workplace culture. Dees denied any sexist or racist behaviors and told the public he was not fired for misconduct, but rather the leaders of the organization had been trying to push him to retire for years (Hassan, Zralck, & Blinder, 2019).

As a leader, Dees was described in both positive and negative ways. Some characterized him as generous and thoughtful, and many former employees stood up for him denying allegations he was racist or inappropriate. He was revered for his marketing and fundraising skills and his abilities to grow and build an organization (PA Pundits – International, 2019). Others described him as inappropriate with women and subordinates, and racially insensitive. After his termination from SPLC, multiple stories of Dees' inappropriate behavior toward women emerged. Many of the stories describe unwanted sexual advancements and innuendos toward women, some of which were reported to the board of directors and were dismissed as 'jokes.' Other stories of racist behaviors also began to emerge in the news media after Dees' termination, although details are slim with the individuals involved citing fear of retaliation if their story were to be told in a public setting. In some cases, individuals had been required to sign nondisclosure agreements (Satija et al., 2019).

Dees insisted he was a scapegoat for the current leadership's mishandling of the organization (Satija et al., 2019). At the time he was fired, Dees said he had "limited involvement with the organization in recent years," despite having been paid over $400,000 a year and continuing to benefit from the prestige of being the SPLC's co-founder (For Purpose Law Group, 2019; Hassan et al., 2019, para 6). Given his more limited role in the organization, the internal turmoil within the organization, he argued, must be the current CEO's doing. As an illustration of his point, within 10 days after Dees left the SPLC, the interim President and legal director also resigned (Koplowitz, 2019; Vollers, 2019).

Dees' case of founder's syndrome is another illustration of conflict between the founder and the board of directors. Like Cindy Lightner of MADD, Morris Dees was a public-facing figure whose identity was closely wrapped into the organization he founded, even when his role at SPLC had decreased. Dees suffered from psychological ownership, in that he felt possessive of his organization and thus did not want to resign even in the face of criticism and scrutiny from both within and outside of the organization. His adamant refusal of any wrongdoing is typical of founder's syndrome behavior, and this is especially true when ownership is coupled with the length of time the individual has been in a leadership role in the organization. As noted in Chapter 1, when a founder struggles with a board of directors, it is often the founder who feels victimized or mistreated. It is also the case that Dees rationalized his corrupt behavior by focusing on his good intentions for the SPLC while minimizing the harmful consequences of his behaviors and actions. With these examples of corrupt behaviors in mind, we turn to our third illustration of founder's syndrome.

Livestrong Foundation

The third case we present in this chapter differs from the other two. Although the previous cases highlight conflict between a founder and its board of directors, this case provides an illustration of how a public scandal can foster founder's syndrome in a nonprofit organization.

In one discussion of founder's syndrome, it is warned that "Powerful founders who fall from grace can take the organization down with them; surviving a scandal requires that the nonprofit's mission is larger than the founder's personality and that the right succession plan is in place" (Hemenway & Barnes, LLP, 2015). This case focuses on Lance Armstrong, the founder of the Lance Armstrong Foundation now known as the Livestrong Foundation. Similar to the stories of Cindy Lightner and Morris Dees, Lance Armstrong's story is one of triumph and inspiration ending in a separation of ties from the organization the individual founded.

Lance Armstrong grew up in a nontraditional household. His mother was 17 at the time of his birth, and soon after his birth his father left the family. Armstrong's mother remarried, but the second marriage did not last. As a boy, Armstrong channeled his energy and feelings into his bike which "gave him a way to escape the sense of being inferior to the 'normal' children" who did not live in broken households but frequented the country club in his neighborhood (Burgo, 2013, para 10). Armstrong began competitive cycling at the age of 16, and in 1991 at the age of 18 won his first amateur cycling championship. One year later, he came in 14th at the Barcelona, Spain 1992 Olympics, turning to the professional circuit one year later. In 1993, Armstrong won 10 titles and finished his first Tour de France. In 1996, he was the number one cyclist in the world (Cycling News, 2005). This same year, at age 25, Armstrong was diagnosed with stage three testicular cancer (Hamblin, 2019). Despite being given a thirty percent chance of survival with cancer having spread to his abdomen and his brain, Armstrong beat the odds and won his battle against the disease (Costas, 2020). Only one year later, he was back to training, then racing again in 1998. Over the next six years, Armstrong won seven Tour de France victories with multiple wins at individual stages and time trials (Whitcomb, 2012).

In 1997, the famous cyclist founded the Lance Armstrong Foundation, whose mission was to serve others affected by cancer. Armstrong and a small team of colleagues built the nonprofit organization from the ground up, and in just over a decade it had grown into a global brand. By

2010, the foundation had served more than 608,000 people. By 2011, the foundation and the organization had grown to $47 million in revenue and 90 full-time employees (Schrotenboer, 2012a). The foundation was built on a governance structure that coveted close personal relationships between individuals in top leadership positions, accessible networks that could be used to the foundation's advantage with fundraising and public exposure, and board members who were close friends with Armstrong. These close relationships and networks worked in Armstrong's favor as he grew the organization and fundraised for the foundation. Over the years, Armstrong filled many important roles in the foundation, including chairman of the board. In this role, he spoke frequently with the CEO, in addition to participating in the organization's work on a daily basis (Landau, 2012).

In 1999, Armstrong was one of many cyclists accused of using performance-enhancing drugs. He consistently denied the allegations until 2012 when the United States Anti-Doping Agency presented evidence that he had been using the drugs for many years. The United States Anti-Doping Agency released over 1,000 pages of evidence backing up their finding which included a statement confirming that Lance Armstrong was part of "the most sophisticated, professionalized, and successful doping program that sport has ever seen" (Pearson, 2012, para 1). Armstrong denied the allegations with his lawyer noting the investigation was a 'one-sided hatchet job' and a 'government-funded witch hunt' (Pearson, 2012, para 3). To back up their claim, the United States Anti-Doping Agency produced scientific data and testimony from multiple teammates of Armstrong who had confessed to having taken performance-enhancing drugs and to having witnessed Armstrong take the drugs as well (National Public Radio, 2012). Coinciding with the United States Anti-Doping Agency's report, major sponsors such as Nike and Oakley were cutting ties with Armstrong (Schrotenboer, 2012b; Whitcomb, 2012). After his refusal to confront the evidence against him, the United States Anti-Doping Agency banned Armstrong from competitive cycling for life and stripped him of his seven Tour de France wins. This scandal ended Armstrong's cycling career (Whitcomb, 2012).

When the United States Anti-Doping Agency's final report was released, an emotional avalanche fell over the former and current CEOs, employees, and board members of the Lance Armstrong Foundation as they wondered whether the foundation could take the hit (Cassie, 2013). To many, Armstrong had become a hero on many levels as a "cancer survivor, humanitarian, and a model of bravery and perseverance" (Burgo, 2013, para 13). But, to others, Armstrong was a person who threatened, sued, conspired against, and drove his competitors out of the cycling world (Burgo, 2013). Contradicting their accusations, Armstrong characterized his behavior as 'controlling the message' (Carroll, 2013).

While Armstrong's scandal was unfolding, the Lance Armstrong

Foundation was being flooded with supportive emails and calls (Landau, 2012). At the time of the scandal, the foundation was receiving between $45 million and $50 million in donations per year (Landau, 2012). In an effort to spare his foundation the negative impacts of his cycling career, Armstrong stepped down as Chairman of the board of directors on October 17, 2012, resigning completely from the board and cutting all ties a few weeks later on November 4, 2012 (Schrotenboer, 2012a). The CEO, Doug Ulman, who had worked at the foundation for 14 years, resigned two years later noting that he could not keep up with the fallout from Armstrong's scandal (Carter, 2014). In an interview, the CEO who replaced Ulman made it clear that the newly renamed Livestrong foundation wanted "nothing to do with its disgraced former namesake" (Schrotenboer, 2012a, para 4).

As a leader, Armstrong is described as having a "narcissistic personality" with a desire for money, fame, and victory. As discussed in Chapter 2, narcissistic personality disorder is an authoritarian style of leadership with a need to exercise power, at times becoming untrustworthy and self-centered (Matos, O'Neill, & Lei, 2018). In one review of Armstrong, he is said to be grandiose, arrogant, and willing to tell ongoing lies. Lying was a

> defense mechanism to ward off unconscious feelings of shame, defect or inferiority. The 'Lance Armstrong' who for so long was adored by the public embodied a carefully constructed lie meant to disprove these feelings of unworthiness. Ongoing lies, in public statements and under oath, helped sustain the central lie of his existence: *I'm a winner, not a loser.* Over the years, whenever someone has challenged those lies, he has responded with swift brutality to protect that perfect image and prevent the return of shame. (Burgo, 2013, para 3)

The goal of Armstrong's lying was to flip the accusations of his accusers by trying to destroy their careers or character (Walsh, 2015). In doing so, the threat to Armstrong might be annihilated.

During Armstrong's 2013 interview with Oprah Winfrey, the cyclist and founder admitted to using performance-enhancing drugs. He expressed sorrow and regret for lying and treating others poorly in his efforts to hide his wrongdoing. Armstrong described himself as "the guy who expected to get everything he wanted, and to control everything" (Carroll, 2013). After years of lying about his use of performance-enhanced drugs, the public response to his doping scandal was not one of understanding and compassion. Rather, it was one of disgust. Friends and associates of the fallen icon said his confession would, in part, exhibit an effort of Armstrong to rebuild his reputation and would help build back his charity (Burgo, 2013).

Armstrong's relationship with his board of directors was mostly positive, but interviews with associates at the charity reveal concerns over the foundation's reliance on Armstrong's reputation and fame. Armstrong's deals with major corporations often resulted in gifts to the foundation, and many business partnerships were questioned as to whether Armstrong had a conflict of interest between his own personal dealings and the benefit of the foundation (Saul, 2013). As the foundation's development officer noted, "There was a conflict. I felt there was, and of course we run into this with nonprofits. Personal interest, personal agendas, should not be greater than the interest of the mission of the organization" (Saul, 2013, para 8). It should be noted that Armstrong was never accused of any wrongdoing with the foundation. Regardless, after the doping scandal, large corporations scaled back donations to the foundation not wanting to associate their corporate name with Armstrong himself (Saul, 2013). Upon his departure, Armstrong relayed on the Livestrong website in his own words that,

I am deeply grateful to the people of the foundation who have done such hard and excellent work over the last fifteen years, building tangible and effective ways to improve the lives of cancer survivors. And I am deeply humbled by the support our foundation has received from so many people throughout the world survivors, world leaders, business leaders and of course, the cancer community itself. We turn to this community frequently for guidance and collaboration to achieve our shared goals. They are unfailingly generous with their wisdom and counsel and I can never thank them enough.

I have had the great honor of serving as this foundation's chairman for the last five years and its mission and success are my top priorities. Today therefore, to spare the foundation any negative effects as a result of controversy surrounding my cycling career, I will conclude my chairmanship. (Livestrong, 2020, para 3–4)

Although the Livestrong case is not one of conflict between the founder and the board of directors, it illustrates the conflict that can arise when a scandal emerges. Despite his work with the foundation, Armstrong's doping scandal revealed a corrupt individual who rationalized his poor behavior to benefit himself and his foundation. For years, Armstrong denied the accusations made against him and in turn questioned the ethical standing of his victims as though the "victim was a lower class of person and thus might have deserved it" (Gannett & Rector, 2015, p. 169). Even after he admitted to taking performance-enhancing drugs and treating his accusers so poorly, he still implied that his actions were in some way forgivable because of the good work he had accomplished through his foundation and his achievements after beating cancer. The fallout from his coercive and abusive power and behavior toward others was catching up with him, and the impacts on his foundation were becoming evident. In the end, Armstrong sacrificed his own reputation for the good of his foundation by stepping down from his board of directors and cutting all ties with the organization. This action alone shows his deep commitment to his mission and the organization he founded.

Conclusion

As a conclusion to this chapter, one might wonder if nonprofit organizations are more likely to experience founder's syndrome than private sector companies. Does the mission of a nonprofit organization make the founder more attached to his or her organization? Does this attachment prevent a founder from wanting to leave, even when it is time to cut ties with the organization? The answer is, yes, probably.

As we have seen throughout this volume, founders start their companies for many different reasons. Although nonprofit founders are working to achieve a specific mission, founders of all organization types put forth their emotional energy to accomplish their organizational goals and vision. The founder has an emotional and financial stake in the success of his or her creation. Conflict or failure experienced by any entrepreneur or founder is traumatic, especially when there is an ideological difference between the founder and his or her board. Given the nature of the nonprofit mission, founders of nonprofit organizations are more likely to feel the emotional pull of staying with the organization they created, and many will have a harder time letting go and allowing their brainchild to be entrusted to others. It is interesting, then, to think about the emotional sacrifices of the three founders discussed in this chapter. Whether deserved or not, cutting ties with the organization he or she founded must have felt like losing a piece of their own identity.

In the next chapter, we offer ideas about the organizational conditions that might lead to the prevention of founder's syndrome and why founder's syndrome might be an inevitable 'fact of life' in many public and nonprofit companies.

Discussion Questions

1. Think back to the three cases of founder's syndrome in nonprofit organizations discussed in this chapter. What are the similarities of the cases? What are the differences?
2. How did the personality traits and characteristics of Candy Lightner, Morris Dees, and Lance Armstrong help generate founder's syndrome in the organizations they founded?
3. What is the relationship between a nonprofit founder and the mission of the organization? Does the mission of a nonprofit

organization make the founder more attached to his or her organization? Explain your answer.

4. Is founder's syndrome more likely to occur in a nonprofit organization than a private-sector company? Explain your answer.

5. Which base(s) of power did Candy Lightner use?

6. In this chapter, we read about founders of nonprofit organizations that lost their jobs. Do you agree with the idea that a founder of a nonprofit organization can be fired by a group of people (that is, a board of directors) that had nothing to do with creating the organization? Explain.

7. In the case of SLPC, Morris Dees was heavily criticized in the press for what some would call fundraising success. Since many nonprofits fail because of an inability to raise money, how is it possible that a profitable nonprofit can be considered inappropriate for raising money?

8. In the case of the Lance Armstrong Foundation (before it became the Livestrong Foundation), its founder had for years been rewarded with fame. What founder's syndrome behaviors can you identify from the case study?

9. In your opinion, which of the cases described in this chapter exemplified Founders Transformational Reaction Syndrome? Explain.

References

Adams, J. M. (1994, January 15). MADD founder Lightner takes a job as lobbyist for liquor industry. *Chicago Tribune*. Retrieved June 14, 2020, from https://www.chicagotribune.com/news/ct-xpm-1994-01-15-9401150133-story.html

American Addiction Centers (2020). Effectiveness of Mothers Against Drunk Driving. Retrieved September 30, 2020, from https://www.alcohol.org/teens/mothers-against-drunk-driving/

Biography (2020). Candy Lightner biography. Retrieved September 30, 2020, from https://www.biography.com/activist/candy-lightner

Brown, M., & Edwards, B. (2019a, March 16). 'Civil rights' movement television evangelist': Dees weathered criticism for decades amidst SPLC's groundbreaking legal work. *Montgomery Advertiser*. Retrieved August 12, 2020, from https://www.montgomeryadvertiser.com/story/news/2019/03/16/morris-dees-splc-southern-poverty-law-center-martin-luther-king-jr-levin-hatewatch-klan-tracy-larkin/3173039002/

Brown, M., & Edwards, B. (2019b). Southern Poverty Law Center fires co-founder Morris Dees. *Montgomery Advertiser*. Retrieved August 12, 2020, from https://www.montgomeryadvertiser.com/story/news/2019/03/14/southern-poverty-law-center-fires-co-founder-civil-rights-lawyer-morris-dees/3164839002/

Burgo, J. (2013, January 28). How aggressive narcissism explains Lance Armstrong. *The Atlantic*. Retrieved July 16, 2020, from https://www.theatlantic.com/health/archive/2013/01/how-aggressive-narcissism-explains-lance-armstrong/272568/

Carman, J. G., & Nesbit, R. (2012). Founding new nonprofit organizations: Syndrome or symptom? *Nonprofit and Voluntary Sector Quarterly, 42*(3), 603–621.

Carroll, R. (2013). Lance Armstrong admits doping in Oprah Winfrey interview. *The Guardian.* Retrieved August 15, 2020, from https://www.theguardian.com/sport/2013/jan/18/lance-armstrong-admits-doping-oprah-winfrey

Carter, W. (2014). Livestrong CEO leaving after 14 years at the helm of Lance Armstrong-founded charity. *The Dallas Morning News.* Retrieved June 16, 2020, from https://www.dallasnews.com/news/texas/2014/09/23/livestrong-ceo-leaving-after-14-years-at-helm-of-lance-armstrong-founded-charity/

Cassie, R. (2013, June). Surviving Lance. *Baltimore Magazine.* Retrieved September 12, 2020, from https://www.baltimoremagazine.com/section/community/surviving-lance/

Coombs, A. M. (2019, March 15). The hate u give: SPLC co-founder sacked over allegations of racism, sexual harassment. *Newsbusters.org.* Retrieved August 12, 2020, from https://advance-lexis-com.coloradocollege.idm.oclc.org/api/document?collection=news&id=urn:contentItem:5VN1-MG91-JCMN-Y22W-00000-00&context=1516831

Costas, C. (2020). Lance Armstrong's doctors say he made a difference for cancer community – Inspiration in spite of the flaws. *Survivornet.* Retrieved September 30, 2020, from https://www.survivornet.com/articles/lance-armstrongs-doctors-say-disgraced-athlete-made-a-difference-for-cancer-community-im-flawed/

Cycling News (2005). The legend of Lance: An Armstrong retrospective. Retrieved June 15, 2020, from https://www.cyclingnews.com/features/the-legend-of-lance-an-armstrong-retrospective/

Dees, M., & Fiffer, S. (1991). *A season for justice: The life and times of civil rights lawyer Morris Dees.* Charles Scribner's Sons.

Fell, J. C., & Voas, R. B. (2006). Mothers against drunk driving (MADD): The first 25 years. *Traffic Injury Prevention, 7*(3), 195–212.

For Purpose Law Group (2019, May 16). The shocking turmoil at the SPLC. Retrieved August 1, 2020, from https://forpurposelaw.com/shocking-turmoil-splc/

Gannett, A., & Rector, G. C. (2015). The rationalization of political corruption. *Public Integrity, 17,* 165–175.

Glaeser, E. L., & Shleifer, A. S. (2001). Not-for-profit entrepreneurs. *Journal of Public Economics, 81*(1), 99–115. doi: 10.1016/S0047-2727(00)00130-4

Gusfield, J. R. (1981). *The culture of public problems.* University of Chicago Press.

Hamblin, T. (2019, November 4). What kind of cancer did Lance Armstrong have? *Verywell Health.* Retrieved June 17, 2020, from https://www.verywellhealth.com/what-kind-of-cancer-did-lance-armstrong-have-3209386

Hansmann, H. (2000). *The ownership of enterprise.* Harvard University Press.

Haque, M. S. (2001). The diminishing publicness of public service under the current. *Public Administration Review, 61*(1), 65–82.

Hassan, A., Zraick, K., and Blinder, A. (2019, March 14). Morris Dees, a co-founder of the Southern Poverty Law Center, is ousted. *The New York Times.* Retrieved August 17, 2020, from https://www.nytimes.com/2019/03/14/us/morris-dees-southern-poverty-law-center-fired.html

Hemenway & Barnes, LLP. (2015). Mission-driven success: Bringing lessons from the family business to nonprofits. Retrieved July 19, 2020, from https://

hembar.com/uploads/1280/doc/Mission-driven_success_-_Bringing_lessons_ from_the_Family_Business_to_Nonprofit_-_FJM,_April_2015.pdf

Hughes, C. (1985, October 12). MADD founder ousted from leadership. *The Associated Press*. Retrieved September 21, 2020, from https://advance-lexis-com.coloradocollege.idm.oclc.org/api/document?collection=news&id= urn.contentItem:3SJR-2RP0-0011-71G4-00000-00&context=1516831

Independent Sector (2020). The charitable sector. Retrieved September 30, 2020, from https://independentsector.org/about/the-charitable-sector/

Internal Revenue Service (2020). Exempt organization types. Retrieved September 30, 2020, from https://www.irs.gov/charities-non-profits/exempt-organization-types

James, E. (2003). Commercialism and the mission of nonprofits. *Society, 40*(4), 29–35.

Koplowitz, H. (2019, March 22). SPLC President Richard Cohen resigns. *AL.com*. Retrieved June 1, 2020, from https://www.al.com/news/2019/03/splc-president-richard-cohen-resigns.html

Landau, E. (2012, August 25). Armstrong's cancer foundation still strong. Retrieved July 19, 2020, from https://www.cnn.com/2012/08/24/health/armstrong-livestrong-cancer/index.html

LeRoux, K., & Feeney, M. K. (2014). *Nonprofit organizations and civil society in the United States*. Routledge.

Lightner, C. (1984). Victims of crime: MADD at the court (Mothers Against Drunk Driving). *Judges Journal, 23*, 36.

Livestrong (2020). Who we are, News. Retrieved September 30, 2020, from https://www.livestrong.org/who-we-are/news/lance-armstrong-step-down-chairman-livestrong#:~:text=Lance%20Armstrong%2C%20founder%20and%20chairman,serve%20people%20affected%20by%20cancer

Madigan, T. (1985). Review of MADD 'routine': California plans audit of group's finances. *Fort Worth Star Telegram*, Jan 5, 21 A.

Matos, K., O'Neill, O. M., & Lei, X. (2018). Toxic leadership and the masculinity contest culture: How 'win or die' cultures breed abusive leadership. *Journal of Social Issues, 74*(3), 500–528. doi: 10.1111/josi.12284

McCarthy, J. D., Britt, D. W., & Wolfson, M. (1991). The institutional channeling of social movements in the contemporary United States. In L. Kriesberg's (Ed.), *Research in social movements, conflict, and change* (Vol. 13, pp. 45–76). JAI Press.

McCarthy, J. D., Wolfson, M., Baker, D. P., & Mosakowski, E. (1988). The founding of social movement organizations: Local citizens groups opposing drunk driving. In G. R. Carroll's (Ed.), *Ecological model of organizations* (pp. 71–84). Ballinger.

Miller-Stevens, K., Taylor, J. A., & Morris, J. C. (2015). Are we really on the same page? An empirical examination of value congruence between public and nonprofit managers. *VOLUNTAS: International Journal of Voluntary and Nonprofit Organizations, 26*, 2424–2446.

Montague, W. (1989, May 2). Dissidents question ties between fundraiser and mothers against drunk driving charity. *The Chronicle of Philanthropy*, pp. 1, 20–22.

Morabito, S. (2017, May 17). 12 ways the Southern Poverty Law Center is a scam to profit from hate-mongering. *The Federalist*. Retrieved July 16, 2020, from https://thefederalist.com/2017/05/17/12-ways-southern-poverty-law-center-scam-profit-hate-mongering/

National Center for Charitable Statistics (2020a). Data. Retrieved September 30, 2020 from https://nccs.urban.org/data

National Center for Charitable Statistics (2020b). IRS subsection overviews. Retrieved September 30, 2020, from https://nccs.urban.org/project/irs-subsection-overviews#publications

National Public Radio (2012, October 12). Doping agency says 11 teammates testified against Lance Armstrong. *NPR*. Retrieved July 3, 2020, from https://www.npr.org/sections/thetwo-way/2012/10/10/162640916/doping-agency-says-11-teammates-testified-against-lance-armstrong

National Public Radio (2019, March 14). Southern Poverty Law Center fires Morris Dees, its co-founder. Retrieved August 12, 2020, from https://www.cpr.org/2019/03/14/southern-poverty-law-center-fires-morris-dees-its-co-founder/

O'Brien, B. (2019, March 14). Southern Poverty Law Center Fires its co-founder, chief litigator. *Reuters*. Retrieved August 15, 2020, from https://br.reuters.com/article/us-usa-splc/southern-poverty-law-center-fires-its-co-founder-chief-litigator-idUSKCN1QV37I

O'Neil, T. (2020). *Making hate pay: The corruption of the Southern Poverty Law Center*. Bombardier Books.

PA Pundits – International (2019, March 19). SPLC, Morris Dees, and their hypocritical facade. *PA Pundits*. Retrieved July 21, 2020, from https://advance-lexis-com.coloradocollege.idm.oclc.org/api/document?collection=news&id=urn:contentItem:5VNW-GY51-F03R-N4RM-00000-00&context=1516831

Pearson, M. (2012, October 10). Evidence of Armstrong doping overwhelming, agency says. Retrieved August 16, 2020, from https://www.cnn.com/2012/10/10/sport/armstrong-doping-investigation/index.html

Perkins, K. E. (1986). A question of power: Why Candy Lightner lost control of MADD. *Sacramento Bee Magazine, Jan 19*, 12–17.

Reinarman, C. (1988). The social construction of an alcohol problem: The case of Mothers Against Drunk Drivers and social control in the 1980s. *Theory and Society, 17*, 91–120.

Sant'Anna, A. M., & Weiss, R. S. (1986). *Mothers Against Drunk Driving in 1986: Problems and recommendations*. Amsa International, Inc.

Satija, N., Lowery, W., & Reinhard, B. (2019, April 5). Years of turmoil and complaints led the Southern Poverty Law Center to fire its founder Morris Dees; Dees' ouster last month marks a stunning fall for a man long regarded as a civil rights icon. He denies any wrongdoing. *The Washington Post*. Retrieved June 15, 2020, from https://www.washingtonpost.com/investigations/years-of-turmoil-and-complaints-led-the-southern-poverty-law-center-to-fire-its-founder-morris-dees/2019/04/05/58717bfc-50fa-11e9-8d28-f5149e5a2fda_story.html

Saul, S. (2013, January 14). Armstrong's business brand, bound tight with his charity. *The New York Times*. Retrieved July 2, 2020, from https://advance-lexis-com.coloradocollege.idm.oclc.org/api/document?collection=news&id=urn:contentItem:57H0-JFJ1-DXY4-X1CG-00000-00&context=1516831

Schrotenboer, B. (2012a, May 4). Livestrong adjusts to life without Lance Armstrong. Retrieved July 17, 2020, from https://www.usatoday.com/story/sports/cycling/2016/05/04/livestrong-cancer-lance-armstrong-donations/83619386/

Schrotenboer, B. (2012b, November 12). Livestrong, resigns from board. *USA Today*. Retrieved August 5, 2020, from https://www.usatoday.com/story/sports/cycling/2012/11/12/lance-armstrong-resigns-livestrong-board-of-directors/1699531/

Silverstein, K. (2000). The Church of Morris Dees. *Harper's Magazine*. Retrieved August 15, 2020, from https://harpers.org/archive/2000/11/the-church-of-morris-dees/

Southern Poverty Law Center (2020a). About us. Retrieved September 30, 2020, from https://www.splcenter.org/about-us/our-history

Southern Poverty Law Center (2020b). Our history. Retrieved September 30, 2020, from https://www.splcenter.org/about-us/our-history

Stevens, S. (2001). *Nonprofit lifecycles*. Stagewise Enterprise, Inc.

Van Slyke, D. M. & Lecy, J. D. (2012). Profiles of nonprofit startups and nonprofit entrepreneurs. Andrew Young School of Policy Studies Research Paper Series, Department of Public Management and Policy Nonprofit Studies program, 12–28. Retrieved July 16, 2020, from https://aysps.gsu.edu/files/2016/01/12-28-VanSlykeLecy-ProfilesofNonprofitStartups.pdf

Ventriss, C. (1997). Toward a public philosophy of public administration: A civic. *International Journal of Public Administration*, 20(4), 1041–1069.

Vollers, A. C. (2019, March 24). SPLC leadership shakeup continues with legal director's resignation. *AL.com*. Retrieved June 17, 2020, from https://www.al.com/news/2019/03/splc-leadership-shakeup-continues-with-legal-directors-resignation.html

Wade, T. (2014). Candace Lightner: Founder of MADD, armijo grad. *Daily Republic*. Retrieved June 20, 2020, from https://www.dailyrepublic.com/all-dr-news/solano-news/local-features/local-lifestyle-columns/candace-lightner-founder-of-madd-armijo-grad/

Walsh, D. 2015. *Seven deadly sins: My pursuit of Lance Armstrong*. Atria Books.

Warr, M., & Stafford, M. (1983). Fear of victimization: A look at the proximate cause. *Social Forces*, 61, 1033–1043.

Weed, F. J. (1993). The MADD queen: Charisma and the founder of mothers against drunk driving. *The Leadership Quarterly*, 4(3–4), 329–346.

Weisbrod, B. A. (Ed.). (1977). *The voluntary nonprofit sector: An economic analysis*. Lexington Books.

Whitcomb, D. (2012, August 23). U.S. Anti-Doping Agency strips Armstrong of titles for cheating. *Reuters*. Retrieved September 1, 2020, from https://www.reuters.com/article/us-cycling-armstrong-doping/u-s-anti-doping-agency-strips-armstrong-of-titles-for-cheating-idUSBRE87N03N20120824

8 The Inevitable Life of Founder's Syndrome

Chapter Objectives

When you finish studying this chapter, you should be able to:

- Identify and explain the three primary etiologies of founder's syndrome
- Explain how organization development (OD) strategies can help a company avoid founder's syndrome
- Discuss how and why an external consultant can help a company address the symptoms of founder's syndrome
- Explain how founder's syndrome is an inevitable occurrence in organizations
- Describe what can be done to try to prevent founder's syndrome
- Discuss what is meant by an OD intervention
- Identify seven organizational impediments that contribute to the challenges of an OD intervention to help rectify founder's syndrome
- Discuss the reasons for incorporating information about founder's syndrome in educational programs designed to increase knowledge and skills in management and organizational leadership and related curricula

Introduction

If we take to heart the meaning behind management guru Peter Drucker's (2007, p. 8) words that "the only choice for an institution is between management and mismanagement," we can conclude that founder's syndrome in its simplest form is a failure of human interaction within for-profit and nonprofit organizations. In the preceding seven chapters, we offered concepts, theories, models, and examples of the social processes that lead to and explain founder's syndrome.

There are now three remaining questions that are essential to completing this book and we embark on those queries and answers in this final chapter:

1. Is founder's syndrome inevitable?
2. Can founder's syndrome be prevented?

3. Once founder's syndrome is observed, are there options for effectively defusing the hostilities, surviving the symptoms, and improving organizational performance?

Is Founder's Syndrome Inevitable?

In his book *King Solomon's Ring*, Lorenz (2002) shared a personal story of an imprinting experiment with ducklings that he conducted outside of his home:

> I was wondering about, squatting and quacking, in a May-green meadow at the upper part of our garden. I was congratulating myself on the obedience and exactitude with which my ducklings came waddling after me, when I suddenly looked up and saw the garden fence framed by a row of dead-white faces: a group of tourists were standing by the fence and staring horrified in my direction. Forgivable! For all they could see was a big man with a beard dragging himself, crouching round the meadow, in figures of eight, glancing constantly over his shoulder, and quacking – but the ducklings, the all-revealing and all-explaining ducklings were hidden in the tall spring grass from the view of the astonished crowd. (p. 42).

From this humorous story of a Noble Laureate quacking like a duck and being observed by tourists who only see him and not the ducklings, we will establish an important lesson about this book on founder's syndrome and begin a systematic answer to the first of the three pressing questions.

Watzlawick, Beavin Bavelas, and Jackson (1967) make an eloquent point that can be applied to Lorenz's embarrassing event that transmitting information in human communication may fail to present a full picture, thus leading the receiver to attribute qualities and characteristics that are simply not present. In their words, "a phenomenon remains unexplainable as long as the range of observation is not wide enough to include the context in which the phenomenon occurs" (pp. 20–21).

Weaving together the experiences of Lorenz and the statement by Watzlawick et al., we want to suggest that up until the writing of this book, the global understanding about founder's syndrome behavior has largely been narrowly focused and not wide enough to fully comprehend this organizational phenomenon. This conclusion becomes particularly obvious when searching the Internet for information and solutions about founder's syndrome. On the Internet, a searcher will find explanation after explanation describing a powerful founder, a Dr. Frankenstein, who has unleashed a metaphorical illness onto the organization that he or she created.

To limit the explanation of founder's syndrome to the scornful and problematic behaviors unleashed by an organizational founder, as thousands would have us accept on the Internet, is like watching a person walk in figure eights and quack like a duck. In other words, to truly grasp the organizational phenomenon known as founder's syndrome, we had to expand the frame of the picture and become more proficient observers of human behavior and social systems, while reminding ourselves to continue to widen our lens.

We discovered from widening the lenses during our own experiences and through surveys, research, and interviews that each case study is its own saga, but its cause can be pinned to one of three separate etiologies of founder's syndrome: One, the traditional malady of a founder engaging in ill-advised behaviors including unsatisfactory decisions; two, founder's syndrome behavior triggered by management staff and/or board members who were eager to dismiss a founder who is an entrepreneurially talented founder but managerially incompetent; and three, founder's syndrome behavior triggered by the jealousies and betrayal of a manager or board member who plots the removal of the founder with the aim of obtaining the CEO position for oneself or a colleague. Indeed, with additional research perhaps other etiologies of founder's syndrome will be theorized, but for now we can at least point to those three.

Once we observed the three pathways to founder's syndrome we were driven to delve further into this complex subject. And as plain as we can say it, complex subjects are easier to present if they can be examined in conceptual parts, as in Chapter 1. Additionally, we found using sociological and psychological theories, models, and logic to be critical tools for increasing cognition and comprehension of the types of social interaction in organizations where founder's syndrome emerged.

As a result of the above activities and putting it altogether as a book, we have come to an answer to the first question. Founder's syndrome is like a virus, some organizations will get it and others will not. There is no inoculation against founder's syndrome. It is endemic to organizations because it is a problem ignited by people working together. Furthermore, its existence is biologically based. Although personality psychologists are engaged in various research studies (Wrzus, 2019), testing for personality stability, personality changes through the lifespan, the ability to purposefully alter personality, and the strength of genetics and environment on the influences of personality throughout one's lifetime, we do know that by the time individuals are old enough to become an organizational founder, their personality and trait characteristics have stabilized during that period of their lifecycle. This means that their personality has a direct bearing on their behavioral tendencies and the decisions they make. The same applies for those managers and board members who will eventually want to get rid of the CEO and for the individual who engages in underhanded activities and seeks the position for their own or a colleague. Consequently, until the day comes when personalities can be programmed to build in good qualities and remove the bad, there will always be some number of founders, managers, and board members whose personality will orient them to behaviors of impatience, poor decision-making, aggression, passive-aggressiveness, and short temperedness. Some will also have strong egos that influence their behaviors in less healthier ways including personality disorders such as narcissism with grandiose views of their abilities or sociopathy with no regard to the feelings of others.

Can Founder's Syndrome be Prevented?

Many who live in the Denver area of Colorado are aware that the most attractive homes designed by award-winning architects who ensure buyers have magnificent views of the Rocky Mountains may not be worth the dollars paid unless the soil has been tested and accommodated because the area contains a great deal of bentonite clay that expands and contracts and can easily destroy the structure of a building. Unfortunately, many sad stories and lawsuits point to builders and homeowners who did not take precautions and preventative measures. The lesson is that careful planning can prevent horrific problems. Because we already concluded that founder's syndrome is inevitable among some organizations, then the objective is to become as close to founder's-syndrome-proof as possible, to encourage prevention by carefully planning the design and development of new organizations, like building houses on solid foundations that won't fall apart.

The only reason that prevention is not factored into new organization planning efforts is a gap in awareness. Filling the prevention gap is necessary because founder's syndrome will occur in some organizations (perhaps in the range of twenty-five percent extrapolating from Block & Rosenberg, 2002). We believe that the topic of founder's syndrome and the importance of prevention planning measures should be included in an array of educational programs. The information should be included in the curriculums of management, organizational theory, organizational behavior, organizational communication, organizational psychology, organizational development, organizational leadership, and similar programs. Students would benefit from learning about the multiple factors that contribute to healthy organizations and what contributes to organizational dysfunction. For example, Okiomoto (2009) presents the following contributing factor to organizational problems and staff reactions:

feelings of injustice elicited by poor treatment have the potential to affect subsequent behavior and attitudes in the context (or group) in which the injustice occurred. Numerous empirical investigations linking poor interpersonal treatment to behavioral reactions and attitudes attest to the strength and importance of interpersonal treatment. (p. 69)

Starting an organization or joining one as an employee or as a board member are major commitments with many potential advantages and conceivable disadvantages. Therefore with so much of our time, money, emotional dependency, and physical well-being tied to organizational life, it would seem wise to assess the potential consequences of starting a company or joining one, and not simply dash in because of the obvious upside. Founders and organizational stakeholders would be better off if they approached organizational affiliation with the same level of pre-cautionary and prudent decision-making they apply to other life events to prevent injurious outcomes: Most individuals get behind the wheel of an automobile and think about buckling seatbelts and driving defensively to avoid an accident; before entering into matrimony, many couples consider what they need to do to have a good marriage and avoid the painfulness of divorce; when entering into a large crowd, some shift their wallets or purses in a way to prevent a purse being snatched or wallet taken by a pickpocket; to the extent possible, families try to pick the best locations they can afford to reside in areas that have better rated schools; in a strange city, individuals are warned not to walk in dark alleys or in places with reports of high crime; some homeowners install burglar alarm systems or place stickers on a window declaring the home is protected by a security firm. The list of preventive activities that people engage in is plenty, but prevention activities for joining or starting organizations are hardly ever considered.

Because we rely on organizations for income and health benefits and spend years tied to organizations to lay the groundwork for future retirement, some precautionary activity before deciding to join or start a company may prove advantageous. We are not suggesting that to make better choices we should all openly announce our personal faults and idiosyncratic behaviors and have our personality traits printed on a tee-shirt during the process of starting a company or when interviewing to join one. To do so would not be rational, although we could suggest *tongue-in-cheek* that potential investors, potential employees, board members, managers, line staff, and founders could learn a great deal about the likelihood of making a sound choice by interviewing the mothers and psychiatrists of all the potential organizational stake-holders! Aside from interviewing mothers and psychiatrists, what is a reasonable approach to prevent founder's syndrome?

One of the lessons emphasized in the Starting an Organization Course described in Chapter 1 is to determine if there is a difference in how organizational founders perceive their roles compared to how they go about performing it. For example, founders or potential founders should be thinking clearly and be conversant about several facets of the design of their organization that is oriented to prevent founder's syndrome. Others considering to join a new organization should be prepared to ask questions, such as:

1. Describe the type of organizational values and beliefs that you will inculcate into the organization and how will you go about it?
2. What is management's philosophy about supervision and what goes on in a supervisory session?
3. You advertise your organization as being family friendly. How will you respond to a staff member who is delayed in coming into work because their child woke up with a fever and they needed to arrange for someone to care for their child?
4. Because your materials state the organization values education and professional development, what type of support do you provide a staff person who wants to enroll in college courses that will enhance their work knowledge and skills? Will the organization pay or co-pay a staff member's tuition for higher education courses, or professional conferences? Are staff allowed paid travel to participate in professional continuing education programs or attending professional conferences?
5. Because the company will focus on metrics to determine merit pay, how do you go about evaluating work outcomes?
6. Your company boasts that its greatest asset is its employees: How do you go about protecting staff from work stress and what benefits do you offer to ensure staff remains physically and mentally healthy?

Clearly, an attempt at reduction of harm offers no guarantees that a new organization will be free of founder's syndrome, but there is a better chance of starting or joining a company that will be free of it if one explores how the stated values, beliefs, and culture will be infused into the organization and its decision-making methods. We would prefer to take a risk with a new founder and company that has spent time thinking about the design of an organization's social systems compared to a founder who only discusses the company's products and services or espouses values and beliefs but doesn't have logical answers to questions about how those stated values and beliefs will be applied.

For example, going back to the scenario of a staff member who comes late to work because they have a sick child, why would an espoused family-friendly company issue the staff member a warning for being tardy? A family-friendly organization's response would be to let the staff member know how difficult it must have been to come to work and it was appreciated that they made the effort to find someone to care for their sick child. A family-friendly organization might even go a step further by creating an informational handout or include in their personnel handbook on what staff should do if a family member becomes ill and it affects attendance at work. The information could offer ideas on how to set up care for those unexpected home emergencies, planning in advance for last-minute childcare for a sick child, or when to use one's own earned sick time when emergency childcare falls through. The staff member who receives a warning is already experiencing stress. They may even feel upset and embarrassed that they did not have emergency backup planned because it is inevitable that a school-aged child will become ill sometime during the year. A warning will feel punitive and harsh, giving no recognition to the hardship for the staff member who came to work despite having a sick child at home. A founder's syndrome mindset is one who worries that a person will use 'the sick kid' excuse frequently and therefore must uniformly give out warnings. It's called the 'nip it in the bud approach.'

A non-founder's syndrome mindset recognizes the difference between a legitimate set of circumstances that cause late arrivals or no shows, and a staff person who periodically takes advantage of the company's good-will. Until there is evidence that a staff member is taking advantage of the company's kindness, why start off with the stance that all staff will take advantage of the company? Loyalty to an organization is built on trust.

A trust equation construct proposed by Maister, Green, and Galford (2000) is a good place to start. It requires credibility, reliability, intimacy, and self-orientation (p. 69). This means that if a company states it is family friendly, the validity of that statement can be determined through the trust equation. Credibility means that the stated values and beliefs are accurate. Determination of credibility is based on staff experiences which will determine believability. These researchers state that 'the emotional side of credibility is' honesty. Similarly, the trust equation includes the concept of reliability or a demonstration that organizational leaders always behave in the best interest of staff. Trustworthiness, according to these researchers also comes from intimacy. This is not meant to mean intimacy in the relational idea of friendship or sexual closeness. These authors use the term to mean "the willingness to talk about difficult agendas (intimacy). ... a willingness to expand the bounds of acceptable topics, while maintaining mutual respect and by respecting boundaries. ... and fewer subjects are barred from discussion" (p. 77). By self-orientation, the authors mean a demonstration of caring. Related to the concept of trust is fairness, and it is worth noting that Diekmann, Sondak, and Barsness (2007) report the existence of a substantial body of research on procedural fairness in the workplace. Organizational fairness furthers company goals including organizational commitment and the reduction of staff turnover (p. 162).

The ideas about truth and fairness can be used for founder's syndrome prevention and to build an organizational social system that leads to employee satisfaction. According to Ahmed and Farooq's (2020) explanation of the current research literature on job satisfaction and organizational stability, there are several elements that must be fulfilled including job design and social relationships. The stability of a workforce is also dependent on a calm working environment and supportive management styles. The researchers determined that other contributing factors include:

respect and honor that are given to all employees, rewards/benefits, compensation and security of job. These contributors act as a baseline for gaining high satlsfaction level. Ensuring these elements can lead to a more stable and well-established organization. (p. 468)

One of the advantages that exists for a founder building a new organization that will be less susceptible to founder's syndrome is the ability to design an organizational structure that is based on organizational strategy. For the sake of clarity and for the benefit of our readers whose discipline is not in the organization and management sciences, strategy is the way in which an organization pursues its targeted goals and objectives within specific time frames. It is how an organization achieves its purpose. It determines what type of skills, knowledge, and abilities are necessary attributes in their managers and line staff. Organizational structure is how the organization is organized, how staff functions are coordinated, and who reports to whom. Structure eliminates uncertainty by assigning activities to identifiable places within an organization such as departments or units, work groups, task groups, or divisions based on specializations.

When organizational founders launch their entity without adequately planning strategy, they are in effect creating an organization that will be prone to founder's syndrome and eventually require reorganization. This happens because of how staff and managers go about their tasks without clear guidance whether working alone, in teams, or ad hoc work groups. Also, without clear strategy, a company's internal and external communication channels cannot be effectively delineated or systematically realized. Thus, available information may be lost or not received leading to diminished decision-making capabilities. Akaegbu and Usoro (2017) add, "without a clearly defined strategy, a business will have no sustainable basis for creating and maintaining a competitive advantage in the industry where it operates" (p. 39). By developing inappropriate structures, founders and their managers ultimately become micromanagers to ensure staff are getting the work accomplished in the way that the founder envisioned. Of course, there are potential consequences and troubling social implications when top managers resort to micromanagement. To avoid structural problems there is sound advice from organizational design experts who declare that "structure always should follow strategy" (Chandler, 1962), and a related concept of "form follows function" (Gellerman, 1990). Both mean that organizational structure should facilitate organizational performance.

Although organization development (OD) interventions aim to achieve a healthy transformative change to existing organizational problems, OD fundamental strategies can occupy a more prominent position in the design and development of new organizations to prevent founder's syndrome. If they are good enough for the cure, why not include them as part of the foundation? Chinoperekweyi (2019) even suggests that "there is need for corporate governance literature and discussions to precisely capture the practice of organization development not as a mere consultant role or peripheral corporate governance function but as a strategic and operational imperative" (p. 36). Because the general framework for fixing organizational problems have been proven effective in both traditional operational areas and protecting the quality of organizational life of employees, then there is merit in the proposition that organizational development objectives should prove to be effective preventative measures by building them into the organizational design:

1. Create communication pathways that build interpersonal trust
2. Encourage a culture that is open to the identification of problems to be solved and not hidden
3. Create a work atmosphere designed to communicate a statement of respect for employees and visitors
4. Encourage and assign personal responsibilities for implementation of plans
5. Share strategic organization plans from the beginning and when bringing on new staff, include information updates and progress analyses with employees in writing or in all-staff meetings
6. Provide orientation training to new staff
7. Provide training to all staff when introducing new ideas, programs, technology, and upgraded systems
8. Encourage staff to develop personal career objectives with an eye toward strengthening knowledge and skills
9. Personnel evaluation systems should be tailored to each employee's job responsibilities with a clear statement of objectives and expectations
10. Make certain that company goals and priorities are clearly communicated and not assume that they are known by all
11. Make certain that new staff have opportunities to ask questions and have adequate support during the onboarding stage
12. Determine which type of work should include teams and provide team building to ensure there are no misunderstandings as to the expectation of team members and how decision-making and conflict resolution should occur among the team

Other considerations for developing organizations that include a measure of protection against founder's syndrome are those that build-in what Lee and Yoo (2019) describe as a 'sensing capability.' This is an ability to recognize changes in an industry's environment, identifying consumer changes to product demand and responses of suppliers and competitors. Instead of relying solely on in-house research and development, the researchers advise "acquiring diverse and in-depth knowledge through external collaborations with various entities" (p. 5). Success also requires strategies that allow for timely decisions that are dependent on organizational structures that "have built a knowledge management system to improve the efficiency of problem solving by allowing various internal and external-origin information to be exchanged and providing necessary information in a timely manner" (p. 5). Any strategy or structure that provides an organizational advantage adds to an organization's stability.

In summary, prevention against founder's syndrome is never a guarantee but its avoidance is more likely when designing a new organization that includes OD principles, clear strategy, structures that support strategy and performance, a culture built on trust, and consistency between espoused values, beliefs, and their application. Furthermore, it is of paramount importance to teach potential founders and students from various management and organization disciplines on how to create a theoretical framework and organizational mindset for designing and effecting functional organizations that can avoid founder's syndrome.

What is the Best Option to Effectively Defuse Founder's Syndrome Hostilities, Survive the Symptoms, and Improve Organizational Performance?

Instructors rely on examples of successful organizations to teach students how to become effective managers, organizational leaders, or organizational development practitioners. Additionally, case studies are used to teach students how to emulate practitioners that have been able to turnaround troubled organizations into productive and effective entities. Along with examining successful case examples, there are supplementary lessons that can be used to teach management and organizational theory and practice, such as studying organizations that have failed. In fact, Dias and Martens (2019) state that,

> entrepreneurship researchers have considered failure as an important source for the development of skills, as well as a stimulus to different forms of learning that is fundamental for the entrepreneur and able to help them in their next business ventures. (p. 108)

By improving one's understanding of organizational failure, organizational consultants and organizational learners may be better positioned to shed some light on the question of what can be done to correct presenting symptoms of founder's syndrome, survive it, and hopefully thrive.

By failure, we are not referring to organizations that are unfortunately harmed by theft, greed, embezzlement, or fraud which may have been prevented had there been effective financial controls in place. According to Kam (2005), the literature on organizational failure has been categorized into environmental reasons and managerial behaviors. Failure that is ascribed to the external environment includes sudden changes in a market environment, consumers switching their preferences to other brands or services, economic conditions that cause a downturn in the stock market, new competition with better advertising, and market know-how, inability to secure outside investment or banker support. There is also an internally focused explanation for organizational failure that is attributable to managerial behaviors. According to Kam,

> Management is also blamed for the misperception of its own competence level and of market changes in dealing with demand and competition, having distracted attention in the face of the real crisis, acting impulsively with little consideration of risk, being narcissistic and myopic, and can make decisions fostered by pride and over-confidence bordering on arrogance, breeding failure from previous success. (p. 401)

Another management related cause for failure can result from communication problems and poor use of information. There are potentially other reasons for organizational failure such as personal distractions. It may be difficult to attend to the business of work tasks when an individual faces relationship problems in one's marriage or other significant issues affecting family life (Dyer, 1994), or when a serious illness strikes a family member. Another factor that can contribute to failure is one's ego that clouds a founder's judgment at critical decision points (Kam, 2005, pp. 412–413). Clouded judgment can result from a fixation on previous organizational success. Sheaffer, Richardson, and Rosenblatt (1998) reported, "past successes are interpreted by management as evidencing adequate internal practices, competence and fortitude" (p. 2), causing decision-makers to misinterpret, underestimate, or even ignore signs of strategic threats.

Researcher Vijfeijken's (2019) essay that highlighted abusive behaviors in three international nongovernmental organizations also identified six reasons for organizational failure. Primarily using the construct of organizational culture as the framework for the explanation of the six reasons, one insight is the effect of power:

> Having power makes leaders also lessen their inhibitions around rules and norms and makes them less aware of how their behavior may impact on others. It thus lessens leaders' ability to take the perspective of other people. Equally, having power makes leaders see

other people in a more instrumentalist manner, as a 'means' to an end. Similarly, power makes leaders focused on abstract, high level thinking rather than the operational details, realities and the 'how' of everyday organizational life – and how staff may be impacted. (p. 3)

Related to power, the researcher asserts that certain types of individuals are drawn to work environments that require a focus on short-term gains rather than the long view. With leadership focused on taking control of "acutely challenging circumstances," it creates an environment that is ripe for abuse (p. 3). The third reason is related to a culture of silence, where staff are fearful of speaking up. The fourth reason is denial of organizational wrongdoing. Related to the last issue are organizational norms of problematic behavior that have become deep-seated and off limits to change. Lastly, is a lack of accountability.

Overall, intervening to fix a founder's syndrome problem may be the most difficult assignment that an organization consultant can face because the presenting problem is about the founding CEO, the key person who holds positional power and prestige. The level of difficulty of an organizational intervention of this type is akin to providing psychotherapy for a dysfunctional family, a monumentally large dysfunctional family. One that is too large to fit in your office and not everyone in the family cares to cooperate.

Given the complexity of the issues and the personality differences among the stakeholders, there is no one-size-fits-all intervention technique. Indeed, there are choice theories and specific steps and problem-solving models that are favored by consultants (Anderson, 2020; Bennis & Nanus, 2003; Cummings & Worley, 2014; French & Bell, 1999; Kotter, 2012; Lewin, 1997), but every OD intervention must be tweaked to fit the circumstances of the engagement. Consequently, the best option, and answer to the third question, is to seek help from an outside consultant or a consultation group that specializes in planned change and OD. Although we recognize the expertise of organizational development professionals that may be employed in organizations and their capabilities in matters of mission, vision, and strategy support, their closeness to other employees can be viewed or perceived as a conflict of interest in matters of founder's syndrome. Moreover, it is a precarious position to be advising on matters that concern the CEO.

Regardless of who is selected to help the organization repair its behaviors and culture, the interventionist may not be able to save the careers of the founding CEO, other managers, or prevent disruption to the membership of the board of directors. It is like the experiences of Relationship Therapists who see couples on the path to marriage dissolution. Just because a couple engages a therapist does not mean their marriage can be saved, especially if one of the individuals is intent on ending the marriage and views the therapy as helping his or her exit strategy.

In addition to selecting a consultant, there needs to be a clearly delineated understanding of what a successful change effort will mean for the organization. For example, in addition to resolving the founder's syndrome issues:

1. Will the outcome include a change in organizational procedures?
2. Will the structure change and reporting lines differ?
3. Will there be a new procedure for approving major decisions?
4. Will the management team change in composition?
5. Will there be a change in products or services?

Organizational changes can be purposeful but sometimes there are unintended consequences with change efforts. Once unintended consequences are recognized, they require an analysis to determine how they affect the intervention and impact the organization's internal and external environments. The consultant and the client can then determine what additional decisions need to occur. No matter what planned change objectives are initially established or added after the intervention begins, there are a few impediments that usually surface that can intensify the challenges of organizational development efforts. The seven hindrances to the intervention process include the following:

1. The etiology of founder's syndrome
2. The length of time the company has been in business with founder's syndrome behaviors
3. The size of the organization
4. Differentiation and integration
5. Escalation of commitment
6. Behavioral science knowledge and skills of the interventionist
7. The attitude, outlook, and objectives of the board of directors

The following explanations about the seven familiar obstacles are intended to illustrate how they add difficulty to an intervention.

Etiology

We know that founder's syndrome behavior can either be endemic to the founder or in response to persons trying to undermine and get rid of the founder. When first being introduced to the organization based on the presenting problem, the etiology may not be clear-cut. However, through the process of organizational assessment, observation, and interviews, the cause for the founder behavior symptoms will become known. The fact that it becomes known is a source of information for the consultant and to be factored in an intervention. It is unnecessary to broadcast the etiology of the behavioral problems. We make one exception. When a staff member or board member has purposefully sabotaged the CEO with the aim of getting the founder fired and an attempt is being made to secure the CEO position for their own joy, we do not remain silent. When unethical behavior is glaringly evident, we follow a protocol similar to what we follow when uncovering unlawful activity. In such a situation, we ask for a meeting with the executive board or full board of directors and present our findings. We believe the board has an obligation to resolve the matter. We will assist the board, but in the interest of transparency, we will not partake in unethical, immoral, or unlawful activities.

Length of Time

The inhabitants of organizations develop patterns of behavior during their daily work. The longer a company has been operational, those patterns of behavior become routinized and established. In her article on organizational learning research, Ferincz (2016) acknowledges this point by quoting Rerup and Levinthal (2014):

> Organizational actions are history-dependent, and the behavior in an organization is based on routines. Routines are based on interpretations of the past more than anticipations of the future. They adapt to experience incrementally in response to feedback about outcomes. (p. 39)

To put it another way, because the behaviors of staff become routine, they evolve into rules of behavior and over time they become the norm that are observed and understood by all involved. One reality for managers operating in an organization with founder's syndrome is the likelihood of unwanted behaviors by their founding CEO. Different founding CEOs engage in undesirable behaviors for different reasons or have their own personal triggers that unleash founder's syndrome behaviors, such as impulsive decision-making, micromanagement, being argumentative, saying degrading comments, and acting like a bully. Managers and other staff may detest the founder's syndrome behaviors but accede to them out of fear of sanctions such as being terminated from employment. According to Schein (2010), "many leaders do allow themselves to get overtly angry and use those feelings as messages" (p. 239).

The length of time that an organization has existed with founder's syndrome behaviors informs us of how deeply rooted the founder's behavioral outbursts have been sowed into the foundation of the company. As a developed norm, subordinates may become conditioned and sensitive to when the outbursts might occur. As a preventative mechanism, managers may "adopt the leader's assumptions" as an attempt to forestall the leader's behaviors (Schein, 2010, p. 239). The challenge for the consultant engaged to intervene is dealing with issues that have become emended into the fabric of the company. Any attempt to undo founder's behaviors that have become powerful and emotional messages will require the consultant to gain the trust of the founder and while not seeking a confrontation, the consultant should also not shy away from the triggers that lead to emotional outbursts. Once the behaviors have been displayed in front of the consultant, it becomes possible for the consultant, using skillful abilities, to discuss the meaning and implications of the behaviors with the CEO.

Organizational Size

Stating the obvious, organizations come in different sizes. The number of managers and line staff and the company's industry determines whether the organization is considered small or large. The issue of organizational size has been the subject of study for more than 60 years. In 1957, Caplow suggested that organizational administration increases to accommodate the size of an organization. However, Coates and Updegraff (1973) report that Blau and Scotts (1962) book on formal organizations came to a different conclusion. Consequently, the literature is rather mixed on the impact that size has on organizations. Some studies have examined size of budget and/or size of staff, some have examined staff size in relation to productivity, compensation, job satisfaction, and management styles (Vaccaro, Jansen, Van Den Bosch, & Volberda, 2012). Also, the differences in size might have certain advantages or disadvantages within similar industries, such as academic research organizations compared to private or federally funded research organizations (Mote, Jordan, Hage, Hadden, & Clark, 2016).

There are, however, some expected differences in larger versus smaller organizations. Although larger organizations may have more assets, available cash, and greater economies of scale, when it comes to the communication of ideas, it is easier to share information in smaller organizations.

Obstacles may exist based on organizational environment with size being a potential constraint. The qualification of 'may exist' is necessary because larger organizations could have multiple locations. Thus, the focal point of an OD intervention may be location specific and not across the entire organization. In smaller organizations, the issues of founder's syndrome have a noticeable systemic impact on the entire organization due to the proximity of workers. However, if founder's syndrome leads to the dismissal of the CEO or a reduction in investor support, the impacts might share similarities regardless of organizational size.

There is one commonality reported in the research literature on organizational size. There appears to be consistency in the findings that the larger the organization, the more formalized and bureaucratic it becomes. That does not suggest that smaller organizations are absent of rules and divisions, it means that larger organizations appear to have more layers of management and reporting requirements that befits its number of employees. The larger the entity the more complex becomes its hierarchy and need for coordination and controls (Josefy, Kuhan, Duane Ireland, & Hitt, 2015).

It would be an unwieldy and unnecessary feat for a consultant to interview a company with hundreds if not thousands of staff. The key in dealing with an organization's size is to determine the boundaries of where the issues exist and then plan accordingly. When Edgar Schein is engaged to facilitate a culture assessment, he works with the organization's leaders to select groups comprised of 3–30 representatives to interview from one department or from across the organization. The key is to select individuals who will be amenable to an open discussion (Schein & Schein, 2016, pp. 297–318).

Furthermore, we are mindful that any intervention may have systemic repercussions throughout an organization. Any changes in one specific geographical location of a large company, according to systems theory and adaptation theory, may require other locations to adapt to the changing environments and opportunities that emerged from the intervention. This is certainly the case when a founder is terminated, and a new CEO is hired.

As a result of an initial assessment in large organizations, it may be discovered that different locations have different sections that could benefit from planned change. For example, one location may have difficulty with the way information is communicated and another may have relationship issues among top or middle managers. The targets for intervention may need to be rank ordered by the board of directors with the help of the consultant who can decipher which of the problematic areas are the result of founder's syndrome.

Differentiation and Integration

It is easy to think of an organization and its environment as a single entity, but that could be a mistake when planning an intervention. Depending on an organization's structure it can have multiple units, divisions, departments, or project teams. Given the specialized functions that occur in each subsystem of the company, each subsystem could have different reporting mechanisms, different approaches to formality, different work schedules, different requirements for rewards, and a different culture. Lawrence and Lorsch (1967) said of organizations that they are,

a system of interrelated behaviors of people who are performing a task that has been differentiated into several distinct subsystems, each subsystem performing a portion of the task, and the efforts of each being integrated to achieve effective performance of the system. (p. 3)

Because of their differences, the OD practitioner must examine how the subsystems interface and connect to the internal and external environments and their overall integration as a company. Consequently, the interventionist must determine how founder's syndrome has affected the various subsystems and determine the best entry points to intervene.

Escalation of Commitment

At what point is enough, enough? For example, when put on hold making a phone call how long should one wait before hanging up? Don't we consider all the minutes that we just sat on hold and think about going through the same process again. Perhaps a few more seconds and the party will come back on. If we hang up, we wasted all that time and energy and we are no further ahead. Perhaps we reach a personal boiling point and hang-up. When we call back, we are in no mood for pleasantries.

The issue of investing more money and time in a decision that appears to be failing is a quandary that managers and board members occasionally face. At what point should a board decide to bring in a consultant to help deal with a founding CEO engaged in founder's syndrome behaviors? At what point should a founder terminate the managers that are plotting action against their CEO? Is it ever the right time to give up, will something change if we hold out a little longer? Do we look foolish if we reverse course and admit to having invested in time, money, and energy in a bad decision? Have we failed by not acting sooner?

When a consultant enters the scene, they may be stepping into an environment where there is still the residual feelings from that earlier escalation of commitment to a bad management decision. They may also face some board members who are still of the opinion that bringing in a consultant was a hasty decision. They may face an angry founder who believes he or she were not given adequate time to correct their management and behavioral actions.

Behavioral Science Knowledge and Skills of the Interventionist

Some companies have their own organizational development practitioner on staff, whereas others rely on bringing in a consultant. Whomever they select to facilitate the intervention, the practitioner will have available an array of diagnostic and intervention models to choose from. Although some consultants tend to favor one approach, other consultants try to select a model based on the presenting problem, and still others customize their approach using bits and pieces of different models and consider their methodology to be an eclectic style.

Although we use the terms interchangeably, some refer to themselves as consultants, interventionists, change agents, or OD practitioners. There are others who present themselves as capacity builders. Millar and Doherty (2016) define capacity building interventions as helping decide on resource allocation. Elsewhere, they state "capacity needs and assets may be characterized by multiple aspects of the organizational dimensions of human resources, financial resources, external relations, planning, and infrastructure" (Millar & Doherty, 2018, p. 349). Regardless of what the individuals call themselves, there are certain factors to consider, such as whether the company seeking help wants a consultant to tell them what the outcome should be or the company wants to inform the consultant what type of outcome they would prefer. Also, it may be important to know how confidential information will be treated and how the consultant involves staff in the change process.

The intervention goal to fix a founder's syndrome problem may also include other objectives such as clarification of governance responsibilities, adapting to newer technologies, improving interpersonal working relationships, increasing workforce diversity, improving group dynamics, improving strategies and performance, reinforcing or creating a culture change, or ensuring that the organization is engaged in sustainable development, among other options (Kuzhda & Gevko, 2018). Because of the various options that might be tagged on to an intervention, the more added, the more skill required. Although consultants have different approaches once they are on-site, our preference is that organizational interventions begin with a behavioral science approach that incorporates a systemic analysis of human behavior. This includes a discussion of the presenting problem and close observation of the symptoms during the assessment, which should reveal the underlying problems.

Additionally, open systems theory provides a mechanism for gaining insight into the organizational environment and what needs to be changed besides the presenting problem. Falletta and Combs (2018) captured the thoughts of Katz and Kahn (1978) about the importance of the organizational environment in the following statement: "The premise of open systems theory is that organizations are social systems which are dependent on the environment in which they operate" (p. 22). If we understand the environment to include staff, board members, consumers, teams, projects, processes, and functions, then we have a better opportunity to identify the source and nature of the organization's problems.

One caution from Schein and Schein (2018) suggests that too much attention in recent years has been paid to individual performance and not enough on group dynamics. They state, "Perhaps the biggest challenge to OD will be the reeducation of our national culture to the reality that the future will depend more on how groups work together than on finding individual leader heroes" (p. 8). The Scheins' comment strikes a chord that consultants have different work styles. Some consultants tend to interpret every problematic detail to the client and barrage the client with questions. We see this occur among novice consultants and interns who have an ego need to demonstrate their expertise. Our view is that being selected for a project already identifies the consultant as an expert, although some are more expert than others. Therefore, we caution our graduate students during their internships that they need not try to prove their intelligence through 'one upping' the client or monopolizing the client's day. Benn, Jones, and Rosenfield (2008) found that "too many questions may inhibit the development of a collaborative relationship. ... and their overuse may make consultees feel as though they are being challenged" (p. 57). We suggest consultants demonstrate their knowledge in their work product especially during the assessment and pre-intervention planning stages. Otherwise, communication can provoke conflict caused by the client's misinterpreting the consultant's jargon, attitudes, perceptions, and values. Because the intervention process is a difficult challenge in a founder's syndrome case, we caution our learning consultants to minimize unnecessary behaviors that can have an unintended consequence of clashing and antagonizing the client.

Because our belief is to demonstrate knowledge and skills during the assessment and pre-intervention stages, the first step in achieving a level of trust will be determined by the way in which the interventionist was invited into the organization. If, for example, the board of directors informs the founding CEO that they heard of problems with his or her behaviors and decided to engage a consultant to help resolve the conflicts, then the consultant's conversation with the founder starts with the problems heard by the board, and the consultant's tone must be nonjudgmental. In other words, when fact gathering as part of the initial assessment, always start with the presenting problem. Rodríguez (2012) mentions, "The presenting problem (like all research problems) quickly softens to unveil increasingly complex questions, uncovering deeper issues not suspected at the onset of the process" (p. 25).

Similarly, if the consultant was invited in by the founding CEO who asked for help with an organizational issue and the consultant determines that part of the problem is the CEO's behavior toward others or the CEO's management competencies, then the first order of business still remains the primary purpose for the engagement. If the intervention can be planned in a way to fix the presenting problem plus the other issues, that would be the best outcome. Otherwise, the other issues will need to be discussed at a more opportune moment and conveyed with systemic neutrality, that means not taking sides and maintaining a nonjudgmental stance, which does require finesse and communicative expertise (Boscolo, Cecchin, Hoffman, & Penn, 1987).

This approach is not like going to a physician to hear the hard truth. Imagine complaining of a headache, and after the assessment the physician tells you that "the problem is really not a headache; it is a brain tumor." Now, imagine a CEO engages you with the presenting problem of conflict in the management team. After your assessment you inform the CEO that the "problem is really not your management team; it is your incompetency." We daresay that your welcome will be cut short! By focusing on the presenting problem, you will have an opportunity to discuss your analysis after a bond of trust has been developed. Addressing the presenting problem lays the groundwork for developing trust because it demonstrates your skill and that you listened to what the client noted as his or her problem. Remedying additional issues at the same time that the presenting problem is addressed may be possible but it may require a second-order approach that was discussed in Chapter 4. Please recall that second-order approaches should be attempted with caution.

The Attitude, Outlook, and Objectives of the Board of Directors

When it becomes clear that an organization is failing it is common for the founder and possibly other stakeholders to feel desperate and begin to respond erratically. Founder's syndrome behaviors are to be expected during moments of desperation. When the operations, programs, and services of a company are deteriorating, the responsibility to ensure some action takes place to fix the organizational concerns can be shared among any of the internal stakeholders who are concerned about the company's continued existence, provided all of the action is organized as part of a coherent plan.

If a founder's behavior is out of control and the condition of the company is worsening, then staff informing the board of directors of this fact is a viable option. As soon as members of the board of directors are made aware of the organizational problems, they have an obligation to introduce corrective action or they may be held responsible by the shareholders or funders for their omissions.

If it appears that the founder has engaged in founder's syndrome during the organizational decline, every option to fix the founder's behaviors should be considered before accepting the reality of failure. Because governing boards of directors are responsible for the health and financial stability of a corporation, if failure occurs, the *typical* reaction of a governing board is first to bemoan organizational failure, and then they will excuse their role by claiming accurate information was withheld from them, or the timeliness of critical information was too delayed for them to know the seriousness of the issues and promptly react. Then, they will blame the CEO and his or her managers for keeping them in the dark. If only they knew sooner, the board will assert, they could have taken appropriate action. Almost everyone looks for a scapegoat, and there is no better one than the individuals responsible for the day-to-day operations; 'we trusted the CEO.'

It is not entirely unreasonable to cast blame on the CEO and his or her managers. After all, the CEO is in charge and should be aware of all operating issues. It can also be the case, however, that the CEO was truly kept in the dark about critical issues from key informers, too. There is no conceivable way that a CEO with more than 25 staff and upwards of thousands on staff can know all of the problems that each department, division, or staff members have with other staff members, with supervisors, with customers/clients, with funders, or issues with services or products or suppliers, unless someone external to the company or inside the organization brings the issues to the attention of the CEO. Like the board, the CEO is dependent on others for information.

In his classic article on double loop learning in organizations, in which a single loop is the typical problem-solving response and double loop allows for its modification as a source of the problem, Chris Argyris (1977) writes about a product that lost a company more than $100 million. The problems leading to such losses were known to a handful of managers several years before the product was discontinued. The information was withheld from the CEO and top management. When details were finally released in memo form by mid-level managers, it came in bits and pieces to soften the news and mask the severity of the problem. Argyris explains that the staff who were knowledgeable about the problems found themselves in a bind from an organizational norm that prohibited them from confronting company objectives. So, the employees hid the errors. According to Argyris, such examples of withholding information is not uncommon. In another example, Benaroch and Chernobai (2017) discuss the actions taken when a company finds that its information technology has been compromised. Although it appears that many companies seek board members with information technology expertise to advise management on cybersecurity issues, CEOs and top management executives are still the first to be blamed and dismissed (p. 755).

For-profit and nonprofit organizations rely on boards of directors to provide oversight and advice and counsel. In publicly traded companies, shareholders count on the boards of directors to make prudent decisions on their behalf. When a consultant is brought into an organization to help address a founder's syndrome and related issues, ultimately the board of directors is responsible for the health and stability of the company. Because board members rely on their CEO to keep them informed of the important events of the company and have legal responsibilities, it is not surprising that they will hold the CEO accountable for the condition of the company, even if the CEO has been kept in the dark by members of his or her management team.

A Final Word

Risk

Throughout the United States and countries of the world, most inhabitants rely on organizational life. We rely on organizations in all different industries for the products and services that keep us fed, clothed, housed, healthy, educated, employed, and safe. The nonprofit and for-profit sectors of the economy also provide most of the sources of revenue from production and services that provide income to pay taxes that support services from government entities.

Because society is dependent on organizations, universities and colleges have established an array of educational degree programs to teach students about organizational leadership and management and certify the competence of their graduates. Educational institutions and professional associations balance their offerings between the science and art of organization management and leadership practices to improve the effectiveness of the methods and skills used to serve society through the construct of organizations.

Of course, not everyone attends an educational program. Some people forge ahead and start organizations. Where would we be without those entrepreneurs who have taken a risk to start organizations? Some are considered heroes for starting companies that employ anywhere from one person to thousands. Regrettably, many risk-takers see their organizations fail and go out of business within the first five years of their existence. As risk-takers, many learn from their mistakes and start all over. Others decide to embark on more formal study believing that much-needed knowledge will give them a practical advantage in their next attempt to launch an organization.

However one chooses to plan and launch a new organization, the better way forward rests on knowledge and a clearer view of all the essential components, concepts, theories, and other relevant propositions to construct an effective organization free of the social phenomena of founder's syndrome.

From the start, we invited our readers to join us in thinking critically about the subject of founder's syndrome and its implications on the health of organizations and the people who are associated with those organizations. We stressed the importance of education, drawing on theoretical frameworks and organizational practices based on knowledge and skills. We also shared some of our documented performance with clients and other cases from the literature as examples of evidenced-based practice.

Our objectives for this book were to illuminate the reality of founder's syndrome, its causes, characteristics, and complications. We are encouraged that this exploration will lead others to generate new knowledge and insights in organizational practices and a better understanding of applied interventive action.

As a final point, because of all the benefits that citizens receive from the organizations in their communities, we hope that the details in this book will lead to a greater understanding and prevention of founder's syndrome and improve the effectiveness of nonprofit and for-profit organizations.

Discussion Questions

1. If you were the Chair of the board of directors, how would you work with the founder to avoid founder's syndrome? What methods and approaches might work best for the board? For the founder? For both?
2. How can OD strategies help prevent founder's syndrome? Who is responsible for developing and implementing these strategies – the board or the founder, or both?
3. You have been hired to facilitate an intervention in a company experiencing founder's syndrome where there is great tension between the founder and board of directors. What process should you follow to gather information? How can different types of information be used to solve or alleviate founder's syndrome?
4. Why would an OD intervention in an organization with founder's syndrome be a challenging experience?
5. What is meant by differentiation and integration?
6. What is the practical value of designing preventive measures when planning a new organization?
7. If applicable, draw on your own experience or that of a colleague and describe the circumstances of an organization with founder's syndrome that could benefit from an OD intervention or had an OD intervention.
8. In your opinion, should a consultant inform a board of directors of attempts by a manager or board member plotting to sabotage a founding CEO?
9. Regarding question #5, does your opinion change if you discover that the founder is engaging in founder's syndrome? Is not a competent manager? Is a competent manager? Has never engaged in founder's syndrome?
10. In your view, is there any value in learning about organizations that failed?
11. Imagine that you are a student that just graduated with a master's degree in management or a related organizational specialty. Unfortunately, you have amassed debt from student loans and are eager to find employment. You have been invited to a large organization for an interview. While seated in the interview room, three staff members walk by and say hello as they get ready to go to lunch. You ask them what it is like to work at this organization. The three spend the next 20 minutes

describing examples of founder's syndrome behavior by the founder and the depressed mood it has caused the managers and the staff that they supervise. You interview for the position and the next day you are offered the position and accept. How will you prepare knowing what the three staff members shared with you?

12. Regarding question #11. You are offered the position and you decline. Later in the day, you receive a call from the Director of the Human Resources Department who wants to know why you decided to reject the offer of employment. What do you say? Is there anything that you want to know from the HR Director that would lead to changing your mind?

References

Ahmad, G., & Farooq, S. U. (2020). Performance related pay and its impact on organizational development: A study of banking sector of Pakistan. *Abasyn University Journal of Social Sciences, 13*(1), 465–475. doi: 10.34091/AJSS.13.1.33

Akaegbu, J. B., & Usoro, A. A. (2017). The place of organizational capabilities in strategy formulation and implementation: An exploratory analysis. *Global Journal of Social Sciences, 16*(1), 39–48.

Anderson, D. L. (2020). *Organization development: The process of leading organizational change* (5th ed.). Sage.

Argyris, C. (Sept–Oct 1977). Double loop learning in organizations. *Harvard Business Review, 55*(5), 115–124.

Benaroch, M., & Chernobai, A. (2017). Operational IT failures, IT value destruction, and board-level IT governance changes. *MIS Quarterly, 41*(3), 729–762.

Benn, A. E., Jones, G. W., & Rosenfield, S. (2008). Analysis of instructional consultants' questions and alternatives to questions during the problem identification interview. *Journal of Educational and Psychological Consultation, 18*(1), 54–80. doi: 10.1080/10474410701864115

Bennis, W., & Nanus, B. (2003). *Leaders: Strategies for taking charge*. Harper Business.

Blau, P. M., & Scott, W. R. (1962). Formal organizations: A comparative approach. Stanford Business Books.

Block, S. R., & Rosenberg, S. (2002). Toward an understanding of founder's syndrome: An assessment of power and privilege among founders of nonprofit organizations. *Nonprofit Management & Leadership, 12*(4), 353–368.

Boscolo, L., Cecchin, G., Hoffman, L., & Penn, P. (1987). *Milan systemic family therapy: Conversations in theory and practice*. Basic Books.

Chandler, A. D. Jr. (1962). *Strategy and structure: Chapters in the history of the American industrial enterprise*. MIT Press.

Chinoperekweyi, J. (2019). Organization development: A strategic & operational corporate governance imperative. *Organization Development Review, 51*(3), 36–41.

Coates, R., & Updegraff, D. E. (1973). The relationship between organizational size and the administrative component of banks. *The Journal of Business*, 46(4), 576–588.

Cummings, T. G., & Worley, C. G. (2014). *Organization development and change* (10th ed.). Cengage.

Dias, T. R. F. V., & Martens, C. D. P. (2019). Business failure and the dimension of entrepreneurial learning: Study with entrepreneurs of micro and small-sized enterprises. *Brazilian Journal of Management/Revista de Administração da UFSM*, 12(1), 107–124.

Diekmann, K. A., Sondak, H., & Barsness, Z. I. (2007). Does fairness matter more to some than to others? The moderating role of workplace status on the relationship between procedural fairness perceptions and job satisfaction. *Social Justice Research*, 20(2), 161–180. doi: 10.1007/s11211-007-0036-x

Drucker, P. (2007). People and performance: The best of Peter Drucker on management. Harvard Business Review Press.

Dyer, W. G. Jr. (1994). Toward a theory of entrepreneurial careers. *Entrepreneurship, Theory and Practice, 19*(2), 7–22.

Ferincz, A. (2016). Adaptation and change in organizational learning research. *Vezetéstudomány/Budapest Management Review, 47*(5), 53–63.

Falletta, S., & Combs, W. (2018). The organizational intelligence model in context: A comparative analysis and case profile. *OD Practitioner, 50*(1), 22–29.

French, W. L., & Bell, C. H. Jr. (1999). *Organizational development: Behavior science interventions for organizational improvement* (6th ed.). Pearson.

Gellerman, S. W. (1990). In organizations, as in architecture, form follows function. *Organizational Dynamics, 18*(3), 57–68.

Josefy, M., Kuban, S., Duane Ireland, R. and Hitt, M. A. (2015). All things great and small: Organizational size, boundaries of the firm, and a changing environment. *The Academy of Management Annals, 9*(1), 715–802.

Kam, J. (2005). Making sense of organizational failure: The Marconi debacle. *Prometheus, 23*(4), 399–420.

Kotter, J. P. (2012). *Leading change*. Harvard Business Review Press (original work first published 1996).

Katz, D., & Kahn, R. L. (1978). *The social psychology of organizations*. Wiley.

Kuzhda, T., & Gevko, V. (2018). Organization development components, process and performance. *Socio-Economic Problems & the State, 18*(1), 61–69.

Lawrence, P. R., & Lorsch, J. W. (1967). Differentiation and integration in complex organizations. *Administrative Science Quarterly, 12*(1), 1–47.

Lee K., & Yoo, J. (2019). How does open innovation lead competitive advantage? A dynamic capability view perspective. *PLoS One, 14*(11), 1–18.

Lewin, K. (1997). *Resolving social conflicts and field theory in social science*. American Psychological Association. (Resolving social conflicts originally published 1948. Field theory in social science was originally published 1951.)

Lorenz, K. (2002). *King Solomon's Ring*. Routledge Publishers. (Original work first published 1949.)

Maister, D., Green, C., & Galford, R. (2000). *The trusted advisor*. Free Press.

Millar, P., & Doherty, A. (2016). Capacity building in nonprofit sport organizations: Development of a process model. *Sport Management Review*, *19*(4), 365–377. doi: 10.1016/j.smr.2016.01.002

Millar, P., & Doherty, A. (2018). You can't just start and expect it to work: An investigation of strategic capacity building in community sport organizations. *Journal of Sport Management*, *32*, 348–361.

Mote, J., Jordan, G., Hage, J., Hadden, W., & Clark, A. (2016). Too big to innovate? Exploring organizational size and innovation processes in scientific research. *Science and Public Policy*, *43*(3), 332–337.

Okimoto, T. G. (2009). The moderating and mediating role of group identification in observers' reactions to intragroup disrespect. *European Journal of Social Psychology*, *39*(1), 69–81. doi: 10.1002/ejsp.474.

Rerup, C., & Levinthal, D. A. (2014). Situating concept of organizational mindfulness: The multiple dimensions of organizational learning. In G. Becke (Ed.), *Mindful change in times of permanent reorganization: Organizational, institutional and sustainability perspectives* (pp. 33–49). Springer.

Rodríguez, K. (2012). *Small city on a big couch: A psychoanalysis of a provincial Mexican city*. Rodopi.

Schein, E. (2010). *Organizational culture and leadership* (4th ed.). John Wiley & Sons.

Schein, E. H., & Schein, P. A. (2016). *Organizational culture and leadership* (5th ed.). John Wiley & Sons.

Schein, E. H., & Schein, P. A. (2018). What is new in OD? Nothing, yet everything. *OD Practitioner*, *50*(4), 6–8.

Sheaffer, Z., Richardson, B., & Rosenblatt, Z. (1998). Early-warning-signals management: A lesson from the Barings crisis. *Journal of Contingencies & Crisis Management*, *6*(1), 1–22.

Vaccaro, I. G., Jansen, J. J. P., Van Den Bosch, F. A. J., & Volberda, H. W. (2012). Management innovation and leadership: The moderating role of organizational size. *Journal of Management Studies*, *49*(1), 28–51.

Vijfeijken, T. B.-V. (2019). Culture is what you see when compliance is not in the room: Organizational culture as an explanatory factor in analyzing recent INGO scandals. *Nonprofit Policy Forum*, *10*(4), 1–9. doi: 10.1515/npf-2019-0031

Watzlawick, P., Beavin Bavelas, J., & Jackson, D. D. (1967). *Pragmatics of human communication: A study of interactional patterns, pathologies, and paradoxes* (1st ed.). W. W. Norton & Company.

Wrzus, C. (2019). Editorial: Does age matter for personality psychology? *European Journal of Personality*, *33*(3), 217–220.

Index

Page numbers in **bold** represent tables.

Printed in the United States
by Baker & Taylor Publisher Services